ROBERT WISE
SHADOWLANDS

Three Roberts: Robert Wise (center) on the set of Blood on the Moon *(1948), with stars Robert Mitchum (left) and Robert Preston.*

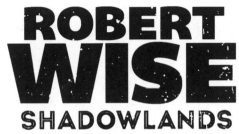

ROBERT WISE

SHADOWLANDS

A WES D. GEHRING BIOGRAPHY

Indiana Historical Society Press
Indianapolis | 2012

© 2012 Indiana Historical Society Press

This book is a publication of the
Indiana Historical Society Press
Eugene and Marilyn Glick Indiana History Center
450 West Ohio Street
Indianapolis, Indiana 46202-3269 USA
http://www.indianahistory.org
Telephone orders 1-800-447-1830
Fax orders 1-317-234-0562
Online orders @ http://shop.indianahistory.org

The paper in this publication meets the minimum requirements of American National Standard
for Information Sciences—Permanence of Paper for Printed Library Materials,
ANSI Z39.48–1984

Library of Congress Cataloging-in-Publication Data

Gehring, Wes D.
Robert Wise : shadowlands / Wes D. Gehring.
     p. cm.
Includes bibliographical references and filmography.
ISBN 978-0-87195-296-7 (cloth : alk. paper)
1. Wise, Robert, 1914-2005. 2. Motion picture producers
and directors—United States—Biography. I. Title.
PN1998.3.W569G46 2012
791.4302'33092—dc23
[B]
                              2011034751

To my daughters, Sarah and Emily,
who suggested I write this book many years ago.

Robert Wise: Shadowlands is made possible through the generous support of Margot Lacy Eccles.

Margot Lacy Eccles (far left) and her mother Edna Balz Lacy (left) joins Robert Wise (center) at Franklin College in 1968 upon the occasion of Wise receiving an honorary degree.

"A Robert Wise Film is . . ."

Where even the best battlers
are told, "You'll always be just
one punch away." *

A setting where desperate characters are
"just trying to find a hole in the fence
like everyone else."

About passionate people who try to make
a difference but often die asking,
"What the hell happened?"

Where even a Christlike character talks
tough, "Live in peace, or pursue your
present course and face obliteration."

Where "the hills are alive with the sound of
music" but the valleys are full of Nazis.

A world where the motto might be,
"Life is like coffee; the aroma is better
than the . . . [taste]."

— Wes D. Gehring

*All quotes are drawn from Robert Wise films and appear in the following order:
*The Set-Up, Odds Against Tomorrow, The Sand Pebbles, The Day the Earth Stood Still,
The Sound of Music,* and *Born to Kill.*

Contents

Foreword

David L. Smith

A film colony worker of some repute once said of Robert Wise, "For all his genius and success, Bob's a very shy man. Sometimes that's the way it is with giants."

When I first met Robert Wise on the set of *Star Trek: The Motion Picture*, I, too, was impressed with his quiet demeanor and his soft voice. At that time he was a double Oscar winner twice and one of the world's foremost film directors and producers. After we began our interview in his office on the Paramount lot, it became apparent in many ways that he was just a grown-up little boy from rural Indiana.

He put me at ease, as he must have put hundreds of actors at ease over the years when he was making such films as *The Body Snatcher* (a horror masterpiece), *The Set-Up* (perhaps the finest film on boxing ever made), and his wonderful adaptation of *West Side Story*. These are impressive credentials for three directors, but the versatility of Wise is mirrored throughout his body of work. Like his fellow Hoosier, Howard Hawks, Wise cannot be pigeonholed.

In an American Film Institute seminar in 1980 Wise told students, "People ask me, do I prefer to do musicals to drama or comedy? I like them all. If it's good, exciting, gripping, original material, that's what's important, what counts."

It is indeed fortunate that author Wes Gehring has at last given us a biography that places Wise in the company of other great and distinguished directors who brought their creativity and skill to projects large and small. Wise brought something more than routine treatment to what would have been otherwise routine pictures. His films have explored a whole spectrum of subject matter, from strong personal drama to movies of mass dimensions, but through it all Wise controlled his films with a sure hand and personal vision.

This book provides us with a serious, comprehensive study of a great director. Gehring is a prolific author and a preeminent scholar of motion picture history. He presents compelling evidence for Wise to take a deserved place in the ranks of auteur directors.

After a long career in broadcast television where he wrote and hosted a pioneering movie series titled When Movies Were Movies, *David L. Smith became a professor of telecommunications at Ball State University in Muncie, Indiana. In 1998 he was designated a professor emeritus and has since written two books on movies,* Hoosiers in Hollywood *(2006) and* Sitting Pretty: The Life and Times of Clifton Webb *(2011).*

Preface

As the following pages document, filmmaker Robert Wise, like most popular artists, had formulated a similar creative philosophy at an equally young age. After all, Wise's favorite childhood moments were spent in darkened movie theaters watching the action-adventure comedies of Douglas Fairbanks Sr. But one component of this Wise biography chronicles how such a seemingly simple entertainment philosophy could, on occasion (when it involved Orson Welles or a musical set in Austria), cause controversy.

My personal catalyst, however, for writing this life, is to thoroughly chart the recurring patterns in Wise's pictures. The standard modus operandi on Wise limits him to being a great craftsman. While having professional proficiency is no small achievement, more important, Wise put his signature upon a large divertingly diverse body of work. The consistent themes and characters that link his films have long been neglected by cinema history. A wordsmith might rephrase the opening sentence of this paragraph to read, "My personal catalyst is to write/ right a representation of Wise's life." Sadly, some otherwise wonderful books about Wise's work have minimized his auteur status.[2] Moreover, like many commercial "name" artists, some critics/historians feel more comfortable elevating misfires over milestones, such as John Baxter calling Wise's *Star!* (1968) the director's "most satisfying musical," instead of either *West Side Story* (1961) or *The Sound of Music* (1965).[3]

The case for Wise the auteur might start with his most iconic movie, *The Day the Earth Stood Still* (1951). This science-fiction classic is a landmark antinuclear weapons warning from a Christlike alien who assumes the earthly name of Carpenter. Playing upon populist Frank

Capra overtones, it is reminiscent of *Mr. Smith Goes to Washington* (1939), with laser guns. But unlike Capra's stereotypical "we can work it out" finale, *The Day the Earth Stood Still* closes with the planet's future very much in doubt.

Wise, however, was involved in creating countless earlier watershed films, starting with his Oscar-nominated editing of Orson Welles's *Citizen Kane* (1941). Because his initial home studio was the modest RKO, Wise was allowed to move into directing at a time when a castelike situation existed at the major film factories, á la once an editor always an editor.

Wise is best known for producing and directing two of the most memorable movie musicals in cinema history, *West Side Story* (codirector Jerome Robbins) and *The Sound of Music*, for which he won four Academy Awards—two Best Picture and Best Directors Oscars. Yet, other than Howard Hawks, Wise was arguably Hollywood's most versatile director of various celebrated genre films. For example, his roots in horror go back to a tutelage under the great producer Val Lewton, with Wise directing Boris Karloff's chilling *The Body Snatcher* (1945) for Lewton. Years later Wise brilliantly adapted a Shirley Jackson novel as a homage to Lewton, *The Haunting* (1963). No less a horror aficionado than Stephen King later gave both Jackson's novel (originally titled *The Haunting of Hill House*) and the film his highest praise in his nonfiction study of horror, *Danse Macabre*.

Other pivotal pictures by Wise often qualified for unique status in multiple genres. For example, *The Set-Up* (1949) is both a compelling example of film noir and the problem film—dissecting the sport's brutality and manipulation by the mob. Paradoxically, *Set-Up* is also possibly the best boxing picture ever made. No less an auteur than Martin Scorsese was a huge fan of Wise's work, and he made his fight film, *Raging Bull* (1980), distinctly different from *Set-Up* in order to avoid comparisons with Wise's movie, which won the Critic's Prize at the prestigious Cannes Film Festival. Later film historians were unanimous in their praise for *Set-Up*. In their study of Hollywood in the 1940s, Charles Higham and Joel Greenberg wrote: "The film was staged at night and haunted by a vivid range of nocturnal characters. . . the boxing scenes have a harshness, a sure feeling for cruelty and mob hysteria that have seldom been surpassed."[4]

Along similar multiple genre lines, Wise's *I Want to Live!* (1958, for which Susan Hayward won a Best Actress Oscar) is both a biography film of convicted murder Barbara Graham and a gutsy problem film

Robert Wise directing Marayat Andriane in The Sand Pebbles *(1966).*

against capital punishment. *Somebody up There Likes Me* (1956, with Paul Newman) excels at biography (chronicling the life of boxer Rocky Graziano), the problem film (Graziano's juvenile delinquency youth), and the sport of boxing.

Wise's *The Sand Pebbles* (1966) is an inspired antiwar film keying upon a cynical sailor (Steve McQueen in his only Oscar-nominated role) on a U.S. gunboat in 1926 China. The anti-American imperialism message was really about the country's 1960s involvement in the Vietnam War. Not since Buster Keaton's casting in *The General* (1927) had there been such an organic connection between a star and a giant prop. McQueen's minimalist acting builds upon his relationship with mechanical objects—a nonverbal way of extending his character. *Sand Pebbles* allowed McQueen to define his figure through the care of the gunboat's engine room, just as Keaton had done with his defining maintenance of the steam engine title character The General. The ironic poignancy for both characters (one tragic, one comic), was that each figure preferred the safety/predictability of something mechanical over relationships with chaotic, hurtful humans.

In these movies and many others, Wise brought a consistent auteur mindset to a wide assortment of genres. Auteur status is more readily apparent if one focuses upon a single genre, such as an Alfred Hitchcock thriller or a John Ford Western. But Wise themes and characters are consistent picture to picture: a noirish world (even his musicals feature street gangs and Nazis); a positive handful struggle against a boorish mob; a championing of the often melodramatic plight of women, minorities, and the young; and questioning of the military and all wars, including the domestic collateral damage that accompanied even the "good war" (World War II). Still, Wise characters fight against their fate, even if it is pointless.

This pointlessness, summed up by McQueen's dying words in the defining movie moment of *Sand Pebbles*—"What the hell happened?"—had movingly surfaced throughout Wise's oeuvre. But since *Sand Pebbles* is one of the director's most personalized projects, it can be seen as a microcosm of the dark side in Wise's movies. Starting with the ongoing antiwar message (including the racist subtext inherent to imperialism), *Sand Pebbles* also examines how prejudice often guarantees heartbreak for biracial relationships.

Sand Pebbles provides viewers with two such couples. The conventional romantic variety is played out between an American seaman (Richard Attenborough) and a young forced-into-prostitution Chinese girl (Marayat Andriane). A myriad of circumstances transpire to make this coupling end tragically. Along the way to this sad conclusion, one sees other classic Wise themes. The director is an ardent feminist and Andriane is yet another Wise woman/child protagonist whose life has been an unending melodrama. Hope briefly surfaces in a new relationship (Attenborough), but his death will leave her even more vulnerable.

Another twist on a biracial *Sand Pebbles* couple keys upon Jake (McQueen) and his Chinese assistant Po-Han (Mako, in an Oscar-nominated performance). Though it was common for American naval ships in the Pacific theater in the 1920s to take on Chinese laborers, there was often a racist attitude toward these workers. But McQueen's loner seamen and Po-Han bond over their shared fascination with the care of the ship's engine.

At this time China was in the midst of a civil war involving Chiang Kai-shek's Nationalists, an embryonic Chinese Communist Party, and assorted regional warloads. The one thing these various factions agreed upon, however, was the need to rid China of foreign powers. American forces, such as McQueen's ship, were trying to be international policemen yet somehow remain neutral. Late in the movie the Nationalists kidnap Po-Han and begin to torture him on the beach near the American ship in hopes of provoking a military incident. The captain (Richard Crenna) commands that nothing be done. But a distraught Jake disobeys and, taking a rifle from a fellow sailor, mercifully shoots and kills Po-Han. This violent death, predicated upon a rare instance of McQueen's character letting his emotional guard down, foreshadows Jake's own violent death when he once again comes out of his loner shell. Like the horror and film noir genres in which Wise started his career, survival in the *Sand Pebbles* world is contingent upon doing as little as possible. To get involved with someone and/or something is tantamount to a death sentence.

Despite a dark realism (bordering upon naturalism) that Wise brought to most movie projects, the private man was charmingly upbeat. A proudly passionate liberal, both on screen and off, he championed the extreme long shot in real life, too. Yet, as a true secular humanist, he respected various perspectives, as long as no one's rights were compromised. For example, the Joseph McCarthy-era blacklisting of Hollywood artists during the 1950s was repugnant to him. He fought against this un-American cancer in every way possible, from resisting pressure to drop an alleged "Red" actor from *The Day the Earth Stood Still*, to the use of a blacklisted writer (via "a front") on *Odds Against Tomorrow* (1959). But later in life Wise was able to accept director Elia Kazan as a friend, despite this filmmaker's controversial "friendly witness" status as someone who "named names." Wise agreed with the comments of former blacklisted writer Dalton Trumbo, who stated upon receiving the Writers Guild Laurel Award (1970) for lifetime achievement: "We were all victims because almost without exception each of us felt compelled to say things he did not want to say, to do things he did not want to do, to deliver and receive wounds he truly did not want to exchange. That is why none of us—right, left or center—emerged from that long nightmare without sin."[5]

To borrow a line from critic David Orr, "It's tough to be a Grand Old Man of—well, anything, really."[6] But Wise managed to fill that role for cinema with the same panache as winning Oscars. He gave back to the industry in a multitude of ways, from encouraging and guiding young talent to playing film historian at large, forever providing insights about past screen classics.

Writer C. S. Lewis once observed, "I never read an autobiography in which the parts devoted to the earlier years were not far the most interesting."[7] This sentiment is also frequently applied to

Elia Kazan (center) and Marlon Brando (left) discussing the stool pigeon scene from On the Waterfront *(1954, Kazan's subtextual defense for "naming names").*

biographies. And whether or not the best part of the book in hand addresses the early years, it was certainly the most fun to research. This involved the assistance of several people from Wise's hometown of Centerville, Indiana. From the Connersville Public Library, Fayette County historian Paulette Hayes was invaluable. In the Connersville High School, media teacher Joe Glowacki was equally important, with librarians Kim Giesting and Kathy Caldwell helping me track down Wise's early writing. Plus, two of the filmmaker's high school classmates, Charles and Jackie Heck, were kind enough to grant me a long interview, as well as answer random questions through correspondence.

A number of special collections immeasurably enriched this study: the Robert Wise Collection in the Cinema Arts Library at the University of Southern California in Los Angeles; the Warner Brothers Archive, USC School of Cinema Arts; the Robert Wise clipping files at the Connersville High School; the Margaret Herrick Library, Academy of Motion Picture Arts and Sciences, Beverly Hills, California; the Performing Arts Library, New York Public Library at Lincoln Center, New York; and the microfilm "Tombs" (dead newspaper) section of New York City's Main Library at Fifth Avenue and Forty-Second Street.

Many people made this project possible, starting with Ray E. Boomhower, Indiana Historical Society Press senior editor. I am forever grateful to his support of my writing. Ball State Emeritus Professors Dave Smith and Conrad Lane provided valuable advice during the writing of the manuscript, with Dave also penning the foreword. In Los Angeles historian Anthony Lane, USC archivist Ned Comstack, and film specialists Joe and Maria Pacino were pivotal to this study. Jean Thurman was responsible for the computer preparation of the manuscript. Janet Werrner was a tireless copyeditor. Kris Scott assisted in additional manuscript troubleshooting. My former chairman, "Dr. Joe" Misiewicz, facilitated university financial travel funds. And friends and family were ever so patient and helpful throughout the long process of researching and writing a book. Thank you one and all.

As a final fitting addendum to my subject, I must include this anecdote. As I was doing Wise research at USC, I asked directions to the university's Warner Brothers Archive, located just off campus. I was told to exit the college's main gate and go to Hope Street, where the warehouse structure would be visable. What struck me about the directions, however, were their poetically appropriate description of my subject's work—"It's just beyond Hope."

Prologue
Shadowlands

*"The beginning and end of the business from the author's
point of view is the art of making the audience believe that
real things are happening to real people."*[1]
GEORGE BERNARD SHAW

When RKO's now celebrated producer Val Lewton gave Robert
Wise the opportunity to direct, Lewton gifted his young friend with
a creative blueprint to follow, an essay titled "The Art of Rehearsal."
Written by the great Irish playwright George Bernard Shaw, the above
quote is the text's first major tenet. Wise, a former college journalism
major and a Lewton disciple, was already predisposed toward realism.
Thus, Shaw's essay immediately becomes Wise's guide to directing.
Plus, with Lewton having already applied the playwright's "Art of
Rehearsal" philosophy to the RKO horror picture department in which
Wise found himself, it is hardly surprising that the young filmmaker's
subsequent movies ooze stylized realism.

Shaw's essay, which originally surfaced as the *Collier's Weekly*
essay, "Make Them Do It Well," also includes several leadership tips
that could now double as a description of Wise's directing methods.[2]
While I would hesitate in calling the document Wise's creative Rosetta
Stone (see the Lewton-related chapters, 3 and 4), Shaw's essay could
be a description of Wise at work. The playwright's great emphasis
on a director's thorough preparation would have reinforced Wise's
workaholic blue-collar mentality. Second, unlike a diva director with
whom Wise had already worked (Orson Welles), Shaw suggested that
leadership is *not* being disruptive. Like any parent, one must be forever
sensitive to the players/coworkers: "If a thing is wrong and you don't
know exactly how to set it right, say nothing. Wait until you find
out the right thing to do, or until the actor does. It discourages and
maddens an actor to be told you are dissatisfied. If you cannot help

him, let him alone."[3] As the following pages document, the congenial
Wise was a democratically friendly force on his films, with a Wise
movie set being known in the industry as a professionally pleasant and
efficient work environment.

Third, Shaw's tone is all about nurturing: create a safe rehearsal
zone where it is all right to fail. On more than one occasion he cites the
danger of being a martinet "schoolmaster," noting: "If you get angry,
and complain that you have repeatedly called attention . . . [to some
mistake], like a schoolmaster, you will destroy the whole atmosphere
in which art breathes, and make a scene which is not in the play, and a
very disagreeable and invariably unsuccessful scene at that."[4]

George Bernard Shaw (right) with Charlie Chaplin (circa 1930).

One is tempted to compare actors to children in Shaw's article, an analogy that has existed since the beginning of "pretend." The stereotypical performer is talented but very insecure and needs constant positive strokes—first from a director and then from an audience. A metamorphosis into another character is a very delicate process, like trying to grow up. Consequently, such an actor/child subtext is a helpful interpretation of the director as thoughtful parent. But it is noted here for another reason. An inordinately large number of Wise films involve a childlike protagonist. Wise was known as an "actor's director" (performers felt safe under his leadership—he would not make them look bad), who was also celebrated for his rapport with child actors. Shaw did not necessarily teach Wise those values. But at the least, the essay further encouraged a soft-sell philosophy, especially when Wise's film mentor (Lewton) was already practicing this approach.

Ironically, given this supportive secular humanist method/environment embraced by Wise, his directing break came in an RKO division specializing in horror films. This is a genre known for its nonpopulist slant on the people. That is, not only are its characters capable of unspeakable acts, a sort of mob mentality/fear governs the rest of the populace. But as the opening chapter demonstrates, Wise had an early appreciation of dark comedy, a component frequently inherent to horror. Thus, he thrived in an RKO/Lewton incubator of horror that made his later transition to the studio's other specialized related genre (film noir) a natural, with dark comedy being a pivotal element here, too.

This biography's subtitle, "Shadowlands," is drawn, in part, from both Wise's dark comedy interests and his early directing in horror and film noir. But to come full circle to Shaw's opening quote on "making the audience believe that real things are happening to real people," Wise's ongoing perspective on cinema stories, regardless of the genre, equated realism with a dark worldview. If one of his movie titles could sum up his filmography it would be *Odds Against Tomorrow* (1959). Yes, there are Wise pictures with happy endings but they are usually long shots made palatable by being anchored in true stories, such as *Somebody Up There Likes Me* (1956) or *The Sound of Music* (1965). Even then, as the former title suggests, it feels like an act of God is necessary for a positive outcome—deus ex machina (Latin for "god out of the machine").

Robert Wise's beloved Douglas Fairbanks Sr. (on top), with Charlie Chaplin (left), director Ernst Lubitsch, and Mary Pickford — the three most popular actors of Wise's childhood (circa late 1920s).

The "shadowlands" moniker for Wise also goes beyond the traditional underdog long-shot story. There is a "problem film" component to many of his movies tied to prejudice based upon gender, age, and race. Henry David Thoreau essentially wrote about "shadowlands" when he said, "most men lead lives of quiet desperation." Wise films frequently up the "shadowland" ante by the various prejudice factors.

"Shadowlands" also works as a moniker for a man, like Wise, who was so consumed by his pictures that his personal life was forever under the radar. Like Lewton, Wise was joyfully consumed by his work. This passion for pictures was originally anchored in his Indiana childhood devotion to the silent films of swashbuckling action comedy star Douglas Fairbanks Sr. The actor once described his athletic screen persona, which openly courted the young, as an attempt "to catch the real spirit of youth . . . [which] doesn't take the time to walk around obstacles but hurdles them."[5] While Wise's movies often explored topics impossible to hurdle, his climb from manual laborer at RKO to a multiple Oscar winner has a certain Fairbanks flair.

The Early Years

Robert Wise's (1914–2005) filmmaking
philosophy was also how he lived his life:
"Mine is a prepared approach with ample
room for improvising as we go along."[1]

Robert Wise's practical homework-orientated mindset came
from a heartland beginning. The Oscar–winning director was born
in Richmond, Indiana, on September 10, 1914, just as Europe was
becoming engulfed in World War I. He was the third son of Earl and
Olive "Ollie" Longenecker Wise, who, like most Americans, were more
concerned with building a strong home for their growing family than
foreign wars. The couple had married in their late teens (April 14,
1904), with Lloyd being born in 1905, and David following in 1907.

Earl found a more lucrative way to support his family when Robert
was eight years old. It was early 1923 and the Richmond butcher
jumped at the chance to establish his own meat-packing plant in larger
nearby Connersville (population 9,901 in 1920).[2] Roughly twice the
size of Richmond, Connersville had a booming economy and was then
known as "Little Detroit," given that several pioneering automobiles
(such as the racing Lexington) were made there. The community's
rapid growth was reflected by the fact that young Robert's first year in
the Connersville school system (1922–23) coincided with the highest
enrollment in the city's history.[3]

Connersville, which Wise pinpointed for non-Hoosiers as "halfway between Indianapolis and Cincinnati," was his beloved hometown

Douglas Fairbanks Sr.'s athletic/balletic persona is caught in this pose from The Thief of Bagdad (*1924*).

for the next decade. Fittingly, given the boy's eventual Hollywood career, his favorite pastime was going to the movies. This phenomenon had dramatically increased for the general population, too, given the box-office bonanza produced by Charlie Chaplin's Tramp persona, introduced to film audiences in a series of short subjects the same year Wise was born.

Though a fan of Chaplin's iconic alter ego, Robert was most taken with the comedian's best friend, swashbuckling screen legend Douglas Fairbanks Sr. The handsome, athletic Fairbanks was the "Indiana Jones" of silent cinema. He brought both grace and humor to such groundbreaking action adventure films as *The Mark of Zorro* (1920), *The Three Musketeers* (1921), *Robin Hood* (1922), *The Thief of Bagdad* (1924), and *The Black Pirate* (1926). To adequately gauge Fairbanks impact upon Wise's generation keep in mind that Batman creator Bob Kane credited Fairbanks with being a pivotal influence for his caped crusader, sort of a modern "winged Zorro."[4] In a 1998 interview Wise recalled his own obsession with the actor:

> I was a big fan of Doug Fairbanks, Sr. in those days. He
> was just marvelous and did all of his own stunts and everything.
> I could not wait for his new picture to come out. As a matter of
> fact, I remember once when I was nine or ten his new picture
> had come out. . . [Fairbanks's only new film during that period
> was *The Thief of Bagdad*], and I went that evening to the movies
> to see it. I decided to stay through and see it again. I was half-
> way through it when I felt a heavy hand on my shoulder; my
> older brother [David] had been sent over to drag me home—
> I shouldn't have been out that late looking at movies.[5]

Besides the obvious escapist fun Fairbanks symbolized for young boys such as Wise and Kane, the action star's righting-wrongs persona is seemingly also reflected in Batman's pursuit of justice, and the social themes frequently at the heart of Wise's pictures. *New York Times* critic and later screenwriter Frank S. Nugent beautifully summarized the Fairbanks multifaceted magic for the young, and the young at heart, in a 1939 tribute after the actor's death: "There wasn't a small boy in the neighborhood who did not, in a Fairbanks picture, see himself triumphing over the local bully, winning the soft-eyed adoration of whatever ten-year-old blonde he had been courting, and wreaking vengeance on the teacher who made him stand in the corner that afternoon."[6]

Years before, on the eve of Fairbanks's greatest triumphs (1921), the actor had described his athletic screen persona in a manner that openly courted the young: "In my efforts to portray the . . . American boy . . . I was trying to catch the real spirit of youth . . . the spirit that . . . dashes impetuously at what it wants, that doesn't take the time to walk around obstacles, but hurdles them—the fine, restless, impatient, conquering spirit of youth."[7]

Both Wise and Kane would, however, later couch their own variations on Fairbanks justice, and/or simply enthusiastically embracing one's personal salvation, in a noirish world that suggested hope might be a commodity on the way out. After his retirement, Wise briefly touched upon this dichotomy when accepting the American Film Institute's Lifetime Achievement Award: "I fell under the spell of the movies [early]. They show us the best we are capable of and the dangers to avoid. I hope I've made a small difference."[8]

In addition to Fairbanks's mesmerizingly athletic movie image, the actor also courted the young with a groundbreaking series of inexpensive popular self-help books for boys. Though actually ghostwritten with his personal secretary, Kenneth Davenport, the practical advice about discipline and being all you can be are consistent with Fairbanks's mindset and movies. With titles such as *Laugh and Live* and *Making Life Worthwhile*, the books entertainingly preached a regimen that played particularly well to Middle America. For example, in the former text Fairbanks encourages an ongoing celebration of "*inner determination*" that "once firmly implanted in one's nature, cannot be destroyed or conquered."[9] But this "seize the day" mentality is alive in various ways on every page of these books, from praising life experience, "horse sense," to encouraging scholarship: "These men [like Lincoln] made eternal friends of certain great thinkers and drank in their learning with all the fervor of their natures."[10] These are sentiments that would not have been out of place coming from the award-winning Wise, such as the director's late-in-life summation of his career: "I think many of my films have an importance to them in what they say about man and his condition and the world around him, how he faces it and overcomes it. I always want my films to have a comment to make."[11]

The young Wise's fascination with Fairbanks, and movies in general, was also fueled by the sheer volume of cinema then available. Unlike today, when new films traditionally open on Friday, the small-town world of Wise's childhood frequently saw *three* movie changes a week. The theater schedule was often prestige pictures playing Sunday to Tuesday, B films and children's matinee serials on Friday and Saturday, and the offbeat, hard-to-pigeonhole films Wednesday and Thursday.

While Wise's childhood screening habit of seeing three movies a week remains impressive, given the period's quick turnover of pictures and Connersville's then three theaters, he had had a great deal of films from which to choose. Three picture houses, however, did give the Connersville film fans some leeway on the weekly schedule noted above. That is, the city's Vaudette theater had a greater propensity to play boy-pleasing action adventure films such as Westerns starring Tom Mix, Hoot Gibson, and Buck Jones—three of Wise's cowboy favorites. Connersville's Lyric theater focused upon prestige releases such as Lon Chaney in *Laugh Clown Laugh*, and King Vidor's *The Crowd* (which both played there in July 1928).[12] The Auditorium's film fare fell between these two extremes, but the theater's special draw was its added attraction of vaudeville acts on Friday and Saturday. All three theaters were within easy walking distance of the Wise home at 520 Eastern Avenue. Providentially, when Wise's oldest brother, Lloyd, and his father opened a meat market in 1928, the shop was on the same block (Central Avenue) as the children's matinee friendly Vaudette. While one can imagine Robert dropping by the family business to panhandle movie money from his father, it might not have been a hard sell. Earl and Ollie enjoyed taking their boys to Indianapolis on Sunday for dinner and a movie.[13]

Though the practical Wise initially decided to turn his creative interest in writing toward journalism instead of the movies, being a Hoosier in Hollywood was then less of a long shot. One could almost say there was an Indiana pipeline to filmland during the silent era, ranging from Wise's Western heroes such as Maynard and Jones, to Fairbanks's *Thief of Bagdad* leading lady Julanne Johnston. Several Hollywood Hoosiers, such as Jones (Vincennes's most famous entertainer until Red Skelton), made a point of working with transplanted Indiana natives, including a young Carole Lombard.[14]

In 1928 this movie migration took on a more personal slant for Wise. That year his older brother, David, went to Hollywood, and his eventual behind-the-scenes employment at RKO ultimately was the catalyst for brother Robert's move west in 1933. Yet, until just prior to Wise's economy-driven exit for California, being a newspaper man had been his goal.

Thankfully, there is a time-tripping window back to young Wise the journalist—his columns for his high school newspaper, *The Clarion*. Moreover, keep in mind this was no ordinary senior high publication. Wise's school newspaper, which also included the nationally syndicated work of prominent columnists and cartoonists, could easily have passed as a medium-sized metropolitan publication. The future filmmaker's humor column, "Wise Crax," was a forum in which the teenager addressed an assortment of subjects, from his beloved basketball (seemingly a basic component of Indiana DNA), to provocative pop-culture references, such as a poem to be recited "to the tune of [Cab Calloway's street saga] of 'Minnie the Moocher.'"[15]

Wise's comic writing was not unlike that of celebrated period humorist Robert Benchley, who was also a popular screen personality of the 1930s and 1940s. In drawing from a sampling (all from 1932) of both these Roberts, several parallels became apparent. Each has a democratic desire to be pleasingly honest, and initially hopeful. Thus, Benchley optimistically begins a piece upon stress between strangers: "Nobody would like to see the Brotherhood of Man come to pass any more than I would, for I am not a very good fighter and even have difficulty holding my own in a battle of repartee. I am more the passive type, and I would be glad to have everybody else passive, too. But I am afraid that can't be done."[16] That same year Wise wrote, "We hate to disappoint some of you. In fact, it is entirely against our policy to disappoint anybody, but the time has come."[17]

Both of these vulnerable antiheroic humorists had, however, a dark side that was often driven by the boorish behavior of others. Wise devoted part of a column to inappropriate audience actions: "After seeing that Jeff [basketball] game we have about decided that a lot of fans could stand a few lessons on 'How to Act at a Ball Game.'"[18] In a later column he then ironically applauded "the new permanent bleachers in the gym. Lots more room to kick the [rude] fellows in front of you in the back."[19] Benchley took his Emily Post payback to a more black humor extreme: "I once heard a woman laugh at that most tragic moment in all drama, the off-stage shot in 'The Wild Duck,' and I afterward had her killed, so there will be no more of that out of *her*."[20] Of course, Wise could be equally surreal in his inspired use of dark comedy: "Our idea of an unpleasant surprise—trying to pull the big roller down at the tennis courts. After an unsuccessful attempt one gets

Robert Benchley, one of America's favorite humorists during the 1930s and 1940s.

the impression that the darn thing must be filled with the dead bodies of every tennis player that ever lived, to say nothing of dead balls and old rackets. Fear not. . . . It is filled with some kind of sand. And what sand!"[21]

Given the topic of boorish behavior, one should note that Wise came of age in an era dripping with satirical commentary on provincial small-town values/prejudices, from the novels of Sinclair Lewis to such iconic Grant Wood paintings as *American Gothic* (1930). Artists such as Lewis, Wood, and critic H. L. Mencken (who christened conservative middle-class Americans the "booboisie") could be called that period's *The Daily Show with John Stewart*. Like today, younger people are often attracted to edgy antiestablishment entertainment. Fittingly, while Wise's later movies, regardless of genre, usually include some figure of hope, his general picture of humanity is often as damning as that of Lewis, Wood, and Mencken, or Wise's favorite humorist, Mark Twain. Wise's Benchley-like dark-comedy musings are his first expression of this shared mindset.

Benchley and Wise also had casually charming manners for refusing to take themselves any more seriously than their target subjects. One might label their technique "parentheses second thoughts." Consequently, more macabre merriment by Benchley had him observing, "People interested in murders (and who, aside possibly from the victims themselves, is not interested in murders?)."[22] Along similarly self-conscious comic lines, the nonworking Wise wrote, "We would have given a week's salary (what salary?) to have seen [track star] Stranahan's face."[23]

All in all, Benchley and Wise were often timid nonathletes emboldened-by-words voyeurs who fought a fifth-column comic action against an insensitive real world. Over time, Benchley, the veteran, focused his amusing defensive diversions in high-profile screen appearances. In contrast, Wise did just the opposite, as a major Hollywood director his future metaphorical "Wise Crax" would be sublimated through social statements in an assortment of film genres.

So what was Wise like away from his newspaper platform? High school classmates Jackie Mabee and Charles Heck, long since married and still living in Connersville in 2009, remembered the director "as a quiet student but easy to talk to."[24] In a lengthy interview with the couple, they described a boy obsessed with the movies, a good student (all three youngsters were in college-prep classes not available to mediocre students), and a family-like social scene where "group dating" was the norm. This small-town casual interaction is borne out in one of the letters Wise later wrote to the Hecks. In chronicling the Washington, D.C., premiere of his award-winning musical *West Side Story*, sponsored by First Lady Jackie Kennedy for the benefit of the Institute of Contemporary Arts, Wise shared a pleasing surprise: "It turned out that the Director of the Institute is our old classmate Robert Richman. When Bob saw the information he immediately called me wanting to know for sure if this was the same Robert Wise who graduated from CHS. We talked by phone and saw each other on a couple of different occasions in Washington for long periods of time."[25]

Then, as now, the formal dance "prom" was the big event for Connersville High School. But the Hecks shared their era's propensity to throw numerous informal parties, especially around scavenger and/ or treasure-hunt themes. When I asked the couple about popular hangouts, they both mentioned a downtown ice cream parlor, the "Ideal." But in a later letter, Jackie added: "a more popular [meeting place] was the 'Elliott-Hood' Drugstore, which was across the street from the high school. There was also a [nearby] drugstore named 'Spicely's.' Both of these were very popular . . . after school was out. Not having cars of our own we couldn't do much running around."[26]

Besides shared free time at the drugstores, the Hecks and Wise had other common interests. All three were members of the Aeneid (poetry) club, with young Robert and Jackie also being in the various school choruses. Given that the musical genre later led to four Academy Awards for Wise, the Hecks revealed a telling entertainment fact. The theatrical event of the 1920s was the visit by a world-famous European singer, which the city's front-page newspaper coverage chronicled as the "Golden Voice and the Woman Make Schumann-Heink [a] Truly Great Artist."[27] With a repertoire ranging from "Erlkonig" (Schubert) to "Danny Boy," the capacity audience at the then new high school auditorium gave Madame Schumann-Heink almost "a continuous ovation."[28]

Equally beloved for her lack of ego and earthy humor, something Wise would also undoubtedly have appreciated, one such Schumann-Heink tale from her Connersville visit was told and retold locally through the years: "When she appeared here . . . she was trying to get her well upholstered bulk through a narrow doorway and was advised, 'Try it sideways,' she exclaimed, 'Mein Gott! I haf no sideways.'"[29]

Wise's fascination with performers, from cinema's Fairbanks to road-show visitors such as Schumann-Heink, belied his own thespian fears about being in front of an audience. Nearly sixty years after the director's graduation, when the Connersville School Board decided to name the high school auditorium after him (1990), Wise shared these anxieties with a media instructor at his alma mater: "Joe Glowaski said Wise talked about when he never thought he was good enough to be on stage. Instead, he worked behind the stage all the time. Wise said he regretted [not acting] . . . because having the experience of being directed by someone on stage may have helped him along as a director."[30]

While one cannot change the past, the driven director attempted to keep other young artists from making the same mistake. On the 2005 DVD voice-over track for his film *The Body Snatcher* (1945), Wise advised young filmmakers: "I always tell students who think they want to direct, while you're here [in school], find some time to go over to the theater department and get in some stage plays. And find out how it is from an actor's standpoint to be up there . . . [on the stage]. I think that will help you very much in your directing career."[31]

Still, to play devil's advocate, maybe Wise's acting fears made him more a pure student of performance, teaching him to better appreciate what he would need from his film actors. Regardless, for the consummate professional Wise, it was never too late to play catch up. In the early 1940s, on the verge of directing opportunities (after a seminal RKO editing career that included an Oscar nomination for *Citizen Kane*, 1941), Wise began to audit acting classes.

Coupled with this midwestern work ethic, further encouraged by the Great Depression, Wise and his classmates were given an unexpected tutorial on cooperation. Only four weeks into their senior year, what was described at the time as a "fiery catastrophe" (October 2, 1931) gutted Connersville High School.[32] From October to mid-April, high school students had half-day afternoon sessions at the junior high building, while the largely destroyed structure was rebuilt. This education in shifts was not only a catalyst for the power of making do—travail as the crucible that redeems—but the new, improved facility also produced, according to the student yearbook, both a greater appreciation of and "a more sentimental feeling for their school . . . [and] after six months they were 'at home' again."[33] Still, given Wise's dark sense of humor and prominent involvement on the yearbook staff, the "Wise Crax" columnist probably had something to do with the title selected for the 1931–32 yearbook, the *Senior Siren*.

During this problematic school year, a beautiful, young, dynamic English and drama teacher, Pearl Bartley, joined the faculty. She became a creative arts force at the school and in the community for the next forty years, including being the longtime sponsor and director of the "Strut and Fret" plays.[34] Though Mabee, Heck, and Wise only had contact with Bartley during their senior year, nearly eighty years later the Hecks immediately named her as the teacher who had made the greatest impact upon their graduating class.[35]

In addition to the classroom, Wise worked behind the scenes on at least one theater production directed by Bartley. She might also have given stage directions to the future filmmaker in a Connersville High School production (1931–32) of *Miss Cherry Blossom*, a Japanese comic operetta in which Wise was part of the chorus. This play was "very popular with American High School theatre departments of the 1920s and 1930s, not unlike *Bye Bye Birdie* is today," noted Kim Giesting, present-day librarian at the high school.[36] Bartley would presumably have directed *Blossom*, but surviving records only document Wise's involvement.[37]

The full extent of this teacher/director's influence upon Wise is undoubtedly lost in the proverbial "cracks of time." But it seems safe to assume that, at the very least, Bartley would have reinforced Wise's interest in the dramatic arts, and possibly even impacted the decidedly feminist direction of many of his later films, including Valentina Cortese moving from World War II refugee to film-noir survivor in *The House on Telegraph Hill* (1951), or the Jane Wyman teacher who raises her son to be self-sufficient in the 1953 adaptation of Edna Ferber's novel *So Big*. Regardless, one might couple this Bartley connection with a comment Wise made near the end of his life: "[Success is a combination of talent] and the people we meet along the way, that help us . . . [grow, and] I had that throughout my career."[38]

Interestingly, maybe Wise's signature feminist movie, *I Want to Live!* (1958) had another tie-in with the future director's senior year, besides the influential Bartley. *Live* was a strong anti-capital punishment picture based upon the true story of Barbara Graham, a promiscuous party girl habitually tied to petty crime. Implicated in a drawn-out murder case that ultimately sent her to the San Quentin gas chamber, criminal law experts are still debating Graham's innocence. (The Los Angeles police department even put pressure upon Wise to drop the project.) The director's acclaimed biographical melodrama stressed that no one deserved to go through the cruel and unusual punishment of the death penalty, especially with the frequent eleventh-hour stays of execution.

Wise's passionate feelings about this subject (*Live* was one of his two favorite films, along with *The Set-Up*, 1949[39]), might date from two murder trials that paralleled his graduation from high school. Both cases were given front-page coverage in the *Connersville News-Examiner*, and each was a heartland tragedy (Crown Point, Indiana, and Rockford, Illinois). One of the men/boys sentenced to death was Wise's age (seventeen, the other only twenty-three), and the "news" factor for both was not the question of guilt or innocence but rather the death penalty itself.[40] Indeed, the convicted seventeen-year-old (Russell McWilliams) was sentenced to death in the electric chair despite the fact that the famous and much honored lawyer Clarence Darrow "had pleaded his cause and eminent social workers had interceded because of his youth."[41] An added connection with Wise's later problem film was that McWilliams had also been given a temporary high-profile stay of execution.

Granted, these potential links to *Live* are conjecture. But the two cases generated a great deal of public interest/sympathy at a very impressionable time for Wise. Moreover, despite his love of film and theater, at this point Wise wanted to be a journalist. He was just a few months away from being a freshman at nearby Franklin College. This hardworking student would have been all over these capital punishment news stories. Fittingly, *Live* is just one of many Wise films that has a muckraking journalistic tone.

If one were looking for a more overt connection between the Connersville of 1932 and Wise's later liberal tendencies, the much-admired commencement address that year would be a better starting place. The popular Hoosier speaker, Purdue University's Louis M. Sears, took the bicentennial of George Washington's birth (1732 to 1932) as his focus. He discussed the importance of both friendship and humor to the first president. But toward the speech's conclusion, Sears "called attention to [and expanded upon] the deep affection Washington had for his colored servant, Billy Lee, and whom he regarded as a friend rather than a servant."[42]

Wise's later pictures often showcased the tragedy of racism, such as the underrated crime film *Odds Against Tomorrow* (1959, with Harry Belafonte), the Nazi evil of *The Sound of Music* (1965), and the doomed interracial couple in *The Sand Pebbles* (1966). It would be simplistic, though hardly outside the realm of possibility, to suggest that one memorable speech to an activist-orientated teenager would make such a racial tolerance impact. However, the importance of said speech

resonates more if one simply scores its racial tolerance theme as yet
another example of the culturally open-minded community in which
Wise was reared.

I am reminded of an observation by film critic David Thomson
in his book *Try To Tell the Story: A Memoir*: "Handling fear is a step
towards art."[43] Wise loved to fold a message into a movie. But he
was not a starry-eyed populist, à la a young Frank Capra. Wise often
portrayed *the people* with all the frightening negativity of which they
are capable, from the angry hateful faces of a ringside fight crowd in his
other favorite film, *Set-Up,* to a film noir femme fatale (Claire Trevor)
responding to a murder scene into which she has stumbled (*Born
to Kill,* 1947) with no more surprise than discovering someone had
rearranged the magazines on her coffee table. Wise acknowledged man's
dark side very effectively. But he realized bad things often come out
of fear—reacting violently to what is different, misunderstood, and/or
simply perceived as a threat.

One could argue that Wise also felt that "handling fear is a step
towards art." The trick for the filmmaker, which he navigated so
successfully when playing the racial card, was a challenge with which
all socially conscience artists wrestle: "How do you make an adventure
out of a sermon?"[44] Wise often sold these "adventures" by playing them
realistically. That is, most of *the crowd* is neither fully cognizant of the
pain they cause, nor how they propagate the suffering. Consequently,
unlike Capra populism (whose basic supposition was that people are
inherently good and deserving of a redemptive second chance), Wise's
often noirish film world, at best, merely allows such insight to a select
few. Even then, there is no guarantee of redemption.

So where is the feel good, take-a-stand payoff for the art of this
former journalism major? One might liken it to secular humanism—
you act accordingly because it is the right thing to do. Given that
Wise's most iconic film was the hopeful science-fiction classic *The Day
the Earth Stood Still* (1951), maybe an H. G. Wells analogy would be
appropriate. The literary father figure of serious science-fiction/fantasy

was a firm believer in Charles Darwin's writings on evolution. But Wells felt man's inherent prejudicial fears sentenced him to an eventual self-destructive fate. Yet, Wells still wanted to believe in hope. At the end of his watershed novella *The Time Machine* (1895), the time traveler has returned to a distant nightmare future on an almost suicidal mission to somehow alter one possible "survival of the fittest" scary scenario. The story's narrator then rehashes the traveler's previous reservations, ironically, about man's iffy future. If so, why did the traveler go? The narrator's poignant conclusion might have doubled as a mantra for Wise's work: "If that is so [man's prejudices and superstitions will eventually destroy him], it remains for us to live as through it were not."[45]

2

A Career Detour: 1930s Hollywood

*Robert Wise later described his teenage (1933) visit to RKO
in search of a job, "I was a little kid from the middle of Indiana;
my eyes were like saucers. I took advantage of the fact that I got
inside for the interview just to walk around the studio."[1]*

The teenage Robert Wise wanted to be a journalist. Although
fascinated by the movies and the dramatic arts, his shyness made
it easier for him to be creative via the printed page. In 1978 he
remembered: "I'd worked for my father first in his meat packing plant
and then in his store, and I decided right then I didn't want to get into
anything where I had to deal one-on-one with the public."[2]

Wise was sports editor of his high school newspaper, wrote a
humor column for the same publication, and was a member of both
the yearbook staff and the poetry club. Coupled with his dark sense of
humor and liberal-cause nature, being a muckraking journalist seemed
a natural career for the college-bound youngster.

Wise left Connersville for nearby Franklin College (in Franklin,
Indiana), twenty miles south of Indianapolis, at arguably the darkest
point of the Great Depression (fall 1932). After the stock market crash
of late 1929, Herbert Hoover's presidency had struggled with all facets
of this worldwide economic collapse. Like Jimmy Carter, Hoover is
now rightfully celebrated for his humanitarian work while *not* residing
in the White House, such as orchestrating the feeding of a starving
Europe after both world wars.

Sadly Hoover did not seem up to the bold new measures called for by such drastic times. Worse yet, his actions sometimes made his administration seem blunderingly callous. For example, during the spring of Wise's senior year in high school, thousands of World War I veterans from across the country marched on Washington, D.C. Years before (1924) Congress had overridden a presidential veto to grant these men a bonus in the form of a paid-up twenty-year insurance policy. Now this unemployed "Bonus Army" was demanding either early payment, or asking for loans against the value of the certificates. While waiting for action, these men and their families proceeded to camp out in the capital, creating another "Hooverville" (the satirical Depression-era term for the muddy shantytowns of the unemployed that peppered the nation). Decades later Albert Marrin movingly described Depression migrants with further irony as "tin-can tourists," who became "refugees in their own lands."[3]

In 1932 the U.S. Senate voted down the bonus bill, though Congress allowed the veterans to borrow enough money for transportation home. By July this so-called army had dwindled to between 7,000 to 10,000 in size. Hoover, anxious for this ongoing in-the-shadow-of-the White House embarrassment to go away, ordered the squatters evicted. When violence broke out, the administration called in the army under General Douglas MacArthur. With machine guns, tanks, and tear gas, the veterans and their families were driven from the area, with all the makeshift housing and possessions therein burned to the ground. Whatever one's feelings about the legality of the veterans' demands, or their mere squatters' rights in the capital, this incident became a metaphor for Hoover's seeming indifference and even hostility toward America's Depression poor.

The resulting media Waterloo for Hoover further guaranteed the election of liberal Democrat Franklin D. Roosevelt to the presidency in the fall of 1932. Roosevelt carried Indiana and most of the nation in one of the country's most sweeping landslides. Even before the election, Roosevelt had dramatically broken precedent by accepting his party's convention nomination in person (a proactive gesture for desperate times), in heartland Chicago. His pledge for progressive change to those delegates soon became America's mantra: "Let it . . . be symbolic that. . . I broke traditions. Republican leaders not only have failed in material things, they have failed in national vision, because in disaster they have held out no hope . . . . I pledge you, I pledge myself, to a new deal for the American people."[4]

The Roosevelt backstory merits belaboring because Wise was already coming out of a progressive community and school system with decidedly liberal views. The New Deal philosophy, therefore, would have further encouraged a climate of thinking outside the box for all citizens on a myriad of subjects. If history teaches us anything, it is that drastic change in one venue, be it social and/or political, inevitably spills into another, from public mores to the popular arts. Wise started college during the most intellectually stimulating of times. (As a footnote to these developments, the mere origins of Roosevelt's phrase "New Deal" would have caught Wise's interest. Like this young humor-loving Hoosier, the president was a great fan of Mark Twain's 1889 novel *A Connecticut Yankee in King Arthur's Court.* The phrase "New Deal" comes from this novel.)

Being a Depression-era Franklin College student would have been another catalyst for open-mindedness, since this small liberal arts institution had forever accented the term liberal. For example, Franklin was the first Indiana college to admit women as students (1834), and only the seventh to do so in the nation. The school recognized Wise early as one of its own by providing a modest scholarship for his freshman year. Unfortunately, tough times sabotaged the boy's long-term college career. Wise later recalled that, besides the Franklin funds, "My family managed to scrape together enough money [his mother's savings] to help me through the first year, but the second year it looked like it was going to be impossible. It was mid-Depression, my father's [meat] business was kind of on the rocks and there wasn't any money for that second year of school."[5]

A backup career plan soon presented itself courtesy of a visit from
Wise's brother, David, an accountant at RKO. This was the young
man's first visit home since heading west in 1928. Though David's
initial filmland job was simply as a day laborer, his rapid ascension was
no doubt assisted by the father of a high school friend, Joseph Schilling,
who managed Connersville's three film theaters at a time when the
various Hollywood studios controlled America's movie theaters. (The
U.S. Supreme Court negated this type of chain monopoly immediately
after World War II.) Schilling provided several effective letters of
recommendation for his son, Harry, and for David. After a family
meeting, it was decided that Wise's brother would attempt to continue
this Hollywood Hoosier pipeline. By late July the two brothers were
Hollywood bound. "After we were out in LA," Wise later recalled, "my
brother got me an appointment with the head of [RKO's] property
department. And fortunately, as it turns out, he couldn't use anybody
right then and the next week he got me an appointment with the head
of the film [sound] editing department. . . . [After a a stint in studio
shipping] editing was my break—getting into that department."[6]

Not surprisingly, David would be the brother with whom Wise
remained the closest. In later years Wise bankrolled a Hollywood
restaurant partnership with his brother. Ever the methodical research-
oriented director, Wise spent a great deal of "study" time at their
eatery while preparing to make *Remember the Night* (1957), a movie
about a soft-hearted tough guy's (Paul Douglas) restaurant/nightclub.
Interestingly, Douglas's age and appearance at this time were similar to
Wise's, with the character actor's ingratiating screen persona matching
the occasional Wise testimonials that surface in this book.

Before Wise jumped at a chance to direct in the 1940s, this
break in RKO's sound-editing department led to the transplanted
Hoosier receiving an Academy Award film editing nomination for
Orson Welles's groundbreaking movie *Citizen Kane* (1941). But a
greater break was simply landing at RKO. Besides RKO's newcomer-
friendly approach and small studio status, it did not have the caste-like

department rigidity that was the norm at the prestige picture factories such as Metro-Goldwyn-Mayer and Paramount.

Given RKO's not quite A-picture reputation, moreover, the studio's unofficial production philosophy had evolved into something not unlike the survivor instincts of this young midwesterner who had just dropped into their midst—a strong work ethic, creative with the materials at hand (such as maximizing RKO's rare expensive A film sets for the studio's B pictures), and a willingness to take artistic risks. In fact, RKO's signature example of the latter point involved Welles. His controversial Halloween Eve 1938 radio adaptation of H. G. Wells's science-fiction classic *War of the Worlds* put the young artist on the national map.

Welles moved the original novel from turn-of-the-century England to contemporary East Coast America. But *the* provocative twist involved presenting this invasion of Martian monsters as if it was really happening. Using a live dance music dummy radio program as a front, fake "news" bulletins periodically interrupted the orchestra with unfolding alien attack updates. While an announcer had opened the production with the bald statement this was a *War of the Worlds* adaptation, many listeners tuning in later, or merely sampling the various radio dial offerings, were frighteningly fooled. Panicking a nation got the attention of RKO.

The studio gave movie novice Welles a carte blanche contract to create similar magic in the movies—a then unprecedented roll of the dice by RKO. The watershed *Citizen Kane* was the result, and another memorable filmmaker, French New Wave pioneer Francois Truffaut, later beautifully articulated how important it had been for Welles to succeed, given both RKO's faith in him and how the rest of veteran Hollywood was actively rooting against this rookie: "[He] must have felt that it was necessary to offer the public not only *a good film* but *the* film, one that would summarize forty years of cinema while taking the opposite course to everything that had been done, a film that would be at once . . . a declaration of war on traditional [Hollywood] cinema and a declaration of love for the medium."[7] Welles and Wise, also a pivotal part of the *Citizen Kane* production, worked for a studio that inspired artists to greatness.

Ironically, the 1933 Hollywood arrival of the liberal young Wise paralleled the push for tougher film regulation by the Catholic Church's powerful Legion of Decency censorship organization. Initially, movies had seemed to be "Depression Proof," since the economic collapse had caused people "to seek out escapism more ardently than ever."[8] But by 1931–32, Hollywood's box office had dropped. Thus, in search of an increased audience, film content became more provocative, from the violence of a new genre (the modern gangster picture), to the sexual innuendo of a new star (Mae West). Couple these developments with the added pressure of policing "talking pictures," a technological development that coincided with the stock market crash, and middle America started demanding more restrictions on the content of Hollywood pictures. Granted, the progressive Wise was already predisposed to bristle at such desecration of the artistic process. But one can only assume that his arrival in Hollywood, just as a censorship code was forced on an industry fearful of federal intervention, would have made Wise even more passionate about the subject. Many years later Wise noted, "I abhor any kind of censorship in films. I feel that films, books and plays should all be presented at whatever level the creator deems necessary. I think that those who wish to go to pornographic films should have the right to; nobody makes them go to see them."[9] For an artist who later gave the world the ultimate feel good "spoonful of sugar" musical film, *The Sound of Music* (1965), one can safely say Wise had no self-serving agenda linked to his strong anticensorship views.

On a personal level, however, the still teenaged Wise of 1933 would also have been threatened monetarily by a censorship code. After just arriving in Hollywood, and luckily acquiring the most modest of entry-level positions, the morality police were suddenly menacing all movie-related jobs. That is, the studio system, like most other major American corporations during the Great Depression, was in a tenuous situation.

For example, RKO's parent company went into receivership in 1933. Consequently, Hollywood feared that a censorship code would destroy whatever movie market remained.

Wise also would have been aware of how even precode morality issues were beginning to restrict the screen persona of a favorite actress, West. Who or what was West? She most resembled a female impersonator, with the verbal wit of Oscar Wilde. Armed with this repartee, West, a small, pleasantly plump, over-forty physical form (through platform shoes and padded 1890s gowns of hourglass proportions), somehow metamorphosed into an inventive parody of sex, transforming an appearance into a performance.

Mae West and Cary Grant in She Done Him Wrong *(1933).*

Though conservative America was offended by early West pictures
such as *She Done Him Wrong* (1933, which prevented Paramount
from going broke), the film industry got it, as well as appreciated
her Depression-era boost to a sagging box office. While *Wrong's*
controversial success helped to fuel the reinvention of the American
censorship code in 1934, which attempted to homogenize West, the
enlightened left continued to celebrate her comic artistry throughout
the 1930s. Late in the decade, pioneering cinema historian Lewis
Jacobs even championed in his seminal work, *The Rise of the American
Film*, an early argument for a feminist defense of the actress (which
would have resonated with Wise) along sexual lines: "Mae West averred
that women get just as much pleasure out of sexual contact as men . . .
[and] that the female can reverse the old custom and cajole the male . . .
Mae West eyed a man from head to foot. All the time you knew she
was evaluating him in terms of virility, as James Cagney eyed a woman.
Neither had any use or time for camouflage. . . . Both knew what they
were after, let you know it, and were intent in their playfulness."[10]

While Wise was never remotely in a position to work with the
legendary West during the 1930s, he never gave up on the possibility.
Decades later (1968) he helped orchestrate a University of Southern
California salute to the actress. Around this time Wise also signed West
to an exclusive contract for a television special. This was no small task,
since West had reservations about the medium, noting: "I've never
liked the idea of television, because people can turn you off."[11] Though
funding issues kept the special from being produced, West and Wise
hit it off. Two of her biographers later said of this friendship, "She
concluded he understood what she was all about," and then shared the
actress's own humorous third-person take on Wise: "'Going from [*The
Sound of Music's* almost nun] Julie Andrews to [brothel broad] Mae
West—he's certainly versatile.'"[12]

Another tangential link between Wise and the 1934 code involved
several of his predirecting assignments at RKO, including being an
apprentice sound effects editor on *The Gay Divorce* (1934, the first

major movie pairing of Fred Astaire and Ginger Rogers), moving to film editing assistant on *Carefree* (1938) and *Bachelor Mother* (1939), and being promoted to film editor on pictures such as *My Favorite Wife* (1940). All these films have farcical/screwball overtones, with the latter a definitive example of the genre.[13] Moreover, producer Pandro S. Berman, who teamed Astaire and Rogers, later even described their musical collaborations as screwball comedies set to song and dance.[14]

So how does screwball comedy connect to Wise and the first year (1934) of the code? The genre's emergence is now seen as having direct links to these restrictions. No one is suggesting that Hollywood bosses called an industry huddle and created screwball comedy. But American censorship, even then, has always been more concerned with sexuality than with violence. So it hardly seems a coincidence that a genre (screwball) later referred to as "the sex comedy without sex" (safe titillation) should blossom the same year the code appeared. Benchmarks include Howard Hawks's *Twentieth Century* and Frank Capra's *It Happened One Night* (both 1934). But there were screwball overtones in assorted genres, from the aforementioned musical *The Gay Divorce*, to the sleeper hit adaptation of Dashiell Hammett's celebrated comic couple-driven murder mystery novel *The Thin Man* (1934). Wise's Hollywood arrival not only paralleled this censorship transition, his early work was often in farcical films that were a response to the code. (Coincidentally, several prominent screwball players were from Wise's home state. For instance, the aforementioned *Twentieth Century* was directed by Indiana-born Hawks and launched the career of Carole Lombard.)

To further play devil's advocate, one could argue that this screwball influence was even a factor in Wise's later film-noir work as a director, such as his cult classic *Born to Kill* (1947, from the novel *Deadlier Than the Male*). Noir is a first cousin to screwball comedy. Both genres often focus on a controlling woman. But whereas the screwball female manipulates the male out of an obsessive love, the noir femme fatale's obsession is deadly self-interest. Each genre is also anchored in a showcase of the wealthy good life, and how all those riches seem to make people crazy funny in screwball and crazy killers in noir. Fittingly, Wise's natural dark comedy tendencies further complement both genres.

Regardless of these big-picture thoughts on Wise's career, there were a number of fundamentals he learned during his early RKO years. One of the most basic came from being an assistant to the studio's head sound-effects cutter, T. K. Wood. The veteran sound man eventually rescued Wise from his foray in RKO's shipping room. Though shipping large film cans was essentially manual labor, Wood admired Wise's work ethic and invited him to join the sound-effects department. The two men became instant friends, a link forged in their mutual workaholic natures. Starting with Wood in 1934, Wise relished the film overload RKO threw at the department, especially one memorable blitzkrieg to prepare for the sneak preview of George Stevens's *Alice Adams* (1935). The pace was always busiest during RKO's first three months of the year—the most hectic time for postproduction departments such as sound effects. During these ninety days, Wise worked "seven days a week, twelve to fourteen hours a day. In some instances, he would literally toil around the clock."[15] Undoubtedly, such nonstop attention to detail would have been great training for the overwhelming demands of being a film director. At this time Wise learned a key lesson from his first RKO mentor: "Raw film, Wood told him, is the cheapest component of a motion picture. Wise says he has never hesitated to shoot 10,000 feet a day if he felt that much footage might be needed for a proper result."[16]

Such an admission might seem odd coming from a director who had graduated from editing. One might assume a former cutter would have such a heightened notion of individual shots that he or she would have a sense of economy with regard to the amount of film footage needed. Ironically, this tip about raw stock being the "cheapest component of a motion picture" seems to be true of several editors-directors. A Wise contemporary, acclaimed British filmmaker Sir David Lean, who also worked his way up the 1930s production ladder to editor, including the occasional farcical material (*Pygmalion,*

1938), eventually embraced shooting a great deal of footage as a director, too, such as for *The Bridge on the River Kwai* (1957) and *Doctor Zhivago* (1965). The added shot selection made possible by extra reels of raw film increased an artist's chances of editing the material into a masterpiece. But exposing miles of film can sometimes lead to pictures that seem equally long. Critic David Thomson wrote, "Lean [eventually] became lost in the sense of his pictorial grandeur . . . [a] prisoner of big pictures."[17] To a certain degree, this same fate hampered Wise's own later "big pictures," such as *The Andromeda Strain* (1971) and *Star Trek: The Motion Picture* (1979).

A sense of Wise the editor always remained. Paradoxically, this is best demonstrated by an affectionate anecdote from novelist Michael Crichton, whose book was the basis for *Andromeda*. The always sensitive Wise avoided having writers adapt their work to the screen, given the sometimes painful reality that the movie medium often necessitates changes in telling the story. Yet, the thorough director usually attempted to consult with the original author. In Crichton's case, he was then a medical student struggling over whether he should commit to his writing full time. Flown to Los Angeles for talks with Wise, Crichton relished soaking in the excitement of being on the set—his first novel transferred to the big screen. Like the youngster he was, Crichton requested an *Andromeda* cameo from Wise. The generous director was immediately receptive to the idea. But his thinking-out-loud response spoke editing volumes to the novelist: "Let me see where I can put you so you won't be cut out."[18] Crichton later recalled this was the precise moment it "really kicked in" that this was the editor of *Citizen Kane*. (The six-foot, nine-inch Crichton's cameo is as a seated technician in a shot where one of the scientists is being pulled out of surgery.)

Wise's initial RKO teacher, the aforementioned Wood, was also responsible for the Hoosier getting his first screen credit. Given their movie-obsessed working relationship, and the studio's mantra of maximizing materials, Wood and Wise worked intermittently over a year on what a later movie generation called a "found film." The men

fashioned a ten-minute short subject from RKO footage shot for an
abandoned South Seas feature. The "new" short was called *A Trip
through Fijiland* (1935). This something-from-nothing project pleased
the studio, which gave both men bonuses, but more importantly it was
an epiphany for Wise. The fun he had fashioning a film from random
footage made clear to him he preferred editing picture content, versus
his normal sound-effects editing assignments with Wood. There was,
however, a practical side to Wise's decision, too. The director later
recalled: "I looked around [my sound-related department] and saw guys
who had been doing that for eight or ten years. And I didn't want to
stop there, so I asked my boss to put me over on the picture side, so I
could become an assistant film editor, which he did."[19]

Once again Wise was teamed with an RKO mentor he came to
greatly admire, veteran William "Billy" Hamilton. Like a youngster
on a farm, Wise was given a great deal of early responsibility, which
was part of Hamilton's gift to him—demystify the process and just
do it. Wise later recalled an exemplary situation on his first film with
Hamilton, Alfred Santell's *Winterset* (1936): "I used to break the film
down [by scenes], put it [the separate spools of film] on the [editing]
bench for him to cut. He would stand at the movieola [viewer] and I
would stand at the synch machine [keeping the picture synchronized
with the second track] and he'd mark while I cut. So he came in one
day, we had a small sequence . . . and he looked at it and said, 'Why
don't you throw that together? Let's see what you can do with it.' I
stumbled through it somehow and he came down and showed me how
it could be improved and . . . in about two more pictures I was doing
all the first cutting in the room, and he would be up on the set with the
director."[20]

Wise went on to assist Hamilton on Gregory La Cava's *Stage Door*
(1937), Mark Sandrich's *Careful* (1938), and Alfred Santell's *Having
Wonderful Time* (1938, which introduced Hoosier comedian Red
Skelton to the movies). Wise's editing workload continued to increase
for Hamilton on H. C. Potter's *The Story of Vernon and Irene Castle*
(1939). By the time of their editing collaboration on *The Hunchback*

Irene Dunne in a scene from My Favorite Wife *(1940), with Mary Lou Harrington and Scotty Deckett. Wise's future wife, Patricia Doyle, was Dunne's stand-in.*

of Notre Dame and *Fifth Avenue Girl* (both 1939), Hamilton had his assistant share the screen credit—the first time Wise's name appeared on a feature film. Just as his working relationship with sound-effects editor Wood produced a pivotal lesson for Wise (concerning raw film footage), the young man received another central axiom from Hamilton: "Always make the scene play when you're cutting it, even if it isn't exactly the director's concept when he shot it. The editor's job is to make it play at all costs."[21]

This directive to always have energy/movement in a film scene became a fundamental tenet for Wise's later work. But the fifth-columnist tone to Hamilton's advice—"even if it isn't exactly the director's concept when he shot it"—also would have been good training for someone (like Wise) aspiring to direct movies. In other words, one should always be aware of how each piece fits into the story puzzle, but be forever prepared to improvise.

Receiving a screen credit on *Hunchback* was a major boost to Wise's career, given that this adaptation of Victor Hugo's novel is one of the acclaimed movies of Hollywood's most magical years, 1939. His quality assignments continued, with his first solo editing jobs on Garson Kanin's *Bachelor Mother* (1939) and Leo McCarey's *My Favorite Wife* (1940, with Kanin stepping in as director when an automobile accident sidelined Leo McCarey). Both were critical and commercial hits, with the latter being a sequel-like follow-up to the smash screwball comedy *The Awful Truth* (1937, for which McCarey won his first directing Oscar).[22] As Wise later recalled, working with Kanin also provided more preparation for a future director: "Because Gar[son] was new to films, he always wanted the editor on the set with him to help him with the camera setups, to be sure he got enough coverage. So for *Bachelor Mother* and *My Favorite Wife*, my assistant Mark Robson was down in the editing room doing the first cuts while I worked with Gar up on the set."[23]

But another major influence, or a creative force of nature, was about to enter Wise's life—Orson Welles.

Orson Welles

"Orson Welles was as close to a genius as anyone I've ever met. There'd be some outrageous piece of behavior and you'd want to tell him a thing or two and then he'd get an idea that was so brilliant that your mouth was gaping open. It was a tremendous experience."[1]
ROBERT WISE

By July 1939 Robert Wise had been in Hollywood for six years. Through hard work and a natural affinity for film, he had climbed the RKO ladder from shipping clerk to being on the verge of industry recognition—a solo editing credit on the prestige picture *The Hunchback of Notre Dame* (released late 1939). That same July, Orson Welles, RKO's hope for a major box-office future, arrived in the film capital. Though the studio was betting he could create something with the pop-culture punch of his previous year's radio adaptation of *War of the Worlds*, RKO had not factored in Welles's more intellectual tendencies, such as his revolutionary modern staging of *Julius Caesar* on Broadway (1937). Unfortunately for the studio, though the pattern was not yet obvious, this wunderkind had an aversion to making anything conventionally commercial. Fittingly, Welles later described his best box-office movie as a director, the excellent noirish thriller *The Stranger* (1946), as "my worst film."[2]

RKO wanted Welles to get something into production quickly, however, there was no rushing this Hollywood rookie, who took the time to give himself a crash course in the movies. The "boy genius" was especially taken with the watershed Western *Stagecoach* (1939).

The director was one of Wise's heroes, John Ford. Though there is not necessarily a natural visual link between Ford and Welles's subsequent work, other than maybe a certain stylized realism, Welles was appreciative of Ford's kindness at a time most of jealous Hollywood was shunning the novice. Welles later honored this generosity with a witty comment much enjoyed by Wise, and presumably by Ford: "[I most admire] the old masters. By which I mean John Ford, John Ford, and John Ford."[3]

Wise did not, however, meet Welles until early the following year. The Hoosier-born editor and his assistant, Mark Robson, had just shipped the completed negative of the Leo McCarey production *My Favorite Wife* (1940) to New York. The two men were preparing to go out for a celebratory supper, their postproduction routine, when Wise received a call from RKO's editing chief James Wilkinson telling him that Welles was interested in having him edit what became *Citizen Kane* (1941). Wise later recalled: "Orson had been shooting scenes that were thought to be tests for the picture but they turned out to be sequences [used] in the final picture. Orson had an older editor assigned to him for those tests and evidently he was not too happy with the particular assignment. I was roughly Orson's age, so I went down to Pathe in Culver City and met him; we had a chat between set-ups. He liked me and wanted me to come on the picture."[4]

Welles and Wise had more in common than their youth. Both were midwestern and passionate about pictures. Appropriately, however, while Wise the boy had been fascinated by American silent cinema's most popular swashbuckling star, Douglas Fairbanks, the young Welles was drawn to a signature art-house movie, German Expressionism's *The Cabinet of Dr. Caligari* (1919), whose fatalistic use of shadow and light is replicated in *Citizen Kane*.

While Wise was receiving on-the-job film training at RKO, Welles was sporadically improvising in film, too. Much is rightfully made of the classic *Kane* being his first feature, but the teenage Welles had done an inventive short subject, *The Hearts of Age* (1934), which both includes many *Kane*-like shots and has Welles aping the aging title character of *Caligari*, which brings one full circle back to Welles's elderly Kane. (Wise's memory of Welles during their first visit is also a freeze frame of the geriatric Kane, since that was how Welles was made-up at the time of Wise's interview.) Later in the decade, like Sergei Eisenstein in the 1920s, Welles experimented with incorporating film in a staged play, particularly with his production of the William Gillette farce, *Too Much Johnson*.

Another Welles-Wise link was each man's ability to become so focused upon a project that he pushed the boundaries of human endurance. This book has already chronicled Wise's Herculean efforts at RKO, a key reason for his rapid advancement. Thus, he was obviously drawn to this trait in Welles, especially given their follow-up *Kane* collaboration on *The Magnificent Ambersons* (1942, with Wise as editor), with Wise noting: "The whole latter part of *Ambersons*, he was not only directing in the daytime, he was also many nights shooting [acting] all night on *Journey Into Fear* [1943]. . . . And sometimes he would come in to run rushes in the morning after a night's work of acting. I don't know how he kept going!"[6]

Though Welles and Wise had midwestern roots, they were both also drawn to a realistically darker perspective on the nature of man. The European angst of a *Caligari* had already been applied to the American scene in such pivotal pictures as German Expressionist director Fritz Lang's first films in this country, *Fury* (1936), and *You Only Live Once* (1937). Consequently, part of the groundbreaking nature of Welles's *Kane*, and his follow-up RKO movie, *Ambersons,* was revealing fatalistic flaws in characters anchored even more in mainstream Americana—the initially populist Kane and the Indiana Ambersons of Booth Tarkington's novel, a family whose success was born of Yankee ingenuity.

The power of Welles's personality and artistic vision effected Wise's later work. Yet, their aforementioned parallels were already in place. Given the observation that opens the chapter, Wise was still breathless with admiration over Welles's sheer genius forty-plus years after RKO brought them together. But this same Wise quote hints at decisive

The Orson Welles ego captured on film in this staged photograph of a Citizen Kane *opening.*

differences: "there'd be some outrageous piece of behavior and you'd want to tell him [Welles] a thing or two." Wise embraced film in a manner that was the embodiment of renowned French novelist Gustave Flaubert's approach to art—live as bourgeois a life as possible and put your wildness in your work. In contrast, a wild life and an attempt to juggle too many artistic balls often got in the way of Welles's greatness. Though his *Kane* is almost universally acclaimed as cinema's greatest movie, the personal freefall of a life that followed is a tale to rival his masterpiece.

Like F. Scott Fitzgerald, another boy genius who hit an artistic home run his first time at bat and then failed to fit into Hollywood, the public's fascination with Welles is forever linked to his fall from grace. Though Welles and Wise were born only a year apart, there was a Jazz Age-like hedonism to Welles that was the antithesis of the more Great Depression-molded, hardworking Wise. In Budd Schulberg's autobiographical novel *The Disenchanted* (1950), the author's surrogate figure summarizes the two positions in a lecture-like comeback to a character (Manley Halliday) based upon Fitzgerald: "Our machine [society] had been in a smash-up too [the Depression]. But we wanted to remain on the scene of the accident and see if we could fix it. We thought we could save it. Instead of . . . [the 1920s] *lost* generation [so demoralized by the millions of lives lost in World War I they stopped caring], I guess you might call us a *found* generation. We found out what was wrong. We were pretty damn sure we'd have something new out of all this mess that would be better than anything you had before."[7] Interestingly, the greatest works by both Fitzgerald (*The Great Gatsby*, 1925) and Welles (*Kane*) would be about flawed business tycoons.

One might also draw a Welles-Wise analogy with two iconic contemporaries from the world of baseball—New York Yankee greats Babe Ruth and Lou Gehrig. Ruth rivaled Fitzgerald for the poster child of Jazz Age excess, yet Ruth is arguably baseball's greatest player. Gehrig was the unselfish blue-collar alternative to Ruth, a quiet company man who approached his job with the same loyal happy-to-be employed dedication of any Great Depression worker. Consistent with this dichotomy, despite Hall of Fame numbers as a hitter and fielder, Gehrig's defining achievement as a player was his time-clock passion to never miss a day of work, playing in a then record 2,130 consecutive games. Though Woody Allen later joked, "Ninety percent of life is just showing up," for Gehrig it was a 100 percent of the time. If Welles was Ruthian, Wise was definitely in the Gehrig mold. Fittingly, Wise was an admirer of the Iron Horse, particularly after the dying player's poignant 1939 "luckiest man on the face of the earth" farewell speech, today now sometimes referred to as "baseball's Gettysburg Address."[8] As the Yankee teammates eventually had a falling out, the RKO duo would, too. But first one needs to examine *Kane* and *Ambersons*.

On the surface, *Kane* is both a mystery and a fictionalized biography of media mogul Charles Foster Kane, patterned loosely upon newspaper publisher/powerbroker William Randolph Hearst, who created a print journalism empire built upon sensationalized reportage, colorized comic strips, and "yellow journalism" (manipulatively melodramatic prose). The film starts with the aging Kane's dying last word, "Rosebud," and then follows a reporter's attempt to determine that term's significance. This quest involves scrutinizing private papers, newsreels, and interviewing various people from Kane's life. A mesmerizing mosaic unfolds that correctly sums up his life: "[He] got everything he wanted, and then lost it." Yet the reporter never discovers the word's meaning. However, at the picture's conclusion, as many of the seemingly lesser possessions of this wealthy man are being incinerated in a giant furnace, the viewer realizes "Rosebud" was Kane's childhood sled—symbolizing not only some universal angst over the lost innocence of youth but also a pastoral period before Kane's sudden inheritance of a fortune ended his childhood.

Such a bittersweet chronicling of a great American's life as essentially hollow was groundbreaking for Hollywood cinema. Movie heroes did not yet have feet of clay. While Frank Capra, the ultimate auteur of feel-good populism, had revealed the potential for fascist fissures in

America with *Meet John Doe* (1941), Gary Cooper's title character still manages to save the day and convert Capra's favorite villain (Edward Arnold). Moreover, with the country on the verge of World War II, a nationalistic fervor had jump-started a demand for patriotic pictures, such as the critical and commercial blockbuster biographies *Sergeant York* (about *the* American World War I hero) and *Pride of the Yankees* (Lou Gehrig). Both of these 1941 films starred America's quintessential populist hero, Cooper, who also won a Best Actor Oscar for the former

The Lou Gehrig (Gary Cooper) "Luckiest Man" scene re-created for the screen in the moving biography film Pride of the Yankees *(1941).*

film. Naturally, this jingoistic wave continued throughout the war years, with James Cagney succeeding Cooper as the Oscar-winning actor with another patriotic biography, *Yankee Doodle Dandy* (1942, about song-and-dance man George M. Cohan).

Even without the war driving popular culture's retrenchment to traditional values, a natural knee-jerk need to define and/or underline what one is fighting for in any conflict, *Kane's* art house questioning of a seemingly Horatio Alger-like character would have been a hard sell for RKO. As a seminal film historian observed: "*Citizen Kane* was both shocking and confusing to its audiences in 1941. Instead of Hollywood's flat gloss, the film was [realistically] somber and grotesque. The action sprawled over more than sixty years, requiring its performers to make tremendous transitions in acting and appearance. There were no last-minute changes of heart, no romantic reconciliations. *Citizen Kane* followed its tragic premises to their logical, gloomy end."[9] Factor in the heightened period patriotism, and the viable chances for a commercial success were a long shot. *Kane* was essentially a modern (post-1965) antiheroic picture that arrived in theatres a quarter-century early. Being ahead of the times is good for one's historical legacy, but it does not guarantee box-office success.

Coupled with this less than mainstream audience subject matter, *Kane* was also handicapped by the anger of mogul Hearst. This Depression-era Ted Turner was livid over being the indirect model for a movie, especially as it related to his long-term relationship with mistress Marion Davies. In Welles's movie the Davies character (Susan Alexander) is a talentless singer pushed beyond her skills by Kane. In reality, Davies was a gifted comedian whose screen career was sometimes hurt by Hearst's attempts to showcase her in serious historical epics. But Welles's invasion of Hearst's privileged private life—underwritten by newspaper stories feeding upon other people's private lives—proved to be more combustible for the publisher. Between Davies's nephew, Charles Lederer, having married Welles's first wife, and *Kane* being coscripted by a Davies drinking buddy, Herman J. Mankiewicz, a Welles biographer noted that the filmmaker "had

Young Kane (Buddy Swan) and the then unidentified sled, as he shakes hands with a wealthy future (George Coulouris) but loses his childhood and his parents (Anges Moorehead and Harry Shannon) in Citizen Kane.

found out the secret name that Hearst used to refer to Marion Davies's genitalia: Rosebud. To Hearst, it was bad enough that Rosebud be mentioned throughout the picture but even worse was the idea that Kane died with Rosebud on his lips."[10]

Making "Rosebud" a sled was satirically suggestive. This bombshell, unknown to the general public at the time, better explains the extremes to which Hearst went to derail the movie. The coast-to-coast Hearst press "refused to print [*Kane*] ads, publicity or [later] reviews of the film"[11] Behind the scenes, Hearst put pressure on RKO not even to release the film. When that did not work, Hearst threatened the whole movie industry, from revealing scandals Hollywood had paid to go away, to documenting to anti-Semitic America just how Jewish filmland was. Over a half century later Wise recalled just how tenuous the film's future had been: "I was told [by RKO] . . . to take the print of the picture to [New York's Radio City] Music Hall . . . [It was to be seen] by the chairmen of the boards of all the major studios and their lawyers. The purpose was, after looking at the picture, whether the companies would say to RKO: 'In the interest of our film industry, put this film on the shelf, don't release it.' That was the first time I realized the film was really in danger. Orson was there; he knew what was up. He wasn't there just by accident. . . . And he spoke to them for a few minutes before we started. I always have to laugh to myself; I was the only person of Hollywood to see Orson give one of his greatest performances."[12]

At a time when foreign dictators were trampling all over any sense of an international bill of rights, Welles shamed these movie money men into not capitulating to this homegrown fascist. Given Hearst's great wealth and power, this was no small accomplishment. As George Bernard Shaw once described Hearst, à la his castle estate San Simeon, which was called Xanadu in *Kane*, "This is the place God would have built, if he'd had the money."

For a time *Kane* was a cause célèbre, with acknowledgeable picture people lucky enough to see it (Hearst's newspaper chain made theatrical bookings difficult) coming away with the same feelings Wise had had early in the production process: "You couldn't look at those rushes coming in, every day . . . without realizing you were getting something quite extraordinary, the photography, the angles, the shooting, it was marvelous."[13] For Wise, the key reason *Kane* was Welles's greatest film, and arguably cinema's most memorable movie, was tied to it being "the only film Orson ever made that he had complete concentration on. . . . *The Magnificent Ambersons* was a different cup of tea; he had many other distractions."[14]

Welles had courted controversy with the Hearst-Kane connection, something with which he had conquered other mediums, from his all-black staging of a *MacBeth* relocated to Haiti, as a Works Progress Administration production at Harlem's Lafayette Theatre, to his notorious *War of the Worlds* radio broadcast. But in the case of Welles versus Hearst, the verdict might be likened to that old joke about a reactionary Southerner's take on the Civil War, "It was a tie." Yet in the long run, the film won, and ultimately Welles's take on the mogul is what endures.

Though all these factors kept *Kane* from being a commercial success, film reviewers recognized its greatness. One of cinema's watershed critics, the *New Republic*'s Otis Ferguson, wrote: "The things to be said are that it is the boldest free hand stroke in a major screen production since [pioneering D. W.] Griffith and [his cameraman Billy] Bitzer were running wild to unshackle the camera."[15] The now legendary Gilbert Seldes, who basically invented insightful pop-culture criticism, observed in a lengthy *Esquire* piece titled "Radio Boy Makes Good" that while Irving Thalberg was Hollywood's "producer of genius" (a status that has only further solidified through the years), "not one [Thalberg] picture . . . has the unity of *Citizen Kane*—the unity inside, which makes everything in it ten thousand times more effective."[16]

Consequently, though Hollywood had generally scorned the young upstart when he arrived in the film capital, with Fitzgerald even cracking, "All's well that ends well(es)," at Oscar time *Kane* garnered nine nominations.[17] Welles became one of the few artists to simultaneously be nominated as director, writer, and actor for the same picture. But the film's only win was the Academy Award Welles shared with Mankiewicz for best original screenplay. Despite the Oscar recognition, Wise was not surprised the *Kane* team was nearly shut out at the ceremony: "I went to the Academy Awards of 1941 because I was one of 9 [as best editor] nominations the picture got. And I'll never forget that evening. The first time *Kane* was mentioned as one of the nominees . . . there was a certain number of very noticeable boos. Then other people shushed them down. Then we went on to another category or two. The second time *Kane* came up—more boos."[18]

Keep in mind, though, this was not simply a lingering backlash against Welles. The United States had entered World War II shortly before the ceremony, and the sky-high nationalism of 1941 was ratcheted up further. This Oscar festivity even had a military air, from a uniformed Lieutenant Jimmy Stewart presenting several statuettes to Donald Crisp accepting his Best Supporting Actor Academy Award in uniform. The Associated Press's coverage of the event added, "Men wore business suits or uniforms—many army officers were guests."[19] How was this part of *Kane*'s boo-factor? Welles's clay-footed title character was perceived as anti-American. Indeed, an early satirical working title about this flawed figure was *The American*.

So how did working on the greatest movie ever made affect Wise? Presumably, it reinforced the traits Wise already had upon arriving in Hollywood. For example, the importance of hard work, focused behavior, a predisposition toward dark comedy (the real meaning of "Rosebud" is black humor incarnate[20]) and a modern sensibility about man's baser nature.

Since Wise was a muckraking journalist wannabe, *Kane*'s populist first half, in which Welles's young newspaper editor attempts a populist makeover of a New York newspaper, would have resonated with the Hoosier filmmaker. In fact, the hero of Wise's later picture, *The Captive City* (1952), is a passionate reporter (John Forsythe) who engages in a one-man crusade against criminal elements. In a film Wise called a favorite, *I Want To Live!* (1958), a biography picture of convicted murderer Barbara Graham (Susan Hayward), her execution is predicated upon press attacks that sensationalized her shady past and falsely suggested she was a vicious killer. Interestingly, these tactics were directly linked to Hearst's/Kane's lurid journalism legacy, since one of the film's central reporters, Simon Oakland (Ed Montgomery), worked for the *San Francisco Examiner*, Hearst's first newspaper and the spawning ground for his sensationalism. However, in a twist that allowed Wise to be both *Kane*-like in demonstrating how easily the masses can be manipulated, and still portray a positive journalist, the same Oakland reverses himself and works passionately for Graham's acquittal.

Though Graham's ultimate execution is a problem-film message about the barbarous nature of capital punishment (a moralizing Wise), and Kane's death is from natural causes, each picture concludes with the same poignant subtext—is any individual's life ever really understood (only with *Live* there is no tidy last puzzle-piece explanation, à la *Kane's* "Rosebud")? While even a childhood sled could mean many things, there is symmetry to Rosebud resurfacing at the close. That is, the sled was also there at the beginning of the movie, but the name was obscured. *Live* does not have this bookend balance, unless chaos counts. Graham's death in the gas chamber seems as randomly pointless as the life she lived. Added to Wise's ambiguously realistic presentation of her story, Graham's demise further seals this slice-of-life scenario—we will never know for sure whether she was innocent or guilty.

The conclusion to both of these signature productions does reveal one final parallel. Each film chronicles a harsh character—an alleged murderer and a publisher so ruthless he would start a war to sell newspapers. (Inspired from an actual Hearst telegram on the eve of the Spanish American War, Kane dictates to a correspondent, "You provide the prose poems. I'll provide the war.") Yet, just as *Kane* ends with an uncharacteristically sentimental tie-in to a boyhood sled, Wise's finale for *Live* is a letter that puts a movingly positive spin on the face of a death sentence reminiscent of Lou Gehrig's "Luckiest Man" speech.

Graham's letter to her newspaper foe turned ally, Oakland, states: "There isn't much I can say with words: they always fail me when most needed. But please know that with all my heart I appreciate everything you've done for me."

Even Wise's greatest cult picture, the celebrated science-fiction film *The Day the Earth Stood Still* (1951), has a crusading journalist ambience. Given its Capra-like populist tendencies, sort of a *Mr. Alien Goes to Washington*, Wise's dignified visitor (Michael Rennie) is similar to a reporter with a life or death story to tell—Earth must stop its nuclear weapon ways or face its own execution by a higher power. Plus, Rennie does his own reporter-like research on Earthlings, including poignant visits to the Lincoln Memorial and Arlington National Cemetery. As with *Live*, Wise's *Day* is able to show media negatives (the easy-to-fuel hysteria after a flying saucer lands in Washington, D.C.), and the potential for good through Rennie's character.

Ironically, Welles's greatest influence on Wise was to utilize a new technique (by way of cinematographer Gregg Toland), called deep focus, that minimized the need for the Hoosier's then specialty— editing. Film theory's poet of realism Andre Bazin later defined deep focus and Welles's link to this unique development: "*Citizen Kane* can never be too highly praised. Thanks to the depth of field, whole scenes are covered in one take. . . . Dramatic effects for which we had formerly relied on montage [editing] were created out of the movement of the actors within a fixed [all-in-focus] frame."[21]

Instead of an editor cutting to various objects and/or angles of a given film shot (force-feeding the viewer's every perspective), democratic deep focus allows the spectator to choose what is most important to him/her within the film frame. "I've shot many of my films, particularly in black and white, with wide-angle-lenses," Wise later recalled, "so we could have somebody close in the foreground and still have things in the background in focus. I'm sure that came from Orson."[22]

Welles also influenced Wise on the creative use of the soundtrack. For all of *Kane*'s visual flair, this was a masterpiece of sight *and* sound. From early in the movie, when the overpowering blare of the newsreel music could be Kane's theme song, or the sudden disquieting stoppage of this film within the film sounded like a power outage metaphor for Kane's death, Welles was forever inventive in his use of sound. Yet, after all, his prefilm fame was built upon his stage *and* radio work. Wise remembered, "even though I had been a sounds-effects and music editor, I think Orson increased my sense of what a soundtrack contributes to a picture, both in sound effects and in music."[23] Wise was later innovative in this area, too. In *The Set-Up* (1949) Wise limited the music to in-film sources, which became a basic component of the American New Wave cinema movement (beginning in the late 1960s) and featuring such Wise disciples as Martin Scorsese. (Wise's influence on Scorsese is most apparent in 1980's *Raging Bull*.) Conversely, in Wise's *Executive Suite* (1954), he broke realistic Hollywood ground by not using music.

My favorite neglected link between *Kane* and Wise's later directing career involves Welles's genre slant on the picture. The boy genius essentially saw the work as a biography film, though he could not call it *Citizen Hearst*. Indeed, Welles's later thoughts about biography encouraged the profiler to place himself in the story, like the *Kane* reporter searching for the meaning of "Rosebud." That way, for Welles, the degree of difficulty could be underlined by the biographer. Fittingly, an inordinately large percentage of Wise's quality movies could be labeled either biographies, including *Somebody Up There Likes Me* (1956), *I Want to Live*, and *The Sound of Music* (1965), or biography-like profiles of fictional characters such as *So Big* (1953), *Executive Suite*, *Tribute to a Bad Man* (1956), *Run Silent, Run Deep* (1958), and *The Sand Pebbles* (1966). Given the message-oriented predisposition of both Welles and Wise, biography especially lends itself to this goal in one's art. While any genre can double as a life lesson parable, the message anchored in reality often registers more with viewers because the subject is often a known commodity even before the movie.

Paradoxically, maybe Wise's ultimate lesson learned from Welles, grounded equally in their follow-up picture, *Ambersons*, was simply the need to not let the temptations of premature power and privilege distract one from the task at hand. Years later, after rescreening *Kane*, Wise poetically coupled Welles with his greatest characterization: "I suddenly thought to myself, Orson was doing an auto-biographical film and didn't realize it. Because it's . . . rather much the same [the lives of Welles and Kane] . . . a big rise, tremendous prominence and fame, and success and what not, and then [it] tails off and tails off and tails off and at last the arc of the two lives were very much the same."[24]

In a review of *Me and Orson Welles* (2009), a nonfiction fiction cinematic take on a pre-*Citizen Kane* stage production by Welles, *The New Yorker* critic David Denby more broadly summarizes the "tails off" phenomenon noted by Wise: "A theatrical performance can be altered and revised until just before the curtain rises, but a movie, with its thousands of interlocking details, requires long-range planning, consistency, and reliability. In Welles' rabbit-out-of-the-hat victory of 1937 [*Julius Caesar*], one sees the habits that will lead not only to a few peerless films but also to many defeats and tragically abandoned projects."[25]

Welles's fall from grace would begin immediately with his next RKO outing, *Ambersons*. The director again wanted Wise as his editor, but he had to compete with filmmaker William Dieterle for the Hoosier's services. After *Kane*, Wise's editing of another memorable movie, Dieterle's *All That Money Can Buy* (1941, aka *The Devil and Daniel Webster*), had Dieterle wanting Wise for his next feature, *Syncopation* (1942), too. Welles would win the battle, enabling Wise to play his biggest part yet, a controversial part, in a third straight historically notable film.

Ambersons was a fortuitous opportunity for Wise, given that the 1919 Pulitzer Prize–winning novel was by Hoosier author Booth Tarkington. After he won the same prize for *Alice Adams* in 1922, Tarkington was voted the "greatest living American author and one of the ten greatest contemporary Americans."[26] Though flattered by the first recognition, Tarkington felt the latter acknowledgement was "darn silliness," and then he displayed a comic Hoosier modesty that might have been the model for the later multiple Oscar-winning Wise, "You can't say who are the 10 greatest with any more authority than you can say who are 10 damndest fools."[27]

The *Ambersons* story is summarized, in part, by the title of the first screen adaptation, *Pampered Youth* (1925). George Amberson Minafer (played by Tim Holt in Welles's version), is a rich brat set up for a "come-uppance" from the story's beginning. Before his birth, upon the marriage of his parents, a town gossip predicts they will have "the worst spoiled lot of children this town will ever see." Welles's voice-over narration during the opening prologue answers this gossiper's comment: "The prophetess proved to be mistaken in a single detail merely; Wilbur and Isabel did not have *children*. They had only one." George's (Holt's) condescending character makes him entertainingly easy to despise, especially with lines such as: "I don't intend to go into any business or profession. . . . Well, just look at them. That's a fine career for a man, isn't it? Lawyers, bankers, politicians. What do they ever get out of life? I'd like to know? What do they know about real things? What do they ever get?" What was George's career choice? "Yachtsman."

Years later Welles was asked if he considered himself a moralist. The writer/director responded, "moralists bore me very much. However, I'm afraid I am one of them."[28] Thus, Welles's adaptation of the *Ambersons* is a parable about the destructiveness of pride. This epic melodrama follows the late-nineteenth-century rise and fall of George's mother's family, the center-of-society Ambersons, in a midwestern city based upon Indianapolis. While *Kane* chronicled how an initially populist young man of the people was corrupted by power, *Ambersons* documents a moral rot from day one of a silver-spoon birth. Herein lies a problem for some viewers. *Kane* is also a morality tale about the dangers of pride. Yet, there is so much to admire and/or savor about the style of Welles's young Kane that the picture is also a tragedy about what might have been. Because of the dazzling narcissism of *Ambersons*' George, by the time he has his eleventh-hour epiphany, we are past caring about him. *Or*, maybe it is just that Welles the actor is so mesmerizing as the title character of the first picture, that his on-screen presence is sorely missed in *Ambersons* (save for his narrator).

As a footnote to Wise's original desire to be a crusading journalist, *Ambersons* was part of a Tarkington trilogy of muckraking novels (cumulatively called *Growth*, 1927) that also doubled as social histories of the Midwest. Even the author's first novel, *The Gentleman from Indiana* (1899), focused upon a corruption-fighting journalist. Consequently, Wise's involvement with *Ambersons* would have been familiar territory for a wannabe reporter. In fact, Wise's early childhood paralleled the Progressive Era, when liberal legislation was fanned by muckraking novels such as Frank Norris's *The Octopus* (1901) and Upton Sinclair's *The Jungle* (1906). Wise's cause-related tendencies were a natural outgrowth of this period.

Still, there is a sweeping nostalgic charm in how Welles recaptures *Ambersons*' bygone world, revealing a link to *Kane*—a lament for one's seemingly simpler youth and a lost past. Tarkington and Welles couple this affectionate look at yesteryear with a cautionary tale that instructs: as time changes, so must the individual. That is, though the urban sprawl caused by the ugly disruptively noisy automobile industry hastened the decline of genteel families such as the Ambersons, it created jobs and bolstered a growing middle class. Once again, this plot twist from a Hoosier novelist had parallels with Wise, given that his childhood was spent in the Indiana city of Connersville, whose economy was driven by the automobile industry. During Wise's youth, Connersville's prosperity helped fuel a progressive educational system that greatly benefited the future filmmaker.

The good guy in the *Ambersons* story, both in the novel and Welles's adaptation, is Eugene Morgan. He is movingly played by Joseph Cotton in this screen adaptation, an actor whose *Kane* character, Jedediah Leland, was also the conscience of that film. Cotton's Eugene speaks for the future when he answers George's derision of the automobile: "With all their speed forward they may be a step backward in civilization. Maybe they won't add to the beauty of the world or the life of men's souls. I'm not sure. But automobiles have come, and almost all other things are going to be different because of what they bring."

Though set in an earlier era, Eugene is the figure to which Great Depression-surviving fans of *Ambersons* would have related, given his ability to improvise, just as Wise found success in Hollywood after his college-tuition money disappeared. Eugene also oozed an audience-pleasing fatherly wisdom. For example, what follows is an excerpt from Eugene's letter to Isabel (Dolores Costello), George's mother and the love of Eugene's life—although even when she is widowed, her son acts as a roadblock to Isabel's relationship with Eugene. The correspondence, about the insufferable George, is most kind: "At twenty-one or twenty-two, so many things appear solid, permanent, and terrible, which forty sees as nothing but disappearing miasma [vapor]. Forty can't tell twenty about this. Twenty can find out only by getting to be forty."

Paradoxically, shortly before starting work on *Ambersons*, Wise revealed a dark take upon his hometown that sounds like a combination of *both* Eugene and George. Wise was returning to Hollywood by train from his *Kane*-driven trip to New York. Though his parents had now retired to Southern California, Wise stopped to visit some Indiana friends and family. The film editor's comments mix the moving-with-the-times nature of Eugene with George's car-related disgust over the passing of a more genteel time: "I had a favorite Aunt and Uncle who lived in Union City, Indiana, and that was about ten miles from Winchester where I was born. So I stopped there to visit . . . [later] I took the occasion [to] drive down to Connersville to see if I could find any of my old chums. I'll never forget. I was trying to find the president of my senior class. His family ran a tire store in Connersville, and I finally found him there, grumpy and dirty, changing a tire. He was very down-in-the-mouth, not happy with what he was doing. I had arrived in Connersville at dusk. It was midwinter and dirty and sooty and very unattractive. I didn't have much luck in finding anyone else, so I got out of town in about an hour and a half. I did enjoy visiting my relatives, but by that time California was for me."[29]

The ever-playful Welles liked the idea of narrating a tale about a golden child getting his comeuppance, since that was Hollywood's then ongoing wish for him. But as with *Kane*, there were other *Ambersons* basics that felt autobiographical to Welles, such as the overly doting mother. But the filmmaker's plan for his adaptation's conclusion was to be bittersweet, à la *Kane*. In contrast, literary historian Donald J. Gray describes the novel's ending thus: "Tarkington was an optimistic writer—most popular writers are—and he thought that novels ought to give readers something to feel good about at the end. The humbling of George . . . and his [eventual] alliance with . . . [Eugene, planted the] promise that growth need not produce only the dirty city and harried citizens."[30]

Could Welles have pulled his darkly modern antiheroic twist off yet again? The answer is forever lost to history. The war, Welles's wanderlust, and Wise being demonized (as a surrogate for evil RKO) have conspired to cloud *Ambersons'* intended fate.

The United States entered World War II in December 1941. Welles completed shooting *Ambersons* in late January 1942. At the same time President Franklin Delano Roosevelt put Nelson Rockefeller in charge of Inter-American Affairs, an organization that attempted to strengthen ties between the United States and South America, given that there was now a wave of antidemocratic propaganda being pushed by German and Italian groups in the area. Rockefeller pegged Welles as one of several goodwill ambassadors being sent to South America.

Though lip service was paid to a possible Welles lecture tour, the Rockefeller request simply enabled the filmmaker to shoot a documentary of Rio de Janeiro's famed three-day carnival (one of several backburner projects for the multitasker Welles). To be called *It's All True*, the film was to be funded by the government and RKO, with Rockefeller coincidently being a major stockbroker of the studio.

To prepare for this mission, Welles flew to Washington, D.C., for briefings in early February 1942. Then he rendezvoused with Wise in Miami, Florida, for three nearly nonstop days of editing and dubbing of *Ambersons*. (At that time, Miami was the departure point for flying boats to South America.) Wise had been in charge of moving a mountain of film footage to Florida in order to create a rough cut of the movie. Given that the two men and assistants spent an almost comically frantic seventy-two hours editing and rescreening scenes, it seems only fitting that their rented production space was the Fleischer Cartoon Studio! Wise later told filmmaker/author Peter Bogdanovich that while a great deal of editing was completed before Welles went to the capital, "I still had final decisions to be made on certain areas of the preliminary cut of the film . . . there simply wasn't time to get all of this done before Orson had to be in Washington. . . . I went to Miami . . . with a number of reels of the film that needed some additional work. Orson came on to Miami . . . [and we worked] practically around the clock. . . . I saw Orson off just after dawn the 4th morning . . . [and] returned immediately to Hollywood with the film and set about completing the editing as per all of our decisions, and completing the sound and music work to get a print, originally intended for me to take to South America to show Orson."[31] John Lennon later wrote, "Life is what happens when you're busy making other plans." Life was about to sabotage RKO's postproduction plans for *Ambersons*.

Wartime travel restrictions soon kept Wise from being able to join Welles in Brazil, and the *Ambersons* film shipped to the director took an inordinately long time to reach him. Worse yet, telephone and telegram communications between Hollywood and Rio were worse than primitive in 1942. This became a potentially tragic artistic dilemma when RKO, anxious to recoup expenses on an overbudget production, pushed for early *Amberson* sneak previews. When test audiences disliked Welles's dark take on Tarkington's story, Wise was authorized to make extensive cuts to the movie, as well as shoot new scenes to bridge any narrative gaps created by the changes. In this telling of the tale, Wise is sometimes portrayed as a villain collaborating with the evil anti-art, make-a-buck studio. For example, Welles himself said, "they [RKO] let the studio janitor cut *The Magnificent Ambersons* in my absence."[32]

Outside of Erich von Straheim's much-bemoaned loss of final cut on his silent-picture epic *Greed* (1925, from another Frank Norris novel, *McTeague*), Welles has undoubtedly received more sympathy over *Ambersons*'s recutting than any other film maverick ever. But, as one of Welles's favorite directors, Jean Renoir, was fond of saying, "Everyone has their [*sic*] reasons," an axiom also spouted by a character in Renoir's *Rules of the Game* (1939). RKO's reasons involved a studio chief, George Schaefer, about to be sacked, in part, because of controversy surrounding *Kane*, and that *Ambersons* was more than a half a million dollars overbudget—an overrun that would have covered the *total* cost of two or three average RKO features for 1942. The situation does not justify Schaefer's overreaction to two negative sneak previews, but it places the scenario in perspective. One could also "read" RKO's hurry-up action as a left-handed endorsement—Schaefer banking on Welles's magic to save his job.

Still, it was unfair of RKO not to work closely with Welles on the changes the director did send from Brazil, as well as moving ahead so quickly on the previews. Given the situation, though, Welles should have realized his friends on the *Ambersons* production were doing all they could. The following is a letter excerpt sent to Welles by *Ambersons*' nominal star, Cotton, which also detailed the film's "ice-house" reception from a preview audience: "Our cables that fly back and forth I know present everything in a very unsatisfactory manner. They often must be misinterpreted at both ends. Jack [Moss, Welles' business manager], I know, is doing all he can. He is trying his best to get Bob Wise to you [in Brazil]. His [Wise's] opinions about the cuts, right or wrong, I know are the results of sincere, thoughtful, harassed days, nights, Sundays, holidays."[33]

Years later Wise echoed much the same sentiment about *Ambersons*: "As a work of art, it probably was a better picture in its original-length version: as an *accomplishment*. . . . But we were faced with the reality of not art but business, and what to do with something that wouldn't play. But I also think that the fact that it has come down through the years as something of a semi-classic at least means that we didn't destroy the picture, did we? I can tell you, everybody strived as hard as they could to retain every bit of the feeling, the quality of what Orson was trying to do."[34]

Regardless, in a Welles cable to Moss from the same time as Cotton's letter (late March 1942), the director underlines his frustration *and* the importance he gave Wise's contribution to *Ambersons*: "My advice absolutely useless without Bob [Wise] here [in Brazil]. . . . Sure I must be at least partially wrong but cannot see remotest sense in any single [suggested] cuts of yours [Moss], Bob's, Joe's [Cotton]."[35]

At this point, one must wonder why Welles simply did not return to Hollywood. This chapter has already documented Wise's account of how an in-person impassioned plea from Welles rescued *Kane* from a fate worse than drastic cuts. Welles's Svengali-like skills as an actor/salesman might have saved his dark take on Tarkington, had he returned promptly from Brazil. A great irony is generally omitted in the chronicling of the non-Welles happy ending that concludes the *Ambersons* film—it is perfectly consistent with how Tarkington closed the novel.

Even without *Ambersons* pulling Welles back, one has to wonder about his extended stay in Rio. He left in early February to film a *three-day* carnival and stayed for months. His documentary *It's All True* kept morphing into new territory, from staging more carnival footage to flirting with being an exposè of Rio poverty. Ironically, with the possibility of making a controversial movie unflattering to a conservative Brazilian government, he risked both the goodwill-ambassador cover for the trip and the ability to be allowed to keep shooting. Plus, going quickly over budget on *It's All True* would not have helped any Welles/Wise position on *Ambersons*. (Decades later footage from the unfinished *It's All True* surfaced for the home video/DVD market.[36] A film within the film, *Four Men on a Raft*, was an interesting aspect of the once lost picture. This short subject was the core of Welles's exposè footage in *It's All True*—a restaging of a miraculous sea trip by poor fishermen seeking to organize a union. But the Brazilian government's opposition to both this movement, and Welles's attempt to film *Four Men on a Raft*, further demonstrate the director's growing inability to stay on task. By the time of Welles's death, the length of his filmography was rivaled by the number of his unfinished projects. Welles's great imagination made and unmade him.)

Though the negative *Ambersons* previews occurred early (March 1942), the film did not go into general release until the beginning of July. Even an eleventh-hour return by Welles might have helped. But accounts of the "boy wonder" from the late 1930s on, starting with Barbara Leamings's very sympathetic 1985 biography, and including Chris Welles Feder's equally kind *In My Father's Shadow: A Daughter Remembers Orson Welles* (2009), chronicle a brilliantly elusive creative spirit whose appetite for life often derailed his art and personal relationships.[37] Wise, RKO, anyone attempting a collaboration of sorts with Welles would have been sorely tested—long distance or not. Ironically, for all the abuse thrown RKO's way over its ultimate actions on *Ambersons*, Welles probably lasted longer there than at one of the major Hollywood studios. Film historian Joe E. Siegel wrote of this period: "Because the studio [RKO] was never run by a family dynasty, and because ownership changed hands rather frequently, filmmakers tended to have more freedom at the relatively disorganized RKO than anywhere else in Hollywood."[38]

Period reviews for *Ambersons* reinforce Wise's description of a movie "that wouldn't play." *Variety*, the entertainment industry Bible observed: "[Even at] 88 minutes, this emotional downbeat [movie] appears to be endless. On top of the slow [narrative] . . . with a world in flame[s], nations shattered, populations in rags, with massacres and bombings, Welles devotes 9,000 feet of film to a spoiled brat who grows up as a spoiled, spiteful young man."[39] Though *Variety*'s review conceded Welles had given Hollywood yet another lesson in "new celluloid technique," it correctly predicted the movie "will be just as dismal at the b.o. [box office] as the story is on the screen."[40] The same message was reiterated more diplomatically by the *New York Times*: "The Capitol's [theater] new film, however magnificently executed, is a relentlessly somber drama on a barren theme."[41]

Among early critiques, only the *Hollywood Reporter* seemed to completely embrace the movie, from the run-on celebratory title of the review, "'Magnificent Ambersons' Magnificent Welles Film: A Prestige Picture When RKO Needs It," to singling out praise for its editing.[42] But even here there was defensive posturing for Welles against an anticipated commercial backlash and/or disinterest: "It may be difficult to define 'The Magnificent Ambersons' in terms that will sell at the box office . . . lazy exhibitors may fail to capitalize upon the second offering from the man [Welles] who made the N.Y. critics' choice of the best picture of last year in 'Citizen Kane.'"[43]

If Wise had not already been predisposed toward professionalism through his experiences with Welles, the manner in which RKO terminated the director would have pushed him in that direction. That is, a new studio regime sacked Welles, cut their losses by aborting *It's All True*, and devised an in-your-face slam of the indulgent artist with a new studio slogan: "Showmanship instead of genius: a new deal at RKO."[44] The pages that follow document countless examples of the director Wise as that blue-collar Depression-tempered, responsible artist who comes to work. But one example bears noting. In the mid-1950s Wise looked forward to directing the iconic American actor Spencer Tracy on what became *Tribute to a Bad Man* (1956). Unfortunately, when Tracy's unprofessional behavior threatened the production, Wise made the tough choice of having the actor removed. Replacing Tracy with James Cagney, Wise still made a Western classic and saved Metro-Goldwyn-Mayer from a runaway budget.

Any in-depth study of Welles's career cites his colorful appreciation for the great resources of the Hollywood studio system—"the biggest toy train set any boy ever had." But unlike the stereotypical misunder-stood maverick of a poet writing in some drafty garret, filmmaking is such an expensive, responsibly collaborative art form, that playing nice is paramount to this medium, or they take your train set away. Welles spent the rest of his career largely looking in the toy-shop window. In contrast, Wise went on to maximize Hollywood's resources to create a number of memorable movies in an assortment of genres. Maybe the

greatest truth in Welles's toy train metaphor for filmmaking was simply
that, despite his amazing talent, Welles's behavior was rather like that
of George Amberson Minafer—a spoiled brat. *Newsweek* critic Jeremy
McCarter's twenty-first-century slant on the artist offers two perspectives: "To some of his biographers, Welles' descent makes him the
poster boy for a broken culture that grinds up even its geniuses. The
less forgiving call him the author of his own demise, an irresponsible
prima donna who largely got what he deserved . . . an artist [for exam-
ple], who spent plenty of time on his Brazil [*It's All True*] trip partying
with the natives."[45]

It is more than tempting to define Welles as the "author of his
own demise," especially when this pattern of his perceived perse-
cution continued throughout his career. As Henry Karlson, the late
professor emeritus at Indiana University School of Law (Indianapolis) once satirically observed, "There's only so many mistakes you
can make before it starts looking like a plan."[46] But while the verdict
on Welles should be left up to the reader, another example of Welles
losing control of a picture, *Mr. Arkadin* (1955), has special perti-
nence to *Ambersons*. Of the several later occasions in which Welles
(through going over budget and/or missing due dates) lost final cut
of a picture, he saw these two movies as the extremes: "*Arkadin* was
destroyed because they completely changed the entire form of it. The
whole order of it, the whole point of it. [The alteration of] *Ambersons* is nothing compared to [the desecration of] *Arkadin*."[47] Thus,
even if one buys the hoary "world against Welles" enabling defense,
the "boy wonder" himself seems less bothered by *Ambersons'* conclusion than many movie historians.

Wise's work with Welles had a huge impact upon the Hoosier. On
the *Kane* side, Wise was not unlike college student Charlton Heston
after first seeing the movie: "That whole experience was a sort of Saint
Paul on the Road to Damascus thing for me. It opened my eyes to the
possibilities of film."[48] Conversely, *Ambersons* was a study in shooting
yourself in the foot. Decades later Wise summarized what increasingly
handicapped Welles was "self-indulgence and lack of self-discipline

after he made his start."[49] One is reminded of drama critic Ashton Stevens comment about the great actor and self-destructive artist John Barrymore, a Welles friend who died the year *Ambersons* was released, "Nobody can run downhill as fast as a thoroughbred."[50] Consequently, what evolved for Wise was being a creative, commercial storyteller. Given that Wise, the almost journalist, frequently had a message for his movies, he recognized the need to first engage the viewer. But Wise's rise to directing involved working with one more RKO genius—Val Lewton. Yet, this artist excelled within the system while still managing to do his thing.

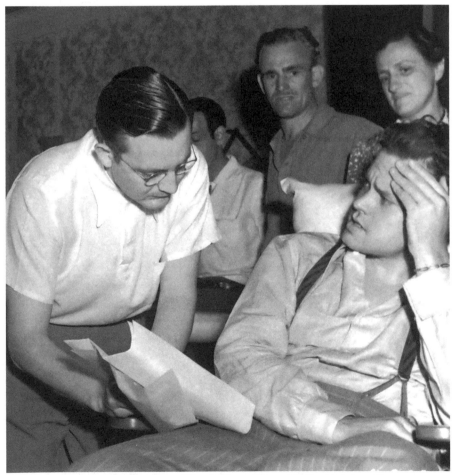

A stormy set session between Robert Wise (left) and Orson Welles (right) on The Magnificent Ambersons *(1942).*

Val Lewton and Becoming a Director

*"There was a time when [the now acclaimed critic]
James Agee [1910–1955], speaking to MGM executive
Dore Schary, called Val Lewton [1904–1951] one of
the three most creative men in American films."*[1]

Amongst the tumult of 1942, Robert Wise was able to experience
one of life's rare gifts—a marriage ceremony on May 25 to a true soul
mate, actress Patricia Doyle, then working as Irene Dunne's stand-in.
The union endured for thirty-three years, until Patricia succumbed
to cancer in 1975. As one of Wise's obituaries later observed, "Unlike
larger-than-life [Orson] Welles, Wise didn't date starlets or allow ego to
overshadow his work. . . . [He simply] made movies that will live on."[2]

Wise had met Doyle in late 1939 after being assigned to edit
Leo McCarey's *My Favorite Wife* (1940, which starred Dunne and
Cary Grant). But Wise's duties went beyond being just the editor. As
noted earlier, injuries McCarey sustained in an automobile accident
necessitated that stage director/writer Garson Kanin direct the movie.
Given his cinema inexperience, Wise acted as Kanin's on-the-set
assistant, with a true love match coming out of this most romantic of
screwball comedies.

Unlike her new husband, who already was more comfortable behind
the scenes, Doyle enjoyed an audience. Prior to her film work she had
been a vaudeville dancer. But while Wise was emerging from RKO
anonymity, she was stalled in small unbilled parts and work as a stand-
in. Though the future couple officially met when she was doubling for

Dunne on *My Favorite Wife*, the majority of Doyle's RKO stand-in work was for Katharine Hepburn, including *Alice Adams* (1935) and *Bringing Up Baby* (1938). Doyle was most proud of being in the cast of John Ford's *Grapes of Wrath* (1940). But with her marriage to Wise she retired from the screen.

Given Wise's workaholic nature, it seems fitting he met Doyle on the job. By late 1939 he had been in Hollywood for more than six years. But between his passion to make good in the movies and RKO's propensity to provide opportunities for him, there had been little time for romance. In a 2005 *Editors Guild Magazine* profile of Wise, author Selise Eiseman shared the artist's extreme film focus at this time, "He said that since he never had any place to go [in his after work hours], he would spend [free] time in the cutting room."[3] For *Grand Illusions* magazine, Wise zeroed in on the exciting intensity of working closely with Kanin on *Bachelor Mother* (1939) and *My Favorite Wife*: "We would spend a day on the [RKO] set and very often have dinner across the street at Lucy's Restaurant and talk about the day's work and the next day's work; so it was a very close and instructive relationship. It was terribly helpful for an editor who aspires to be a director."[4]

Wise's drive for film success could be likened to a comic lyric from a signature song by Johnny Mercer, "Hooray for Hollywood," written shortly before the editor met Doyle: "You might as well try your luck/ you might be Donald Duck." While Wise's slow but steady rise in the movies never quite made him as famous as Donald Duck, he ultimately became a star director. But unlike the patented cartoon duck's comic flights of ego, Wise remained low maintenance. As a Connersville acquaintance recalled near the end of Wise's Oscar-strewn career, "He's pretty much of a down-home-to-earth guy still."[5]

The Wises' only child, Robert Allen, was born the year after their marriage. Parenting is best done through example. Wise's fascination with movies, which, like his parents, involved sharing that interest with a son by seeing new releases, led Robert to work in the industry as an assistant cameraman. Of course, unlike his Hoosier father's childhood, limited to simply haunting local cinemas, young Robert's interest could be further fanned by visiting his father on numerous movie sets. One could also use Wise's child as a metaphor for the director's lifelong encouragement of budding film talent. Along these lines, the celebrated screen historian and critic Anthony Slide recently recalled both Wise's general kindness to beginning filmmakers and how the artist had personally donated money to establish a "special projects" fund for fresh talent through the Hollywood's Director's Guild.[6] Another noted movie historian, Arthur Knight, had linked Wise's support of young gifted filmmakers with the director's belief that one can succeed without becoming an enfant terrible, à la Orson Welles: "Robert Wise believes in young people . . . he feels strongly that the survival of the [film] industry depends upon the encouragement of young people who, like himself, can fashion a modus vivendi within the studio system."[7]

Moreover, unlike many individuals concerned about "humanity" but contemptuous of actual humans, Wise genuinely liked people. This trait is further documented in Wise's private papers, housed at the University of Southern California in Los Angeles. If one were to

Before his marriage, the workaholic Robert Wise (far left) often socialized with his RKO colleagues.

summarize the hundreds of letters in the Wise collection with just
four examples, the starting point would be the director as parent. He
responded to countless wannabe movie stars, such as twelve-year-old
Glenna Boltuck: "Please don't be impatient about getting started on an
acting career. It is a very difficult, frustrating and exacting profession
at best and you will need all the preparation and experience you can
gather along the way. Continue with your schooling—as much of it as
you can possibly acquire."[8]

Second, there was also much *cause*-related correspondence, such as
a letter to Stewart L. Udall, Secretary of the Department of the Interior:
"I have been reading of the proposed Department . . . regulations
which, in my opinion, threaten to gradually destroy Nevada's Pyramid
Lake, the homeland of the Paiute Indians." Wise went on to request
further study be done before any action which would jeopardize the
"economic and social life of the Paiutes."[9]

Third, Wise's correspondence always had time for his many fans,
which also frequently allowed his sense of humor to shine through,
such as his settling of a dispute between Jeffrey Dane and his wife over
the color of the robot Klaatu in *The Day the Earth Stood Still* (1951).
Given that it was a black-and-white film, the Danes were arguing
whether the apparent aluminum-colored robot was really that hue,
or some shade of blue that would better photograph as gray. Wise's
lengthy chatty response that Klaatu was aluminum shaded ended with
this explanation for the quickness of his reply, "I certainly didn't want
you and your wife to lose any more sleep with this matter up in the air
between you. With warmest regards."[10]

Fourth, Wise was always the loyal friend and generous host, such
as the warm invitation to an RKO intimate of years past: "Why don't
you manage, somehow to get down over a weekend . . . [to our beach
house] to be with us for a long, relaxed Sunday brunch? As you know,
[Val's widow] Ruth Lewton lives down the way, and it would be
wonderful for us to all get together after all this time. Just let us know.
Almost any Sunday will be fine and we'll set it up."[11]

Sifting through the mountain of archival material that represents a foundation for any biographer, Wise's youth-oriented sensitivity is a constant, almost as if the director were seeing a younger version of himself. But this nurturing Wise also surfaces in a more high-profile manner—several of his memorable movies prominently feature child actors, including both his first outing as a director, the Lewton-produced *The Curse of the Cat People* (1944); Wise's most iconic picture, *The Day the Earth Stood Still*; and the director's biggest commercial hit, *The Sound of Music* (1965, which also doubled as world cinema's top box-office champion for many years). And most appropriate for this Lewton-related chapter, there is Wise's reincarnation thriller, *Audrey Rose* (1977), whose preteen title character (Susan Swift) has several parallels with *Curse*'s child heroine. When Wise was asked during the *Rose* production if he had any unique method for working with children, he yet again revealed a gentle egalitarian spirit: "I don't know that I have any special procedure. I generally seem to have very good relationships with children. I work easily and gently with them. I don't find the need to trick them into things, to tell them that their pet dog has been run over so I'll get tears out of them—and I understand some directors do resort to this form of trickery. [Children] understand sensible, adult direction. It's just a matter of being patient with them, and willing to try another avenue of approach when one fails."[12] That this degree of sensitivity could be immediately exhibited in the most unlikely of titled pictures, *The Curse of the Cat People*, also owes a great deal to the picture's producer, Lewton.

To properly present the Lewton-Wise connection, however, one must backpedal to the major commercial loss RKO suffered with *The Magnificent Ambersons* (1942). Between this financial fiasco and Welles's aborted documentary, *It's All True*, the director was sacked. Guilt by association also prevailed and several RKO personnel linked to *Ambersons*, including editor Wise, were assigned to lesser follow-up projects. While serving this unofficial punishment, Wise found himself editing such undistinguished fare as *Seven Days Leave* (1942),

Val Lewton at the time of Curse of the Cat People *(1944)*.

Bombardier (1943), and *The Fallen Sparrow* (1943). The best of the trio was *Sparrow*, a World War II domestic thriller starring John Garfield, Maureen O'Hara, and Walter Slezak. But what made it most memorable for Wise was being given the opportunity to reshoot a few scenes when director Richard Wallace was unavailable. Coupled with a similar opportunity on *Ambersons*, Wise was increasingly anxious to move from editing to directing. Though he would theoretically always maintain the methodical mindset of an editor, all movie aficionados realize that power in pictures resides with the director. Unlike the theater, where the writing is more honored, the film script is merely a starting point. Regardless, Wise's banishment to lesser projects continued when he was assigned to edit the Lewton-produced B picture, *The Curse of the Cat People*.

The RKO/Lewton/Wise scenario presents a plethora of paradoxes. The same year the studio fired Welles and publicly mocked the notion of geniuses in the movies, it hired a genius named Lewton. Since RKO's new head of production, Charles Koerner, is sometimes vilified for sacking Welles, does Koerner merit any kudos for almost simultaneously hiring someone who will reinvent the horror genre? Plus, Koerner's directive to Lewton was even to think outside the box, with regard to this genre.

Adding to these ironies, Lewton, as with Welles's original RKO arrangement, was essentially given complete control, as long as he stayed on budget and utilized a series of popular audience-tested titles, ranging from the provocative *Cat People* (1942) to such an over-the-top moniker as *I Walked with a Zombie* (1943). The mind boggles at what Welles's genius and talent might have produced at RKO had he only modestly played ball with the studio. A disciplined Lewton was up to the task, and his success with the studio enabled Wise to escape RKO's proverbial doghouse. The Hoosier's directing break involved another odd twist reminiscent of Welles's exit from RKO. Wise was working with Lewton as the editor of *Curse*, with occasional second-unit directing (uncredited coverage of minor scenes) for other RKO B films, when *Curse* fell way behind schedule. Despite the gentle prodding of producer Lewton, the picture's young documentary-trained director, Gunther Von Fritsch, needed to be replaced. Although Wise had periodically lobbied for a real directing assignment, he had mixed feelings about being selected as the new director on *Curse*. Besides the awkwardness of taking over in midmovie, Wise in his role as an editor and sometimes second-unit director had often worked closely on the set with the novice Fritsch. Being the logical choice to step in made it all the more difficult for Wise. "Gunther and I had planned to do some extra night footage that very [Saturday] evening and I knew he had not yet been told of his dismissal," Wise later recalled. "I couldn't bring myself to go to work with him under those conditions and I called Val to ask his advice. 'Look,' he said, 'if it's not you, it will be somebody else. You're not pushing Gunther out.' So I took over the picture on Monday morning . . . [and] when I arrived on the set that first day, Val gave me a copy of Shaw's *The Art of Rehearsal* which I've kept with me ever since."[13]

In addition to the unusual good fortune of having advanced film apprenticeships with *two* geniuses, Wise was once again given the case for both the blue-collar work ethic and film frugality. But instead of gifted Welles's parable of how *not* to go over budget and burn bridges on *Ambersons*, Lewton was the model of creative efficiency and discipline. Even if Wise had not already been predisposed toward the latter tendencies, two such contrasting examples as Welles and Lewton would have undoubtedly steered him in that direction.

Lewton's pre-RKO accomplishments were many, but he arrived at the studio without the fame and notoriety of Welles. Born in Russia, Val (Vladimir) Lewton (Leventon) immigrated to the United States in 1909, a five-year-old accompanied by his mother, Nina, and sister, Lucy. But before he was thirty, Lewton had written fourteen books, ranging from poetry and potboiler novels to nonfiction on a variety of subjects. The Lewton book that generated the most attention was his naturalistic novel of the Great Depression, *No Bed of Her Own* (1932). Bought by Paramount simply for its erotic title, censors ultimately changed that to *No Man of Her Own* (1932, with Clark Gable and

Carole Lombard). The comedy had little to do with Lewton's serious
novel, and he did not receive a screen credit. But since the shy writer
often used a pseudonym anyway, and enjoyed life's little dark comedies,
simply making some additional movie money was its own victory.

The catalyst, however, for RKO hiring Lewton was anchored more
in his long association with legendary film producer David O. Selznick
of *Gone with the Wind* (1939) fame. The creatively controlling producer
played by Kirk Douglas in *The Bad and the Beautiful* (1953) is often
said to be patterned after Selznick—a character whose ruthless drive for
quality meant any means justified the ends.

Selznick, a former studio boss at RKO, returned to MGM in
1933 as vice president and producer. That same year Lewton came
to Selznick's attention after the writer's mother, employed at MGM's
New York story office, put her son's name on a requested list of Russian
novelists. Lewton was soon hired as a story editor and all-around Man
Friday for Selznick, with the position becoming more multifaceted
as the producer moved to independent production in 1935. Though
Selznick could be a tyrant in his push for perfection, his obsession with
literary-related quality had a profound impact upon Lewton. The result
made Lewton a new and improved Selznick, or as Lewton biographer
Joel E. Siegel described his subject, "a benevolent David Selznick."[14]

When Lewton was given the chance to be RKO's new Selznick,
he created a team operation. Like a Howard Hawks production,
everyone in Lewton's unit was encouraged to contribute ideas to a
project. Lewton was still in charge, and he often wrote and/or rewrote
much of the script material, but there was a true esprit de corps
among his people. And just as Wise had admired Welles's creativity
but rejected his egotism, Lewton was to follow the same pattern after
leaving Selznick. Wise blossomed in the Lewton unit, affectionately
nicknamed "the snake pit," and was soon rewarded with a directing
opportunity. Moreover, the fact that the intensely private and cultured
Lewton befriended Wise was an additional confidence booster for
the young man. A small literary soiree at the Lewtons, which often
included the producer's friend and neighbor, William Faulkner, would

have been heady stuff for Wise. But there was also warmth of humor associated with Lewton's company. "Lewton was a man of great taste and sensitivity," Wise noted. "He was very well educated, well-read, a writer. . . . [But he was also] robust, a rather jolly fellow, [who] liked to sit around evenings and swap yarns and tell stories and anecdotes."[15]

While Wise, the shy former humor columnist, would have savored the laughter, he was undoubtedly also drawn to the accomplished producer's inherent modesty. One gets a sense of both these traits in Lewton's self-deprecating explanation on how he came to head his own cinema "snake pit": "Years ago I wrote novels for a living, and when RKO was looking for producers, someone told them I had written horrible novels. They misunderstood the word horrible for horror and I got the job."[16]

Buried within this self-effacing joke was another trait Wise found amusing. Lewton was a comic fifth columnist. He creatively worked within the studio system by watching the budget *and* getting in his RKO digs at authority by paying lip service to studio policy and then doing it his way. Thus, Lewton's tongue-in-cheek hiring story is also an indirect satirical slap at a RKO leadership that could not differentiate between such basic terms as "horrible" and "horror."

A Wise-related example of Lewton as a comic fifth columnist is tied to Wise's *The Body Snatcher* (1945). RKO producers and studio powerbrokers viewed film rushes at noon each day, prior to the cast and crew. Wise was modestly behind schedule on *Snatcher*, and Lewton was ordered to tell his young director to "pick it up." When the producer later passed this information on to Wise, Lewton made it clear he was merely recycling the words, only to undercut any fears Wise might have by adding, "I saw the rushes. They looked great. Go on and make your picture."[17]

The Lewton snake pit also had its own built-in fifth columnist attitude, even without their producer's outsider tendencies. The catalyst for this view was RKO's demotion of people who worked on *Ambersons*. Wise's close friend and assistant editor on the Welles picture, Mark Robson, later entertainingly explained how a punishment turned to pleasure when it involved Lewton: "Everyone who was associated with Orson [Welles] at RKO was involved in a kind of purge. We were all in trouble because of Orson. So a lot of us, Robert Wise and myself anyway, were . . . demoted to Val's [Lewton] low-budget 'B' unit. The only thing is, Val was an artist, and all his pictures were carefully worked out, even though many of them started out simply as 'Let's make a picture about. . . .' For instance, we saw a painting by [Arnold] Böcklin, called the 'Isle of the Dead' [1880], and someone said, 'Let's make a picture about something that happened on that island.' So we did. . . . We had a lot of fun."[18] As with Wise, Lewton launched Robson's successful directing career, starting with *The Seventh Victim* (1943). More than three decades later, Wise and Robson twice formed joint production corporations, the Filmmakers Group (1971) and the Tripar Group (1974).

Wise's memory of his first official day as a director on *Curse* begins with his own sense of humor, and then morphs into the thoroughness which became a signature of his work. "I was a very nervous cat [that] Monday morning," he recalled. "I was in the studio and [sound] stages at about five o'clock in the morning, before the crew even thought of coming in. [I] went in and turned the stage lights on and went over to the set we were shooting in, which had all the furniture covered with sheets. I took everything off and started to study the set and the scene and walk around and try to figure out what I was going to shoot that morning. Of course, I had one advantage [as a novice]. I knew all the actors. I'd been around the set a lot visiting, as an editor [of the film]. I knew all the crew members. It went all right the minute I started to work with the actors, started directing, putting scenes together, the nervousness left me."[19]

Ironically, while Wise quickly felt comfortable directing, and there was no problem from the filmmaker he replaced (Fritsch, who received a codirector credit on the picture and went on to a successful career as a television director), the Hoosier was briefly blindsided by a disgruntled crew member. But as the modest, unassuming Wise could continually demonstrate throughout his long career, he was not averse

Ann Carter and Kent Smith in a charming dark fantasy with the misleading title, The Curse of the Cat People *(1944).*

to taking tough, decisive actions. "I only had a little problem with the production manager. I guess he was disappointed that he wasn't given the opportunity to take over [the directing] and was a little tough with me the first couple of days," Wise recalled. "So much so that, at the end of the second day, I had to turn on him and tell him that if he didn't like it he could leave the picture. From then on he was fine."[20] During this period Wise also began auditing some acting classes, to assist his directing relationship with performers.

Despite *Curse*'s title, the picture is better defined as an inventively dark fantasy about a solitary child (Ann Carter) who conjurers up an imaginary friend (Simone Simon). But because Simone turns out to be the vision/spirit of her father's (Kent Smith) moody deceased first wife, who was cursed in the original *Cat People* (1942) with seeming transformations (never shown) into a murderous black leopard, Smith's character is concerned about his equally mercurial young daughter. Critics not locked into a simple horror sequel mentality were charmed by the film. James Agee's *Nation* review called *Curse* "a brave, sensitive, and admirable little psychological melodrama about a lonely six-year-old girl . . . [allowing an audience to be] captivated by the poetry and danger of childhood [fears]."[21] *PM* critic John T. McManus observed: "I'd drop that accursed title fast, substituting some beckoning line out of [Robert Louis Stevenson's 1885 poetry text] *A Child's Garden of Verses* and quit scaring nice people away from one of the nicest movies ever made."[22] (Interestingly, a later historian suggested the film was influenced by Stevenson's "The Unseen Playmate"—a more appropriate title.[23]) The *New York Times*' Bosley Crowther stated, "[*Curse*] makes a rare departure from the ordinary run of horror films and emerges as an oddly touching study of the working of a sensitive child's mind."[24]

Given, however, that the picture's title, the horror movie nature of its precursor, and the fact that the high volume of 1940s screen production meant that larger markets often funneled films to specialty theaters, some critics and viewers were not as appreciative as the aforementioned cited examples from left-wing publications. Rose Pelswick's *New York Journal American* mixed review of *Curse* directly addresses why the picture was an immediate disconnect for some audiences: "The new film at the Rialto Theatre isn't the usual type of Rialto presentation inasmuch as it doesn't contain a single mad scientist, diabolical gadget or haunted leopardess [despite its title]. It does have a ghost [Simone Simon] but the ghost is a friendly spirit that even takes time off to do some singing."[25]

The quality of the movie gradually made itself known to the general public, with Agee later heralding *Curse* and *Youth Runs Wild* (1944, another Lewton-produced picture) as "The best fiction films of the year"—an unprecedented honor for B movies.[26] By 1972 film historian Joel E. Siegel would write, "[*Curse*] may well be the most poetically conceived movie about the world of the child ever attempted in Hollywood."[27] George Brown's 1993 *Village Voice* musings about the movie brilliantly capture the timelessness of *Curse*, especially when little Ann Carter collapses in fear on the bridge convinced that the hoof-like horseman have come to claim her crown. But former sound editor Wise helps turn this instance of heart-stopping panic into a "gotcha!" moment. The sound is merely tire chains on an approaching car. Brown's capsulation of the scene, the "automobile as the headless horseman of our age," implies Lewton's central principle—that nothing is as frightening as our own imagination.[28] Critical acclaim was not limited to cinema. The Hollywood Writers Mobilization Committee and the Los Angeles Council of Social Agencies focused upon the film's positive portrayal of little Ann Carter's character during a conference (September 7, 1944) examining the use/misuse of children in cinema. Soon, social scientists would reference *Curse* in their studies of human behavior, such as Yale Press's David Riesman book *The Lonely Crowd* (1950). For example, Riesman cites the scene where the child is supposed to invite playmates to her birthday party: "But believing her father's joke that the big tree in the yard is a mailbox, she puts the invitations there and they never go out . . . [When the party is ruined] her father scolds her for taking him seriously. [Yet, she is later punished for having an imaginary friend.] The parents insist that the child somehow know, without a formal etiquette, when things are supposed to be 'real' and when 'pretend.'"[29] As Wise later observed, "[*Curse*] became a training film for child psychologists."[30] The movie also helped launch Wise the public figure, as he and Lewton were invited to attend other behavioral conferences.

This initial seminar also praised both Lewton and Wise for the progressive treatment of *Curse*'s black servant (played by singer/actor Sir Lancelot). Though this was a hallmark of Lewton's work, a strong sense of equality had always been part of Wise's makeup, too. Unfortunately, such enlightened thinking was still far from the mid-1940s norm. In an Irving Hoffman *Hollywood Reporter* column which, coincidently, appeared the day after the behavioral conference, the journalist cited at length a letter from a concerned serviceman: "Isn't it about time the motion picture industry discovered that it's bad taste to portray Negroes

A little girl (Ann Carter) and her imaginary friend (Simone Simon) in The Curse of the Cat People.

as scared, knee-knocking cowards—while so many of them are giving their lives on America's battlefronts? In recent weeks, particularly in the ghost and mystery pictures, Negro actors are compelled, as they have been for years, to roll their eyes, shudder and hide behind doors when they hear strange noises."[31]

Of course, while Simon was top-billed in *Curse*, the real star is the lovely little Carter, who resembled an undersized Veronica Lake. (Carter played Lake's daughter in *I Married a Witch*, 1942.) Her introspective child in *Curse*, with "the unseen playmate," is part of the story's dual focus, coupled with another misunderstood daughter who lives down the street—the sexy, all-grown-up Elizabeth Russell (Cat Woman of the original *Cat People*). While the child's screen father is almost neurotic in his need to rid her of an imaginary friend, Russell's elderly mother (Julia Dean), for whom she cares, has completely jumped the tracks mentally. The catalyst was a bad accident when Russell was Carter's age, causing the pleasantly potted old lady to think her daughter died as a child.

The link connecting these two narrative strands is the random friendship the daft Dean offers the neighborhood Carter girl— seemingly anchored in maternal feelings the elderly woman feels towards the youngster, as if she were a surrogate for Dean's now grown daughter. Though the positive *Curse* reviews appreciated the film's message to be sensitive to young children, there was little critical attention given to Russell's equally victimized, by another parent, grown child. Yet, Russell's growing instability suggests the young girl's potential plight if her dense father does not respect his child's imaginatively fragile mind. As with Wise's later *Audrey Rose*, a young protagonist comes to represent a child from years before. But while the benevolent "friend"/spirit manages to orchestrate a last-minute rescue for the *Curse* child (when the unstable Russell almost kills her), *Rose*'s reincarnated title character ultimately dies—a victim of a chilling regressive hypnosis that causes Audrey to again fatally experience her own death. In each movie the endangerment of the youngster is tied to an insensitive, controlling father. Interestingly, when Wise was asked if there was violence inherent to the hysterical-nightmare scenes in *Rose*, when child actress Susan Swift replicates the terror of dying in a burning car (from a prior life), the director sounded very much like Lewton on the subject of subtle horror: "It is my feeling that filmmakers should be more creative in their approach to those areas in their films that need violence and leave much more to the imagination of the viewer."[32] Consequently, unlike another twelve-year-old horror victim in the earlier *Exorcist* (1973), the internalized terror of *Rose* is equally effective, without self-mutilation and projectile vomiting.

Pioneering film critic and masterful wordsmith Manny Farber once said of another Wise movie, "The fact that this film is at all commendable is the result of Wise's ability to transform a melodrama into something that mixes terror, geography and truth."[33] This statement is equally applicable to many Wise pictures, especially *Curse* and *Rose*. Besides the director's ability to hone in on a family melodrama scenario tucked away in various genres, Wise films often use a child and/ or a childlike figure, and all that seeming vulnerability, to challenge inherent weaknesses in the blustery whistling-in-the-dark adult world. That is, a child's propensity to make believe, a gift often dulled with age, can also be a prick to the bubble insulating the grownup world. As fantasy film historian J. P. Telotte noted, the imagination of an imaginative youngster often "evokes an ambiguity and even a secret anxiety in the adult realm, for the . . . child reflects many of the fears and insecurities man has managed to dispel or block out."[34] Based upon studying countless Wise interviews, and briefly meeting him for a Charlie Chaplin documentary, one could credit the director's sensitivity to a child's ability to see past the fabric of age by the fact Wise always seemed to be the metaphorically youngest person in the room—an ambassador between the world of Peter Pan and enlightened adulthood. (This might also explain why he worked so well with that brilliant spoiled brat, Welles.)

While *Curse* was a Robert Louis Stevenson-like dark fantasy masquerading as a horror picture, Wise also collaborated with Lewton on a true terror tale from Stevenson, *The Body Snatcher*. The film's

Boris Karloff in a scene from The Body Snatcher *(1945).*

backstory was another example of Lewton's unit being creative with compromise. Despite *Curse*'s critical acclaim, the film's revenue was not close to the original film's box office numbers. RKO brought in a former Universal horror person, Jack Gross, to oversee budgets and make suggestions. At this point, Lewton and Wise preferred putting ordinary American people in realistic contemporary settings, anticipating by well over a decade Alfred Hitchcock's genre-changing horror film masterpiece *Psycho* (1960).

To enhance Gross's then traditional approach to cinema horror, which meant European settings of the past and decidedly unusual sinister figures, the new Lewton supervisor wanted to bring in an actor who ironically embodied all these traits—Boris Karloff. The poetically sardonic critic/film historian David Thomson has written of this pantheon of terror, "[Karloff] shows us monsters . . . who have been isolated by the unthinking cruelty of the 'wholesome' world."[35] This certainly described Karloff's *Body Snatcher* character—a cabman/grave-robber procuring cadavers for a medical school at a time and place (1831 Edinburgh) when legal access to corpses for anatomy classes was severely restricted. Karloff's necessary "monster" was poorly served by the school's director, Doctor MacFarlane (Henry Daniell). Though this director/professor should be the nominal good guy, the story and perennial villain Daniell (see his Garbitsch/Josef Goebbels from *The Great Dictator*, 1940) make him an excellent example of the "unthinking cruelty of the 'wholesome' world." Specifically, the doctor justifies grave robbing for educational purposes, but looks down upon the individual providing the service. Couple this with the ongoing sarcasm of the aptly named Gray (Karloff), who, for example, when called "a malignant, evil cancer" by Daniell's doctor, responds, "You've made a disease of me, eh Toddy?," transforms the heavy into a more likable character. Yet, this was still in the future. Lewton and Wise initially had reservations about using the high-profile, story-distracting Karloff. Gross simply asked the men to meet with the actor. "It was strange," Wise said of that first meeting. "Boris came to the studio for the meeting with Val, Mark [Robson], and me. I had never seen him

except on the screen—and this was before color film [was the norm].
When he first walked in the door I was startled by his [slate gray]
coloring, the strange bluish cast—but when he turned those eyes on us
and that velvet voice said, 'Good afternoon, gentleman,' we were his,
and never thought about anything else."[36]

An off-the-set friendship developed between the literature-inclined
Karloff and Wise, with the director also being bowled over by the
actor's professionalism. Karloff was having severe back problems but
soldiered through the shooting with an upbeat manner. Moreover,
Wise was also appreciative of Karloff's sensitivity and patience with his
frequent screen nemesis (Bela Lugosi in a small role), at a time when his
costar's private life was unraveling. Karloff biographer Paul M. Jensen
felt Wise's direction reinforced the dialogue and created "a strongly
visual atmosphere of evil."[37] This is best demonstrated by Karloff's
almost affectionate smothering of Lugosi, a darkly comic answer to his
sometimes cinema sidekick's question on how the "barking" (murders)
were done. The scene's piece de resistance is then having Karloff's
character kindly stroke his cat.

Years later in correspondence with a fan, Wise described *Snatcher*
as "one of my own personal favorites of all the films I've made." In the
same letter Wise credited much of this joy factor to Karloff: "He was
a very warm, gentle and intelligent person. . . . He was most intrigued
and caught up in the challenge of playing the character of the Body
Snatcher for he felt it would give him an opportunity to show his
quality as an actor that went far beyond the monster roles he was
associated with."[38] Karloff and Wise made the most of the opportunity,
with pop-culture historian Elliott Stein later crediting *Snatcher* as the
beginning of a time when "Karloff enjoyed an artistic resurgence."[39]

Snatcher also helped put Wise on the film map. The rave reviews
for this critical and commercial hit frequently singled out the director
for special attention. Wise was even noted in the *Hollywood Reporter*'s
title for its critique: "'Body Snatcher' All Horror Fans Want; Lewton,
Wise Hit." This notice went on to observe, "As a horror picture, 'The
Body Snatcher' is an unqualified lulu. . . . Robert Wise gave the picture

distinctive direction which developed the quality of convincing realism in the story."[40] The *New York Herald Tribune* added: "Karloff proves that with capable direction and a script to work with he can be a real menace instead of a mere monster. Director Robert Wise has used all of the macabre lighting effects in the . . . [Stevenson tale] to set off the somber story."[41]

New York's *PM* critique was simply a nonstop hosanna, with this opening claim: "After watching the sorry parade of penny dreadfuls streaming . . . through the gory portals of the Rialto Theatre, I am compelled to the conclusion that *The Body Snatcher* is much too good for the lot of them."[42] The box-office monitoring *Variety* indirectly seconded this verdict by predicting *Snatcher* would score in *all* theatrical

Boris Karloff dominated The Body Snatcher *artwork, too.*

settings: "Containing horror in large doses . . . it should do strong biz [business] in both single-feature houses [theaters] catering to this type [of genre] audience and on the duals [double-billed at mainstream theaters]."[43] The *Motion Picture Daily* critic summed up the thrill factor by stating: "Robert Wise's direction creates an unbroken mood of somberness and suspense. . . . Altogether, 'The Body Snatcher' is far superior to the general run of horror films."[44]

One should be quick to add, however, that executive producer Gross had not radically changed the Lewton/Wise game plan to simply overt horror. Yes, he had encouraged a return to the genre's old-school setting, but the hallmark of a snake pit production remained—an understated psychological study of terror grounded in the fears inherent to one's imagination. In William K. Everson's pioneering study, *Classics of the Horror Film*, he observed: "The subtlest and most terrifying moments in Robert Wise's *The Body Snatcher* are achieved through suggestion and sensitive editing rather than an undisciplined charge through a series of shock close-ups and brutalities."[45]

Snatcher's conclusion borrows from Edgar Allan Poe's signature short story, "The Tell-Tale Heart" (1849), where the murderer's own conscience acts as the executioner. For Poe, or for any good storyteller, the payoff lies well below surface events. Consequently, while Daniell's doctor dies from a coach accident after doing some grave robbing of his own, the frightening finale allows viewers to see the corpse from his eyes. Having murdered his nemesis (Karloff) shortly before, Daniell's character hallucinates an elderly woman's cadaver into the body of Gray—come to haunt him. But the Poe-like build-up to the doctor's death in a runaway coach over a precipice is anchored in Daniell's figure repeatedly hearing, in his mind, Gray's earlier caustically mocking threat, "[You'll] never get rid of me." This variation upon the crazed murderer of "The Tell-Tale Heart" still hearing his victim's heartbeat was an opportunity for Wise to utilize his earlier career experience as a sound editor. And this provocative conclusion was a hit with period critics. Even the tony *New Yorker* comically observed: "The scene in which that wicked sawbones, Henry Daniell, plunges over a cliff in the relentless embrace of the corpse of Boris Karloff is especially recommended to your morbid attention."[46]

For the horror aficionado, Wise's *Snatcher* is a tutorial, as well as arguably being one of Karloff's top three films, sandwiched between James Whale's *Frankenstein* (1931) and Peter Bogdanovich's *Targets* (1968). Sadly, the subtle touch is now sometimes perceived as a horror limitation for modern gore fans of the post-*Se7en* (1995) wallow in human depravity offshoots of the genre. Of course, the explanation for this dumbing down might be that many contemporary viewers have the attention spans of a tsetse fly.

Snatcher, like many Wise films, regardless of the genre, reveals the dark side beneath man's thin veneer of civilization. Yet, in real life Wise remained the eternal "mensch"—the good fellow. While there was sometimes a similar sort of person in his pictures, cinema happiness still often seemed a long shot. Farber later wrote, "Wise is inordinately suited to bringing his pessimistic impression of mankind into credible shape."[47] Be that as it may, Wise often found a way of planting at least a modicum of promise in the pessimism. This trait was undoubtedly reinforced by Lewton. The scholarly producer encouraged the addition of literary axioms to his B pictures, particularly in order to wrestle something hopeful from the darkest of situations—a heartfelt belief that was also a welcome metaphorical message for a nation then at war. The Hippocrates quote that closes *Snatcher*, shortly after the violent death of the doctor, is just that sort of maxim: "It is through error that man tries and rises. It is through tragedy he learns. All the roads of learning begin in darkness and go into the light." This is a startlingly positive take on a Poe-like conclusion, but it is consistent with the mindsets of Lewton and Wise.

To demonstrate, however, that the addition of this axiom is not merely some knee-jerk tack-on, with no legitimate ties to the story, one could offer the following footnote. Like *Curse*, there is another dual-focus narrative at work in *Snatcher*. Daniell's doctor, MacFarlane, has a student assistant, Fettes (Russell Wade), implicated in the grave-robbing scenario by way of paying and logging in each of Gray's deliveries. In fact, Fettes is along on the doctor's fatal final ride, having just helped him acquire a fresh corpse from the cemetery—the cadaver Daniell will come to believe is Gray. Fettes, however, has not yet morphed into a MacFarlane, and he is uncomfortable with what they have done, as Daniell had browbeaten him into helping with a professorial "for the sake of science" argument. Fettes survival of the nightmare ride frees him from the doctor's fate, and "through tragedy he learns."

There is also something perversely positive connected to a *Snatcher* subplot involving yet another Wise use of a child. The case of a paralyzed girl, Georgina Marsh (Sharyn Moffett), has been brought to MacFarlane's attention by Fettes. Successful back surgery would allow her to walk again. The doctor initially refuses, but Gray threatens to go public with their unlawful partnership if MacFarlane does not operate. The surgery seems to fail, and in a scene uncharacteristic of the doctor, MacFarlane actually seeks Gray out and in frustrated shock the doctor claims that he had done everything "right" in the surgery. A paraphrasing of Gray's response is a warning all good teachers try to impart: "A lot of knowledge does not represent understanding." While this line would be paradoxical payoff enough, the fact that little Georgina does eventually walk is reminiscent of the something good from someone bad conclusion to H. G. Wells's *The Island of Doctor Moreau* (1896), when one realizes the crazed title character has sculpted one human masterpiece. As the saying goes, "The world turns but sometimes, it doesn't seem to turn at all."[48]

Just as Lewton launched Wise's directing career, the artists' only other collaboration, *Mademoiselle Fifi* (1944), would begin to demonstrate both the genre diversity for which Wise is now best known, and many ongoing themes *not* acknowledged/missed in his future films. *Fifi* is pivotal to making the long-overdue case for Wise the auteur.

5

Lewton and Maupassant: A Template Picture

*Historian Ihor Sevcenko once wrote that historians fell into
two categories: "the brightly colored butterfly flitting about over
a flower bed" and "the crawling caterpillar whose worm's-eye
view covers the expanseof a single cabbage leaf."*[1]

Robert Wise's body of work suggests he was an artist similar to *both*
historian types noted above. His talent for mounting movie classics in
a variety of genres could be called creatively flying over a filmic "flower
bed." And Wise's equal attention to detail on each cinema project was
similar to "the crawling caterpillar . . . [on] a single cabbage leaf." Like
another film realist, the pioneering Erich von Stroheim, Wise quickly
realized movie meticulousness was not just for the viewer. Commenting
on one of his Val Lewton-produced pictures, Wise said: "I believe
that the atmosphere that's created by some of those 'unregistering'
bits of detail is very pervasive and gets to the actors; it influences
them, therefore it influences the whole scene."[2] Thankfully, unlike the
spendthrift Stroheim, Wise's attention to particulars came without the
flying-off-the-rails budget escalations that aborted the older filmmaker's
directing career.

Sandwiched between Wise's two excursions into films of the
fantastic, *The Curse of the Cat People* (1944) and *The Body Snatcher*
(1945), he began to demonstrate his proclivity for genre diversity by
directing the Val Lewton-produced *Mademoiselle Fifi* (1944). The
movie is a melodrama/problem film set against the backdrop of the

Franco-Prussian War (1870). *Fifi* is fashioned from two Guy de Maupassant short stories, "Boule de Suif" and "Mademoiselle Fifi." While the *Hollywood Reporter's* review stated this marked "the first time Maupassant has been given actual screen credit for an original story," period audiences would have been familiar with the framework of "Boule de Suif," given its uncredited influence on John Ford's *Stagecoach* (1939).[3] In Maupassant's story, the title character is the proverbial hooker with a heart of gold. But it is a stereotype which, while if not beginning here, was a seminal depiction of the figure. Maupassant, after all, is considered the father of the French short story, and this is the tale that put him on the cultural map of Europe. Maupassant's pleasantly plump French courtesan ("Boule de Suife" means "ball of fat") is traveling by public stage through the Prussian-occupied countryside. Her coach companions come from assorted social backgrounds united only by their hypocritical actions when a German officer attempts to take advantage of her.

The second Maupassant short story from which Wise's film takes its title, *Mademoiselle Fifi*, is a satirical reference to an especially vindictive, womanizing Prussian officer during this same time period. As Maupassant describes the nickname's origin in the story, the officer's own comrades have tagged him with the "Mademoiselle Fifi" label, in part, because of "his dandified style and small waist . . . [and] pale face . . . [and the habit] of employing the French expression, *Fi, Fi done* . . . when he wished to express his sovereign contempt for persons."[4] The story chronicles the consequences of his abusive behavior toward Rachel, a very young Jewish prostitute. The folding together of these two tales as a movie has Simone Simon playing a composite of both women—Elizabeth, a patriotic laundress. Hollywood censorship would not allow the character to be openly played as a courtesan, but her fellow travelers' comments leave no doubt about her profession. Plus, the brothel-like behavior of her laundry coworkers further reinforces the original Maupassant situation. Still, the payoff edge to the French author's "Boule de Suif," in which the patriotic prostitute is pressured to sleep with a Prussian officer or none of her fellow passengers can

The angelic beauty of Simone Simon in The Curse of the Cat People.

continue on their journey, is blunted by film censorship—the odious demand has been reduced to dining with the man. The film, however, effectively manipulates the scenario to demonstrate how the cinema passengers would believe a tryst had transpired. In either case, the picture or the printed page, Elizabeth is only treated kindly when the others have something to be gained. Once the journey can continue, the passengers again have no time for her. But the underlying hypocrisy goes much deeper. Through the ongoing shared conversations of the travelers, one realizes all but Elizabeth have willingly and profitably collaborated with the occupying Germans. The despised courtesan/laundress is the *only* patriot on the stage.

Wise utilizes Maupassant's "Fifi" story in the second half of the movie, when Elizabeth reaches her hometown. Not unlike the previous pressure placed upon her by collaborating citizens to bed the Prussian, Elizabeth is "encouraged" to attend a German officers' party that will obviously become an orgy. After being pawed by Fifi, including a vicious biting kiss that makes Elizabeth's mouth bleed (shades of traditional horror), and followed by insults to her beloved France, she fatally stabs the German with a small dinner knife. Again, the lowly prostitute, despised by her cowardly hypocritical countrymen, has proven to be the true patriot. As Maupassant himself summarized: "To hear them [her fellow passengers] you would have finally come to the conclusion that woman's [especially a patriotic courtesan] sole mission here below was to perpetually sacrifice her person . . . to the caprices of the warrior. . . . She felt herself drowning in the flood of contempt shown towards her by these honest scoundrels who had first sacrificed her and then cast her off like some useless and unclean thing."[5]

The adaptation of Maupassant is memorable for Wise's career on six counts. First, just as *Curse* and *Snatcher* were anchored in genres (fantasy and horror) conducive to exploring Wise's interest in man's darker and/or weaker side, the Maupassant melodramas set against war were equally rich for showcasing the flaws and follies of humanity. Indeed, one could even apply an early literary description

"Robert Wise Director" (circa mid-to-late 1940s).

of Maupassant's work, a "philosophy of cynicism," to much of Wise's canon.[6] A war backdrop as a litmus test for the feebleness of human values surfaces periodically during Wise's career. For example, early in *Until They Sail* (1957, from James Michener's novel), Jean Simmons's character states: "It [temptation] happens to us in New Zealand the way it happens in other countries where the men went marching off to war."

Coincidentally, the humor-loving Wise was a fan of Mark Twain, who also often addressed the vulnerability of man. While the director's specific thoughts on Twain's satirical short story, "The Man That Corrupted Hadleyburg" (1899), are unknown, one assumes the filmmaker appreciated the tale's conclusion. The smug honest town of the title had formerly embraced the motto: "Lead us not into temptation." But when roundly humiliated by a stranger, the community dropped a single word from its civic axiom—"not." Twain, as was the case with Wise, had ongoing questions about mankind's basic (baser?) instincts, but the humorist ultimately felt it was better to continually test one's values by asking, "Lead us into temptation."

Second, there is a provocative political subtext to Wise's *Fifi*, a shrewd buried-in-a-period-picture suggestion that Wise sometimes revisited in later work. The movie makes some harsh comments about French collaborators during the German occupation of 1870 in a film made during World War II, when another German occupation of France depended upon collaborators—the Vichy government. A later film historian called the picture's wily message "every bit as brave as its heroine," adding: "This playing off of the [French] middle-class collaborations against the cruelty of the Prussian invaders gives the film a [period] . . . moral richness and subtlety no other Hollywood wartime film begins to approach."[7] Wise's most effective later example of a political subtext occurs in *The Sand Pebbles* (1966), a movie ostensibly about a U.S. gunboat policing China's Yangtze River in 1926. But the parallels between what will be a failed example of American imperialism in *Sand Pebbles*, and this country's then involvement in Vietnam, is striking.

Third, Wise's tendency to focus upon children, or childlike figures, is again apparent in *Fifi*. Despite Elizabeth's profession, she is like *Curse*'s little Amy (Ann Carter) in several ways. Both mistakenly assume adults mean what they say. Both are passionate in their beliefs, despite receiving little support for them (Elizabeth's patriotism and Amy's imaginary friend). And both are capable of spontaneous violence when provoked. For example, Amy's unexpected striking of a butterfly-crushing playmate is as unforeseen and startling as Elizabeth's stabbing of the Prussian. One could suggest such outbursts are provoked by the sudden realization of how naturally cruel the world can be. For Elizabeth, the disillusionment with the people around her anticipates Robert Sherrill's observation, "The great war stories do not deal solely with the death of soldiers but with the death of idealism."[8]

Given the importance of the childlike figure to Wise's future work, and their inevitable disillusionment with surrogate adults, one must note that Antoine De Saint-Exupéry's beloved children's novella, *The Little Prince* (1943) first appeared the year before *Curse* and *Fifi* were released. Fittingly, both of Wise's young heroines from these pictures would have been comfortable uttering a pivotal observation by Saint-Exupéry's little protagonist: "Grown-ups never understand anything by themselves, and it is tiresome for children to be always and forever explaining things to them."[9] Jump forward to 1951 and novelist J. D. Salinger's angry adolescent Holden Caulfield is singing a similar song about adults: "I was surrounded by phonies . . . They were coming in the goddam window."[10] Both literary figures were favorites of James Dean, who explored similar angst-ridden youngsters in *East of Eden* (1955) and *Rebel without a Cause* (1955).[11] Wise's early directorial work helped usher this young antihero into mainstream American cinema. And while he often keyed upon a vulnerable girl/woman, there were Holden Caulfield types, too, from Wise's *Somebody up There Likes Me* (1956, Paul Newman in a role meant for James Dean), to *Sand Pebbles* (Steve McQueen in a Deanlike part).

Maupassant and Wise also effectively play the social class card as a further projection of the courtesan as child. The French author's

Steve McQueen in The Sand Pebbles *(1966).*

description of the scheming hypocritical Count (a fellow stage passenger) reads as follows: "He adopted that familiar, paternal, somewhat contemptuous tone which elderly men affect towards such girls, calling her 'my dear child,' treating her from the height of his social position and indisputable respectability."[12]

Wise accents, even improves upon, this class/child phenomenon in the casting of the schoolgirl-like Simon as the prostitute. Obviously, she is no "ball of fat." But Maupassant's age was still taken with the full-figured Rubenesque exuberance of the female form. The porcelain-doll perfection of Simon's youthful appearance better fits a modern age's take upon sexuality. In fact, to play devil's advocate, one could argue she flirts with being suggestive of child pornography, given that her character is a prostitute. Moreover, Wise was a firm believer that successful filmmaking was all about the casting, a frequently repeated axiom of Leo McCarey, for whom Wise had edited *My Favorite Wife* (1940).[13] Whether or not the Hoosier was pushing the sexual envelope with Simon in *Fifi* (she did appear in his first three features), Wise's frustrations over Hollywood censorship would have made him a prime candidate for some fifth columnism toward industry blue noses. As it was, he was being forced to label the poignantly drawn courtesan of Maupassant's most famous story a "laundress." But then, as late as Blake Edwards's adaptation of Truman Capote's *Breakfast at Tiffany's* (1961), the film capital missed the memo about Holly Golightly being a call girl.

Wise's later films occasionally revisited this parental controlling-class theme in relationship to a childlike prostitute, such as in *Two for the Seesaw* (1962, from the William Gibson play). Though Shirley MacLaine's sweetly naïve New York eccentric is not a call girl, she is very free with her body. When her struggling character meets a transplanted lawyer (Robert Mitchum) from the Midwest, there is often a sense of condescending parent-to-child attitude mixed into a relationship driven by his wanting to take care of her. Unlike the *Fifi* Count, Mitchum loves the girl, but his privileged class (and gender) orientation remains grating, even when he tries to compliment her, "You're a gift, infant . . . the way people were meant to be."

A fourth link between *Fifi* and other Wise pictures involves the compromisingly collaborative nature of people, even when signature villains (such as the Prussians) are not around. For example, Wise's noirsh *The Captive City* (1952), about a crusading small-town newspaper editor (John Forsythe), opens with a quote from U.S. Senator Estes Kefauver: "Ordinarily, Americans don't think much about the existence of organized crime; they know vaguely that it is there, and they let it go at that . . . UNLESS PRODDED BY SOME UNUSUAL CIRCUMSTANCES." This indictment of the majority is most damning in *Captive City* when the editor asks for help from the local clergy. Their spokesman, Reverend Nash (Ian Wolfe), says the problem is not so much with the Mafia bookies but rather with the collaborating "respectable elements." More tellingly, Nash says no to getting involved because, "We'd need to take on our own congregations."

Many of Wise's film figures do not want to metaphorically rock the boat, others are so desperate they will do anything to just get into the boat. As a character in Wise's aptly titled *Odds Against Tomorrow* (1959), poetically taunts another, "You're looking for a hole in the fence like everyone else." Or, on some occasions, as in Wise's boxing picture, *The Set-Up* (1949), the have-not fight fans are essentially an angry audience/mob desirous of distracting bloodbath entertainment. While this is hardly feel good Frank Capra territory, Wise does often provide the viewer with a likable and/or positive person with which to identify, whether it is Simon's patriotic courtesan in *Fifi*, or Forsythe's straight-arrow editor in *City*.

Of course, the downside to many of Wise's sympathetically central figures is that, as Mitchum's character describes MacLaine in *Two for the Seesaw*, "you're a born victim . . . of yourself." Frequently, things are simply not thought through, such as the absurdist anger in the dying last words of Steve McQueen's *Sand Pebbles* character, when a good deed is about to cost him his life: "I was home [safe]. What happened? What the hell happened?" But Wise's select few sometimes have an inherent goodness in them despite life's abuses, over which they have little control. In an observation that is applicable to many of Wise's soft-touch characters, starting with Simon's Elizabeth, MacLaine's *Seesaw* figure confesses that if a disagreeable past lover called: "I'd make a face. I'd think who needs it, and I'd talk to him. It's another human being. Maybe they're sick. Maybe they need something. At least you find out why they're calling."

Is this a sap or a saint? Wise sometimes gave viewers bona-fide examples of the latter, too, such as the Christlike alien (Michael Rennie) of *The Day the Earth Stood Still* (1951), or the almost nun (Julie Andrews) of *The Sound of Music* (1965). Ironically, part of the reason these two uniquely positive figures work is that their stories are drawn from incredibly negative, hate-filled periods of history—the Cold War fear and paranoia of the early 1950s, and Nazi Germany's late 1930s swallowing of Europe.

Fifth, as the earlier points have suggested, there is often a feminist slant to Wise's work, regardless of the genre he explores. While the female stage passengers are just as condescending to *Fifi*'s Elizabeth as their hypocritical husbands, Simon's character is a pivotal example of Wise's championing of victimized women. Though the director's seamless stitching together of Maupassant's stories complements the French writer's accent on satirizing the collaborative moneyed classes, Wise's future feminist-tinged films often simply keyed upon relationship melodrama. Regardless of who was at fault, his movies chronicle how women often pay the greater price in affairs of the heart. Thus, several Wise pictures, such as *Three Secrets* (1950) and *Until They Sail* (1957), are about unwed mothers during times when that was tantamount to being a whore. Despite the most exemplary of men, such as *Sail*'s sensitive American officer Captain Richard Bates (Charles Drake), a courtly Rhodes Scholar (who even does the dishes!), bad things happen. Bates's death during a World War II battle leaves his intended New Zealand bride (Joan Fontaine), their marriage delayed by military red tape, in the lurch. Even Wise women who are calculatingly cold, such as Claire Trevor's film-noir spider lady in *Born to Kill* (1947), and Susan Hayward's prostitute-party girl in *I Want to Live!* (1958), are ultimately executed by even less sensitive men and/or the legal system. In Wise's *So Big* (1953), some prostitutes have a brief positive walk-on appearance as they defend a woman's (Jane Wyman) right to be a truck farmer. In the director's *Tribute to a Bad Man* (1956), the companion to James Cagney's title character (Irene Papas) had earlier been forced into prostitution by war and poverty. Whether it is a tough girl broken, or a more traditionally victimized woman, Wise evokes a depth of sadness over mere sentiment. Within the genre confines of melodrama, he attempts to mirror what it is to be human. This is yet another variation upon the aforementioned Hippocrates axiom that served as the epilogue to the Wise/Lewton *The Body Snatcher*, ending with: "All the roads of learning begin in darkness and go into light."

Wise's technique of methodically detailing how people seldom measure the consequences of their actions is especially applicable for the plight of his melodrama women. Dancer turned author Toni Bentley might have been describing several of these Wise films when she wrote, "Like love, living is so often done blind."[14] Thus, if Wise had started directing about a decade earlier, his melodrama inclinations would have labeled him, in the Hollywood parlance of the 1930s, a frequent creator of "women's pictures."

A sixth and final connection between *Fifi* and Wise's future films involves the chase sequences near the conclusion of the picture. Maupassant's story promises that Elizabeth will eventually find an appreciative patriotic love interest. The adaptation actually makes it happen. Cornudet (John Emery), a cowardly revolutionary and sometime sympathetic fellow stage passenger to Elizabeth, is inspired by her patriotism. After he also kills a Prussian soldier, both of them are on the lam. Given the fantasy/horror norm of working for Lewton's "snake pit" unit, thriller sequences tied to the fear of being pursued, whether real or imagined (such as *Curse*'s little girl imagining that the headless horseman of Washington Irving's "The Legend of Sleepy Hollow" was after her) were a natural in these movies.

Fifi, however, anticipates how Wise will apply such a fear-factor component to movies outside the genres of the fantastic. For example, when Robert Ryan's boxer goes against a gambling fix in *The Set-Up* and attempts to exit a dark, empty arena, the ambience effectively replicates the standard haunted-house paranoia about potential dangers in every shadow. When Forsythe's journalist and his wife (Joan Camden) attempt to escape in *Captive City*, their anxiety over the ominously implicit but rarely seen monster-like Mafia foreshadows the fears of the couple running from the insidious pod people transformations of *The Invasion of the Body Snatchers* (1956, with both couples also attempting to warn the outside world). The numerous other Wise demonstrations of these running-in-place, wide-awake nightmares ranged from the director's later horror homage to Lewton, *The Haunting* (1963), to the real-life boogie men (Nazis) of *The Sound of Music* getaway.

Consistent with *Fifi* being a template picture for Wise, the film's summer 1944 release generated assorted positive notices, from the *Hollywood Reporter* calling Wise a "rare talent," to James Agee's *Nation* endorsement: "I don't know of any American film which has tried to say as much, as pointedly, about the performance of the middle class in war. There is a gallant, fervent quality about the whole picture . . . which gives it a peculiar kind of life and likeableness."[15] *Time* magazine said of *Fifi*, "Maupassant . . . would almost certainly have saluted this film . . . [and despite its limited budget], it makes most of its better-barbered, better-fed competitors look like so many wax dummies in a window."[16] The *Motion Picture Herald* best summarized the proceedings: "Direction by Robert Wise preserves a pace that benefits all aspects of enterprise, from the carefully contrived script . . . to the well-balanced performances of the many principals."[17]

Paradoxically, like the luridly misleading RKO-enforced titles that would routinely hamstring the Lewton unit, such as a sensitive exploration of a child's imagination being called *The Curse of the Cat People*, this time Maupassant's own moniker, "Mademoiselle Fifi," dampened the movie's box office. Less literary-minded viewers, expecting some sort of farcical French can-can, were disappointed. Still, over time, the picture's reputation has grown. *Fifi* also demonstrated one of the basic Wise skills that were further honed by his association with Lewton—maximizing every penny. Critic Manny Farber later described Wise's talent to make these "sleepers," "so called because they had somehow turned out to be believable, skillful feature films, though made on little more than it now costs to feed the lions in [Cecil B. DeMille's Oscar-winning circus Best Picture] *The Greatest Show on Earth* [1952]."[18]

Lewton fought hard for Wise across the boards on *Fifi*, both for more artistic freedom and a higher budget.[19] Though a picture's financial restrictions were always a challenge at RKO, Lewton made it possible for Wise and company to replicate a French setting by shooting some of the picture on location in northern California (Big Bear). The phenomenon of leaving the film capital for a more slice-of-life authenticity increased dramatically in the postwar period, fueled by everything from Italy's Neo-Realism Movement to the decline of the studio system. Wise relished this increased naturalism. Indeed, Wise's later fight film, *The Set-Up*, was even praised by period reviewers along those lines. *Cue* said, "The picture is reminiscent of the finest of the French [early Jean Renoir] and Italian films of realism."[20]

Had more been known during World War II about Vichy France's collaboration with the Nazis concerning its Jewish population, one feels this subtext also would have been accented in Wise's adaptation of the two Maupassant stories. Besides Lewton's quietly iconoclastic tendencies, and Wise's social cause nature, Maupassant was writing at a time (1880s) of increased anti-Semitism in France, which explains why one of his sympathetic heroines, upon which Simon's *Fifi* character is a composite, was Jewish. Though Maupassant died before France's infamous Captain Alfred Dreyfus case, his "fiction" anticipated both the harsh truth of this racist travesty of justice, and the even more virulent anti-Semitism to come.

The college of "one" education/opportunities Lewton provided for Wise had a profound impact upon the young director. "I think

I probably learned more from him about screenwriting and screen structure than from anybody else I ever worked with," Wise said. "The other thing, Lewton was very special in the sense of being . . . a really creative producer. But he never imposed himself or seemed to be trying to overshadow the director or take away the director's role or talent."[21] One might further explain Lewton's impact upon Wise by linking it to the director's innate drive. "Starting at about 10 years old," Wise noted, "I would work on Saturdays for my dad, then during the summer I'd work all week. So I was used to a strong work ethic. When I came to Hollywood in 1933, I just stepped into the film business and kept on working hard."[22]

Couple those comments with Wise's equally son-like comments about the blue-collar mentality of Lewton. Wise recalled Lewton passionately saying: "Man should have hands that dig in the soil . . . to work, to build things. I've never had a manicure in my life." After an epiphany-like pause, Wise shared, "I've never had a manicure in my life; that stuck with me."[23] Life lessons come easiest from those who are already predisposed to a given direction.

Sadly, just a few years later (1951), after both men had moved on to different studios, Lewton died of a heart attack at the age of forty-six. Ironically, though Lewton had a preexisting condition, Wise always felt that the tragically premature death was tied somehow to the producer's passion for perfection, coupled with the added stress involved in a collaborative art form such as film. Thankfully, Wise's similar workaholic tendencies had a built-in safety valve that allowed him seemingly to circumvent the pressure. A later fan of the director's RKO work, Warren Beatty, entertainingly described in a Wise-like manner the stamina necessary for the "detail, detail, detail" push of being a successful filmmaker in any age: "When . . . the person you are working with [on the set] has to go home and return a call to his press agent, and lunch is being served, and the head of the union says, 'Well, you have to stay out there for another 10 minutes because they have to have coffee,' and then the camera breaks down, and there is noise, a plane going over, and this wasn't the location that you wanted . . . are

98

Robert Wise: Shadowlands
you going to have the energy to devote to the detail of saying, 'That license plate is the wrong year?' That's where the stamina, the real fight comes in."[24]

One feels compelled to note some random yet poetically appropriate links between Lewton's last movie assignment and his ties to Wise. Only a month before his death, Lewton had "joined Stanley Kramer Productions, where he was preparing 'My Six Convicts.'"[25] This offbeat comedy, about making prison time more than tolerable, might have been a darkly comic metaphor for how Lewton brought creative fun to the restrictions of RKO, and in turn helped launch the directing careers of young filmmakers such as Wise and Mark Robson.

Kramer was, moreover, a producer interested in social issues. Later doubling as a director, he became best known for racially groundbreaking films such as *The Defiant Ones* (1958) and *Guess Who's Coming to Dinner* (1967). Given Lewton's pioneering efforts in encouraging that people of color be sympathetically cast in his RKO-produced pictures, such as *Curse*, the Kramer-Lewton teaming had great unfulfilled promise. Still, one can argue that Lewton's legacy of racial tolerance lived on most effectively in the careers of his RKO protégés Wise and Robson. Wise's films frequently teach racial tolerance: *Two Flags West* (1950, Native Americans), *This Could Be the Night* (1957, Muslims), and *The Set-Up* and *Against All Odds* (African Americans); and Robson's best picture, the Kramer-produced *Home of the Brave* (1949), is a hauntingly hard-hitting look at the abuse suffered by a black soldier (Indiana's James Edwards) from his fellow GIs.

Sadly, the much later documentary, *Val Lewton: The Man in the Shadows* (2007), suggests through narration that Wise and Robson's late-1940s decision to drop Lewton from their plans for an independent production company contributed to his demise: "It was business as usual for Hollywood but it hit Lewton like a death blow."[26] Paradoxically, as the producer's son, Val E. Lawton, had noted in an earlier documentary, *Shadows in the Dark: The Val Lewton Legacy* (2005), the new company did not include the senior Lewton because of his serious health issues: "[My father] was quite ill and he couldn't put the energy into it that they [Wise and Robson] were demanding."[27] One could also argue that it was an act of mercy to not subject a beloved but sickly mentor, already a victim of several heart attacks, to even more stress. Both Wise and Robson were driven artists, with the latter, like Lewton, dying prematurely of a heart attack. Regardless, there was a great mutual-admiration society going on between Wise and Lewton that was best demonstrated during the making of *Fifi* by a Lewton note (also touching on health) that Wise kept in his personal script of the movie: "Dear Bob: . . . the main thing is that I've had a chance to think over the film you've made so far. I think it's grand. You and Harry [Wild, director of photography] are doing a hell of a good job. Keep it up—don't run yourself down physically—and we can't miss."[28]

Wise learned a great deal from his work with Lewton and Orson Welles, which showed almost immediate fruition, from an Oscar nomination for the editing of *Citizen Kane* (1941) to the individual critical acclaim he received as the young director of several Lewton-produced B films. But his contributions to these films would forever be qualified by their association with the names Lewton and Welles. What would Wise accomplish outside these sizable cinema shadows?

Wise's First Noir Classic: *Born to Kill*

*Lloyd Bridges taught his children acting as a
kind of playtime with dad. His son Jeff summarized,
"That's basically what acting was—Advanced Pretend."*[1]

For Robert Wise, moving beyond Orson Welles and Val Lewton
represented "Advanced Pretend." Ironically, escaping their shadows
involved immersing himself in a genre, film noir (synonymous with
"tough-guy fiction"), defined by shadows. But on the way to becoming
a director of A films, Wise was forced to play cat and mouse with
RKO about assignments. His first two features after leaving the
friendly confines of Lewton's "snake pit" were B films, *A Game of
Death* (1945) and *Criminal Court* (1946). Wise's later memories of
the films demonstrate both his drive to make movies, and his ability
to reframe every experience as an opportunity to learn—a philosophy
that anticipated the message of his 1953 adaptation of Edna Ferber's
novel *So Big*. Regardless, as a B director at post-World War II RKO,
Wise recalled: "When you're under contract like I was, you may turn
down one or two films until finally they say, 'Now come on, you're
under contract here and you have to do it.' I did have layoff periods. At
one time . . . I spent almost five months sitting around the house and
climbing the walls. . . . That's why I did films like *A Game of Death* and
Criminal Court. Also, I was still learning. You don't learn when you're
sitting at home. Everything you do should add to your repertoire, your
knowledge of how to do things."[2]

Despite Wise's apologetic tone, both films are tight, well-made B movies that set the table for *Born to Kill* and other noir movies by the director. *A Game of Death* was a remake of the durable Richard Connell short story, "The Most Dangerous Game," which had been originally shot under that title in 1932. The tale is about an unhinged big-game sportsman who decides to hunt humans shipwrecked on his middle-of-nowhere island. Filmed yet again a decade later as *Run for the Sun* (1956), the story has also inspired countless variations upon the theme, such as *The Running Man*, (1987, a science-fiction thriller in which Arnold Schwarzenegger's character is forced to be part of a "Most Dangerous Game"-type television show in 2019).

With a horror plot involving a madman on a remote Pacific island who initially seems a cultured benefactor to shipwrecked "guests," *A Game of Death* is, at first, reminiscent of H. G. Wells's *The Island of Doctor Moreau* (1996). Fittingly, the close of Wise's *The Body Snatcher* (1945), has subtext ties to this same Wells novel. Since the young Hoosier cut his directing teeth in the world of Lewton-produced thrillers, it seems logical RKO would assign him this sort of project.

Wise's unhappiness with the material was heightened by his distaste for remakes. His feelings on the subject also reflected those of his friend, writer/director Billy Wilder: "I'm against remakes in general, because if a picture is good, you shouldn't remake it, and if it's lousy, *why* remake it?"[3] Wilder, one of the first Hollywood insiders to praise the noir quality of Wise's work, also admired the Hoosier's quiet, professional sets. But then, this was a norm with many of the great old-school filmmakers. For example, veteran assistant director Howard G. Kazanjian said, "I didn't like people shouting and bells ringing. Nor did [Alfred] Hitchcock, Billy Wilder, and Robert Wise. They were all very quiet souls."[4] However, despite being a remake, Wise's directing of *Death* garnered rave reviews. The *Hollywood Reporter's* critique appeared under the headline "'Game of Death' Masterful . . . Direction Makes Everything Count." The notice went on to comically add that "the understated and relentless direction of Robert Wise . . . [created] such a well-knit and cumulative suspense that it would require a moron or a nerveless individual to sit back and relax."[5] *Variety* concurred: "Robert Wise has directed in a tempo that sustains suspense and accentuates the chillerdiller motif."[6] Wise effectively created a haunted house-like atmosphere, à la the Victorian mansion of his *The Curse of the Cat People*, in the island castle of *Death's* villain (Edgar Barrier). Plus, as with the *Mademoiselle Fifi* heavy (and lingering World War II stereotypes), Barrier's militaristic figure is a sadistic German. Though simply a programmed thriller, *Death* is also consistent with Wise's propensity to often accent the dark side of human nature. But unlike the bleak thematic norm of a Wise artistic contemporary such as novelist William Golding, author of *Lord of the Flies* (1954), where base instincts invariably override good intentions, Wise is more apt to offer a sliver of hope.

Death's greatest limitations, then and now, are B actors without range and a limited budget trying to replicate an exotic location. While Wise's follow-up B movie, *Criminal Court*, also labored under financial limitations, the money is more effectively utilized upon nightclub and courtroom settings. But that picture's biggest bonus was a strong male lead, Tom Conway, who entertainingly plays the theatrical wannabe district attorney. Conway, the older brother of the suavely cynical actor George Sanders, had a touch of Errol Flynn swagger to his screen persona. Though he achieved neither the A-picture success of Flynn, nor the critical acclaim of Sanders (an Academy Award winner for his venomous drama critic in *All About Eve*, 1950), Conway still lent a certain sophisticated charm to his low-budget leads. Moreover, like both Flynn and Sanders, the force of his cultivated British air often elevated even pedestrian dialogue.

The noirish *Criminal Court* melodrama was also a hit with the critics. *Variety* said, "Robert Wise's direction keeps a tight grip on events to make this one come out better than average for such budget films."[7] The *New York Times* even punned its praise: "[*Criminal Court*] calls forth a favorable verdict from this jury."[8] Wise creates tension/

suspense within the film frame by unobtrusive camera placement and his orchestration of actors within that space. *Criminal Court* anticipates the Wise noir classics that followed.

When writer/director Paul Schrader suggested that some of his favorite noir directors, such as Wise, were never better than their early work in the genre, his starting point for the Hoosier was *Born to Kill* (1947), Wise's follow-up picture to *Criminal Court*.[9] Based upon the James Gunn novel, *Deadlier Than the Male*, the story involves a murderer (Lawrence Tierney) who marries the wealthy foster sister (Audrey Long) of Claire Trevor's bad girl. The frustrated lust of Trevor for Tierney will eventually lead to a body count. As Martin Scorsese later summarized the genre: "Film noir revealed the dark underbelly of American urban life. Its denizens were private eyes, rogue cops, white-collar criminals, femmes fatales. As Raymond Chandler put it: 'The streets were dark with something more than night.' [Noir] combined realism and [German] expressionism, the use of real locations and elaborate shadowplays."[10]

The ambience of the genre is comically summarized by a line from Edward G. Ulmer's bargain-basement B noir *Detour* (1945): "Whichever way you turn, fate sticks out its foot to trip you." Period censorship, however, often necessitated the genre's overtly sexual nature be sublimated by violence. Crime movie historian Carlos Clarens used *Born to Kill* as a model of this noir development: "To deal with forbidden matters, the best recourse was to deflect sexual behavior toward criminal behavior, which was easier to justify in the eyes of the Breen [censorship] Office. . . . [Plus,] According to Breen logic, a criminal going to his doom could indulge in illicit sex, since he was doomed anyway, and punishment for a criminal act implied punishment for unacceptable sex."[11]

The Eve Green and Richard Macaulay screenplay for *Born to Kill* does a meshwork of sex and violence. For example, shortly after the first killing: "The excitement generated by the murder is still on Sam [Tierney], so that there is a keyed-up feeling about him. It is indefinable, evidencing itself externally in nothing more tangible than a glint in his eyes, perhaps . . . it steps up his feeling for Helen [Trevor] into an overwhelming desire and arouses an urgent need to win a response from her."[12]

Wise's take on such behavior in this film, as well as an apparent auteur-worthy Rosetta stone-like link connecting such violence throughout his movie milieu, occurs in a note the director added at the close of his *Born to Kill* script. Wise wrote that Sam's aberrant behavior was a product of having "convinced himself that he was a superior being."[13] This ties innumerable Wise heavies together, starting with Henry Daniell's surgeon in *The Body Snatcher* and the sadistic title character of *Mademoiselle Fifi*, and runs through the military and political leaders of *The Day the Earth Stood Still* (1951), the racism of Robert Ryan's *Odds against Tomorrow* (1959) character, and the Nazis of *The Sound of Music* (1965) and *The Hindenburg* (1975).

Yet, a *superiority* decoder card for Wise becomes even more provocatively interesting if one applies it to the controlling parental males peppered throughout the director's filmography. With children and/or childlike characters at the heart of so many Wise movies, who is more naturally superior sometimes to an almost sinister fashion than a parent (especially from the child's perspective). Two career bookend examples from Wise's work are the dictatorial dads of the *Curse of the Cat People* and *Audrey Rose* (1977). While this topic is further fleshed out in later chapters, one might punningly suggest that if there really was some "curse" attached to these, or other Wise stories, it would be the paradox of a parental figure whose protectiveness has become detrimental to a child/childlike character. The application of this suffocating dad-to-daughter phenomenon increases substantially in Wise's work when metaphorically applied to many of his melodrama-based movie couple relationships, whether in *Three Secrets* (1950), *So Big* (1953), or *Two for the Seesaw* (1962).

While the sadistically superior-feeling Tierney character is no father figure, attempting, however misguidedly, to do the right thing, he is yet another Wise example of a dominating male. And beyond any twisted never-had-a-daddy sexuality Trevor's character might attach to Tierney, part of his appeal for her is what attracts most fans of crime-related genres—characters that simply do what they want, without fear of consequences. Trevor's Helen knows the territory because she is using her femme-fatale nature to land her own wealthy meal-ticket spouse, Fred Grover (Philip Terry). The dysfunctional world of film noir is often a first cousin to the dysfunctional family melodrama, with some pictures, such as Joan Crawford's Oscar turn in *Mildred Pierce* (1945, from James M. Cain's novel), qualifying in either category. While *Born to Kill* fits all the visual and psychologically warped story cues for noir, the movie can also be reduced to the more broad-based titillation factor of a woman having a thing for her brother-in-law, standard melodrama fare. As the film's down-and-out detective (Walter Slezak) satirically chides Trevor, "I suppose even a sister-in-law has sufficient acquaintance to succumb to his [Tierney's] charms." This is a more understandable family taboo "hook" with which to attract audiences than all the vague nihilistic implications inherent to film noir, which is also more difficult to put on a poster. (Recently, the brother-in-law temptation was used to market a problem film about the less commercial subject of post-traumatic stress, *Brothers*, 2009).

The noir/family melodrama connection is important to make, because Wise frequently slides back and forth between the genres, with some of his films, such as *Three Secrets*, and *Against All Odds* (1959), straddling noir/family melodrama lines. In fact, even his problem film (anti-capital punishment) biography of convicted killer Barbara Graham (Susan Hayward), *I Want to Live!* (1958), is essentially a real-life noir/melodrama—the tough "good-time gal" who tries for the white picket fence, only "fate sticks out its foot to trip [her]." These links between Wise films must be belabored, because for decades many critics have denied they existed. But the reoccurring genre themes and character types are hard to miss if one takes the time to look at all forty of his films.

Wise's noir/melodrama tendencies were not unusual for the period. For example, Nicholas Ray, ironically a favorite of auteur cultists, often performed the same genre two-step. His noir classics, such as *They Live by Night* (1949) and *In a Lonely Place* (1950), doubled as melodramatic or tragic love stories. Yet, Ray was equally celebrated for his over-the-top family melodramas such as *Rebel Without a Cause* (1955) and *Bigger Than Life* (1956). Of course, both Wise and Ray benefited from the increased popularity of family melodrama in 1950s America spawned, in part, by a genre makeover in which children, instead of the parents, were more likely to be the victims. Thus, in the traditional melodrama *Mildred Pierce*, Crawford's single parent, working mother is constantly victimized by an ungrateful daughter. Whereas, Ray's *Rebel* and *Bigger Than Life* place the blame for family problems squarely on the parents. (Wise's place in this ever-evolving genre is examined later in the book.)

While Wise's noir/melodrama cinema nature became obvious over time, period fans of *Born to Kill* were more cognizant of another dual genre link—noir/horror. The movie's two signature scenes owe a

Claire Trevor (right) lusting after her foster sister's (bride Audrey Long) soon-to-be husband (groom Lawrence Tierney) in Born to Kill *(1947).*

great deal to Wise's horror film background in Lewton's "snake pit." These shadowy, atmospheric sequences both occur early in the movie: Tierney's Reno murder of a girlfriend (Isabel Jewell), and Trevor's discovery of two bodies. Isabell Jewell's character has been stepping out on Tierney. He kills her date (Tony Barrett) in Jewell's kitchen, next door to the boardinghouse where Trevor lives. When Jewell goes to investigate what is taking Barrett so long with the drinks, she opens the door to a darkened kitchen and his body on the floor near the back entryway. Unable to initially process a murder, she enters the room unaware that Tierney is hiding behind the door. Halfway to the body the horror finally registers with her, and she begins to back away from Barrett. But like the proverbial car wreck, she cannot take her eyes off the victim and slowly retreats, reaching back with her left arm to find either the light switch or the door. Naturally, her stiff arm eventually touches Tierney. Startled, Jewell turns, and in a brief moment, her face poignantly records a rapidly changing litany of emotions: relief (a lover she knows), shock (as she realizes he is the killer), and stark terror (when it becomes apparent she is next). Jewell had been an overnight success on Broadway in 1930 and had had memorable parts in high-profile prestige pictures, such as the simple-minded seamstress of *A Tale of Two Cities* (1935). But though her career began to decline in the 1940s, a revisionist "reading" of Jewell credits is bolstered by her parts in two Lewton-produced B movies, *The Leopard Man* and *The Seventh Victim* (both 1943), and her brief acting tutorial in *Born to Kill*. Like Wise, the Lewton stint helped prepare her for noir horror.

The second pivotal *Born to Kill* scene, Trevor's discovery of two bodies (Jewell and Barrett), is a provocative new variation upon the sequence just examined. Trevor, in Reno for a divorce, knows Jewell through her elderly boardinghouse landlady (Esther Howard). Jewell was a party girl who drank beer with her neighbor in the afternoons, allowing Howard's character to live vicariously, not unlike the confession made to Raymond Chandler's watershed noir detective, Philip Marlowe, by General Sternwood in *The Big Sleep*: "A nice state of affairs when a man has to indulge his vices by proxy."[14] When Trevor returns that night to the boardinghouse, shortly after the double homicide, she sees Jewell's pooch, Romeo, has gotten outside. (The dog had slipped out when Tierney left the murder scene.) Trevor retrieves Romeo, still by Jewell's backdoor porch entrance to the kitchen, and attempts to tuck him back in the house. But opening the door, Trevor is immediately stopped by a medium shot of Barrett's hand and arm. Though modestly taken aback by this revelation, there is neither the shock first exhibited by Jewell when discovering a body, nor that woman's foolishness in then entering the room. Wise next cuts to her view of the other victim—Jewell, with her legs protruding from the darkness. In cinematically reducing the victims to mere body parts, Wise has metaphorically permeated the sequence with the torment of a horror-film dismemberment, without the gratuitous violence of the *Saw* series (started in 2004). Trevor puts the dog through the half-open kitchen door, closes it, and quietly leaves.

The staging, editing, and lighting for both of these sequences is on a horror-film par with the snake pit productions produced by Lewton. Moreover, an examination of Wise's working script for *Born to Kill* suggests how he creatively embellished such scenes. For example, the original script for Trevor's kitchen sequence briefly notes a man's hand but then suggests, "Keeping bodies out of the shot."[15] Wise's overruled this suggestion and his double murder visually defined through body parts makes the scene. Wise's contrasting directions of the two actresses (Jewell and Trevor), in similar story situations, was also stellar. The former plays her money scene with the over-the-top shock of an average person stumbling into a murder scene. Conversely, Trevor's minimalist response to this macabre situation tells the viewer everything one needs to know about her. And this wrong-side-of-the-tracks take on Trevor's character is immediately borne out by her actions upon returning to the boardinghouse. Instead of calling the police, she makes arrangements to catch the next train out of town. Wise recognized early the duality of directing—watching and guiding his actors like a film critic on the set, while simultaneously imagining the technical polish to be added. "You're sitting and judging [during rehearsals] as an audience," Wise noted, "responding to what the actors are giving. You think about how you're going to stage it—but also how it will be enhanced in post production."[16]

Wise's interest in dark comedy goes back to his days as a columnist for his high school newspaper. Given that he campaigned to make *Born to Kill* ("I pushed [RKO] very hard and was very instrumental in getting it done"[17]), part of the attraction was undoubtedly in the black humor inherent to both this script and to noir films in general. For example, at some point each of the picture's major characters waxes poetic about this genre's perpetual dark side. Tierney's sidekick, Elisha Cook Jr. (a noir talisman), is forever giving comically obvious advice: "You go nuts about nothing. . . . You can't just go around killing people whenever the notion strikes you. It's not feasible." Slezak's gumshoe is a compendium of worldly wise axioms on acid, ranging from his understated aside on reading about Trevor's murder—"The way of the transgressor is hard"—to his advice to a total stranger in the location that doubles as the office of a poor detective, the Coffee Pot [Café]: "As you grow older you'll discover life is very much like coffee. The aroma is always better than the actuality. May that be your thought for the day." Even Tierney's square-jawed thug occasionally sounds like Woody Allen's wiseguy ghostwriter (Chazz Palminteri) in *Bullets over Broadway* (1994): "I don't like gambling very much. I don't like being at the mercy of those little white squares that roll around and decide if you win or lose. I like to have the say so myself."

Like Boris Karloff's darkly comic performance in *The Body Snatcher*, however, it was not just in the writing. With a strong cast, which *Born to Kill* had, Wise was able to finesse some wonderful performances from his actors. Wise also enhanced the roles with small visual bits of business that showcased his constant attention to detail. For example, before Slezak's skid-row detective attempts to talk his way into the servants' quarters entrance of the suspect's mansion, he finds a way to save his half-smoked cigarette. He tucks the cigarette into a brick mortar crevice of the building's exterior wall for easy retrieval. With such casual economy, like slipping a paper napkin into the plot,

Wise's fleeting footnote to a life becomes an encapsulation of that life. Fittingly, the realistically focused Wise is also like a detective (or a reporter) himself—a seemingly modest detail can be a defining moment.

Wise's later comments about the now celebrated *Born to Kill* reveal one of art's great paradoxes—inspired work is often not fully appreciated upon initial release. "*Kill* was a middle-ground film, someplace between a 'B' and an 'A' picture," he said. "[Because of *Game of Death* and *Criminal Court*] I had more money, more time, and a very good cast. It got pretty badly attacked [critically, for violence] . . . but by today's standards, it is very mild."[18]

There were also many solid period reviews, but Wise's memories were probably most seared by some negative heavy hitters, such as the *New York Times*' Bosley Crowther, who wrote: "[*Kill* is a] clear

The love-hate relationship between Claire Trevor and Lawrence Tierney (right) in Born to Kill *(with film noir's favorite character actor Elisha Cook).*

illustration of why the movies are sometimes held in low esteem by
people. . . . [The film] is also an apt demonstration of why critics
sometimes go mad. . . . [*Kill*] is an offense to a normal intellect."[19]
Few reviewers have ever matched either Crowther's capacity for moral
indignation, or his ability to misread a picture's importance. Pauline
Kael, the later *New Yorker* critic and National Book Award winner (for
Deeper into Movies, 1974), observed, "Bosley Crowther . . . can always
be counted on to miss the point."[20] Indeed, Crowther's *Kill* comments
are not unlike his miscalculations over another memorable crime movie
twenty years later, *Bonnie and Clyde* (1967). But while Crowther's latter
misstep translated into the unraveling of his career, *Kill*'s characters did
upset some other period reviewers. For example, the *New York Journal
American*'s Rose Pelswick opened her critique: "The writers of 'Born
to Kill' must have been trying to see just how many unscrupulous,
completely unsympathetic individuals they could crowd into one
script."[21] The *Hollywood Citizen News*' Ann Helming satirically opined,
"For people who enjoy contemplating the lives of mentally-twisted
criminals and women of questionable character, however, it should
prove quite satisfactory."[22]

In contrast, *Film Daily* recommended *Kill* as a sexy, suggestive
yarn of crime with punishment [but] strictly for the adult trade."[23]
Variety predicted solid box office and said: "Both stars [Tierney and
Trevor] are equal to the demands of their unsympathetic roles and
get considerable out of them . . . in keeping with unsavory mood of
principals as developed by Robert Wise direction."[24] If judged as a
B-movie offering, the *Hollywood Reporter* called *Kill* a "heads-up above
ordinary [production]," and praised several of the performances, such
as, "Walter Slezak has a grand time playing the private eye, and Isabel
Jewell is swell as the murdered girl."[25] Even the picture's split-decision
reviews zeroed in on Wise positives, such as the *Los Angeles Daily News*'
Virginia Wright noting: "Robert Wise has been chiefly successful . . .
in the direction of Esther Howard, who gives a striking portrait of the
beer-drinking landlady who determines to avenge the death of her
friend."[26]

Maybe the most telling insight to be gleaned from the pages of these various publications, with regard to *Kill*'s provocative reception, was directed at another 1947 picture—Charlie Chaplin's pioneering dark comedy *Monsieur Verdoux* (1947). The writer/director/star plays a dapper former bank clerk who marries and murders little-old ladies for a profit. This "Lady Killer," the working title of the script, was loosely based upon the "career" of Frenchman Henri Landru, better known as the "Modern Bluebeard," who was guillotined in 1922 for murdering ten of his girlfriends.[27] *Verdoux* and *Kill* opened simultaneously in many markets and were even reviewed in the same issue of the *New York Times*. Both Chaplin's black comedy and Wise's film noir (literally "black" film) are now celebrated examples of two genres that often upset critics and audiences of the 1940s. Since noir movies are also liberally laced with dark comedy, as previously demonstrated with *Kill*, it is hardly surprising some period reviews had such visceral reactions about both films.

Revisionist critics soon covered *Kill* with kudos, starting with Francois Truffaut's early 1950s praise for both Wise and his movie, describing it as being "the most Bressonian of American films."[28] That is, Wise reminded Truffaut of the great French director Robert Bresson, whose modus operandi was such an astute attention to detail that the viewer sensed a character's inner reality. Today, the laudation of *Kill* is nearly universal. The program notes for the acclaimed "Melbourne [Australia] film festival of 1995," said "*Born to Kill* is [a] knockout noir . . . [and] indicates Robert Wise's gift for profoundly clever character analysis couched in seemingly typical examples of genre film." *Los Angeles Times* critic Kevin Thomas's seminal article, "In Noir Heaven" (1999), states, "*Born to Kill* is a superb demonstration of Wise's wry control over lurid material."[29]

Wise followed *Born to Kill* with another noir picture, the more pedestrian *Mystery in Mexico* (1948). A standard B-movie thriller, without a name cast, the film was a production experiment for the studio. "At the time, RKO owned forty-nine percent of the Churubusco Studios in Mexico City," Wise recalled. "I was asked to go down and

make a film using all their [production] people. . . . It was a very
enjoyable experience for me, my first living out of the country and
my only one working with an almost exclusively foreign crew. . . . The
studio wanted to know if it could make more reasonably priced movies
in Mexico, and it turned out not to be so."[30]

Mystery is about an insurance investigator who goes missing
in Mexico City with a priceless necklace. Both the agent's sister, a
nightclub singer (Jacqueline White), and another detective (William
Lundigan), fly south to solve the puzzle, though White's character
initially thinks Lundigan is just a flirtatious passenger on the
commercial flight. Wise is handicapped by a so-so script and cast, but
what elevated this beyond standard B-movie status is his refreshing use
of the Mexico City location. *Variety* coupled praise of Wise's direction
with this heightened sense of realism: "[The] Story gets a scenic lift
from locale, and meller [weak] elements are made stronger as played
against some of the rawer sections of Mexico City."[31] The *Hollywood
Reporter* seconded this verdict, and also praised Wise's direction of local
talent: "[The Mexico City] environs is intriguing to watch. A point
for attention is the clever use of Mexican actors. . . . [Ultimately, the
production has] camouflaged the deficiencies of the screenplay with
atmosphere and color."[32] Although *Mystery* is a minor picture, Wise's
attention to foreign locale's detail would be yet another example of why
Truffaut called the director "Bressonian."

Along personal lines for Wise, the *Mystery* production gave
the driven director a new lifelong passion—travel. Wise's later
correspondence is often peppered with references to various trips
abroad. But like any certified workaholic, many of these exotic
expeditions had a career connection. Wise could scout locations and/
or make a movie overseas, and invariably take the longer globe-trotting
way back home. An excellent summary along those lines occurs in a
letter from 1974: "When [my wife Pat] and I made our trip home [Los
Angeles] around the world in 1963, after our stay in London during
THE HAUNTING [production], the high spot of the whole trip was
our 5 days in Israel. We were absolutely caught up by the whole place,

Charlie Chaplin as the bluebeard title character of Monsieur Verdoux *(1947).*

by the people, by the atmosphere . . . that we both agreed that if we had an opportunity to re-visit any of the 13 or 14 countries we did go to on that trip, the number one choice for another visit would be Israel."[33]

Wise and his wife's job-related travel became more of a norm from the mid-1950s on, starting with *Helen of Troy* (1955, Italy) and *Until They Sail* (1957, New Zealand). But to attain the directorial clout to orchestrate such international productions, Wise needed to demonstrate he could bring his highly acclaimed B-movie game to cinema's version of baseball's "Big Show" (Major Leagues), A pictures. Wise's next two movies more than demonstrated that the director was up to the task. And as with *Born to Kill*, both pictures fell under a film-noir umbrella.

7

Signature Cinema: *The Set-Up*

"[The Set-Up, 1949, is] like an Edward Hopper painting of skid row—a rendering of what I knew to be real." [1]
MARTIN SCORSESE

While American cinema of the 1940s is credited with birthing film noir, the decade was fairly oozing with artistic variations of this train wreck of a genre, from Edward Hopper's defining Nighthawks (1942, a depiction of a late-night diner that the artist described as "painting the loneliness of a large city" [2]), to Sir Carol Reed's haunting Cold War noir The Third Man (1949, in which "you can smell the sewers, the fear, and the mistrust in Vienna" [3]).

In addition to the noir-oriented legacy already delineated in this book (Robert Wise's early years with Orson Welles and Val Lewton), one can even trace components of this genre in later Wise movies not normally penciled in as noir. For example, Wise's anti-imperialism war picture *The Sand Pebbles* (1966, from Richard McKenna's novel), hauntingly ends with the dying Steve McQueen uttering, "What the hell happened?" Years before, one of the literary architects of the genre, Philip Marlowe creator Raymond Chandler, had written that the pivotal question to be asked by this new twist on the crime story was "What the hell happened," rather than "whodunit"? [4] That is, in Chandler's first and defining novel *The Big Sleep* (1939), Marlowe does *not* give the story a Sherlock "brain in a tweed coat" Holmes ending,

Gary Cooper, Grace Kelly, and the clock in High Noon *(1952).*

where his deductive reasoning suggests this is a rational and just world. No, Marlowe's monologue on death addresses the inherent chaotic finality of noir and life in general: "What did it matter where you lay once you were dead? In a dirty sump or in a marble tower on top of a high hill? You were dead, you were sleeping the big sleep."[5]

Another example of a noir sensibility, in a Wise film not normally pigeonholed as such, is the director's summary take on his melodrama *Until They Sail* (1957, from the James Michener novel). Wise's key notation on his copy of the script reads: "*Until They Sail* is the theme underlying the whole story—It's what makes everything happen—the shortness of time for human relations—Each man sails away in his turn and the screw turns tighter & tighter—it has the element of suspense—it is the clock ticking around to *High Noon* [1952]."[6]

Although *High Noon* is famous for unfolding in "real time," with numerous on-screen clocks to prove it, Wise had been one of the pioneers of both techniques with *The Set-Up.*[7] Moreover, *Noon* was also predated by Wise's own excursion into this compound genre, *Blood on the Moon* (1948). Regardless of how one examines Wise's career, noir-thriller components frequently link his pictures.

After being a loyal RKO company man (taking a so-so assignment) on *Mystery in Mexico*, Wise was excited to be working on an adaptation of the Luke Short novel, *Blood on the Moon*. With a strong story and a legitimate star, Robert Mitchum, Wise was on the verge of directing his first A picture. Ironically, a real-life twist, befitting of a film noir, almost kept this from happening. The talent agency representing Wise was Famous Artists, an organization with which he signed during World War II because the agency also represented his friend and then frequent leading lady, Simone Simon. Going behind Wise's back, Famous Artists attempted to sell RKO on another director/actor combination that would have been more profitable for the agency. "They were trying to make a package deal with James Stewart and somebody else, with [fellow Val Lewton alumnus] Jacques Tourneur directing it," Wise recalled. "But [Dore] Schary, who was then head of production at RKO, wouldn't hear of it. He said, 'It's Wise's picture. He's been working on it; he's going to do it.' That's the kind of man Dore Schary was—very straight, very honest. Of course, I left Famous Artists right away."[8]

Blood on the Moon is the story of a cowboy drifter (Mitchum) caught between two feuding factions. But given this is a noir (it must be a complicated story) Western, the dichotomy is not the genre's normally simplistically basic rival groups, such as rancher versus rustler (best exemplified by Owen Wister's pioneering Western novel, *The Virginian*, 1902), or the epic rancher versus the settlers as in *Shane* (1953). No, Wise's *Blood* has an epic rancher (Tom Tully) battling an unscrupulous wannabe epic rancher (Robert Preston), as the latter uses his oily charms to have the local homesteaders (led by Walter Brennan) assist him. Plus, this Western takes on another noir twist by having Preston's entertaining villain secretly romancing Tully's daughter (Phyllis Thaxter), merely so he can keep tabs on her father. Factor in another Tully daughter (Barbara Bel Geddes) falling in love with Mitchum's caught-in-the-middle cowboy, who will ultimately bring Preston down, and Wise has another variation on the battling noir sisters of his *Born to Kill* (1947). Yet, for the time, this was hardly standard Western fare, and one can understand the *Los Angeles Times*' reviewer, Philip K. Scheuer, asking, "what are they [the women] doing in the midst of such rough, uncouth types?"[9] But Scheuer caught the tenor of this new compound genre when he wrote, "The film, directed by Robert Wise in the new realistic [noir] manner, . . . establishes a mood of ominous violence early and sustains it . . . to the bitter end."[10] The *Hollywood Reporter* critic more fully fleshed out *Blood's* revisionist nature: "[The picture] veers sharply off the beaten Western track to form itself into a suspenseful outdoor drama whose successful motivation is more the result of characterization, production atmosphere [the West at night] and tensely keyed direction . . . [by] Robert Wise, fully aware that his subject is somewhat different, [he] concentrates on performance and the result is arresting work from the top flight cast."[11]

Robert Mitchum and Barbara Bel Geddes in Blood on the Moon *(1948).*

Still, the inherent violence of noir, even filtered through the most American of genres, is jarringly apparent in the *Blood* reviews, from the rave *Hollywood Reporter* critique being titled "'Blood' Brutal Western," to the *New York Sun's* Eileen Creelman's positive notice warning that "Mitchum and Preston stage one of the most vicious screen fights I've yet had the horror to witness."[12] But Creel had inadvertently highlighted *the* scene. "We tried to do something for the first time in a Western: a barroom fight that was at least realistic," recalled Wise. "We said, let's have these men go at it all the way, as hard as they can, and let's have them exhausted at the end, which they would be. And I think it worked. Mitchum and Preston liked the idea very much, and I think it's the most distinctive scene in the whole film."[13] The *High Noon* fight sequence between Gary Cooper and Lloyd Bridges is sometimes given "first time" Western realism kudos, but it occurred *four years later*!

Noir pictures are an "opposites attract" marriage uniting slice-of-life realism (random violence, minimalist acting, attention to detail) to stylized realism—atmospheric use of light and shadow. The latter component suggests that noir/life is not simply a hard-edged "rough cut," but an irrational out-to-get-you maze. Consequently, film historian Frank Thompson later also credited the look of Wise's aforementioned fight: "low-key, moody lighting" (on deep-focus enhanced interior sets with visible ceilings), as an artistic link to Orson Welles' technologically pioneering *Citizen Kane* (1941).[14] But true to the *Moon* portion of the title, *Blood on the Moon*, the most visually stunning scenes in Wise's picture are the exterior night sequences. These ranged from a breathtaking long shot of Mitchum in the saddle framed against distant mountains at dusk (anticipating the later noir Westerns of Anthony Mann and Budd Boetticher), to a dark alley night scene, where Mitchum is nearly run down by a villain on horseback.

The latter sequence is an almost spoofing emblematic of a standard noir scene—an on-foot hero about to be run over by a speeding car. Critic/director Francois Truffaut received kudos for parodying just this kind of noir component in *Shoot the Piano Player* (1960), twelve years *after* Wise's more provocative variation (with a horse!). While the latter sequence is referenced in the script, Wise embellishes it, starting with the handwritten staging directions he added to the screenplay—directions that demonstrated yet again his Lewton legacy: "[Add a] Shock cut of [the] rider put in black for [a] double silhouette."[15]

Not surprisingly, period reviews for *Blood* were strong. But when critics did not fully appreciate the noir blanket Wise was throwing over the genre, a few dissenters complained about the film being overly melodramatic, or suffering from a "confused script."[16] The *Variety* critique was positive—"Performances are all above average, fitting ably into the [noir] mood sought by Robert Wise's direction"—but the review insightfully acknowledged the box-office dangers of any genre that embraced narrative complexities: "For the connoisseur of adult [noir] Western fiction there is appeal, but the average fan isn't likely to go for the understatement and gradually developing plot."[17]

As with *Born to Kill*, the passage of time earned *Blood* almost universal acclaim, and a special niche in genre history. For example, the revisionist (1998) critique of *Blood* in the scholarly *Pacific Film Archive* stated: "Wise's critically acclaimed Western predicted by two decades the darkly existential ["Spaghetti Western"] swing the genre would take in the late 1960s. . . . Wise used his Val Lewton sensibilities to create the closest thing to film noir the Western had seen yet: terse, realistic, moody, and moonlit."[18]

The bridge from *Blood* to the existential Westerns of the 1960s has more direct roots than has been previously noted. Italian director Sergio Leone, whose trilogy, *Fistful of Dollars* (1964, released in the United States in 1967), *For a Few Dollars More* (1966/1967), and *The Good, the Bad, and the Ugly* (1966), are essentially the foundation of "Spaghetti Westerns" (dark "horse operas" made by Italians, often shot in Spain, and starring Americans), was once a production assistant for Wise! Leone worked for Wise on *Helen of Troy* (1956), which was largely shot in Italy. The two men "struck up quite a friendship," according to Leone. "We talked a lot together," Leone added. "He spoke French, and was keen for me to learn English. He wanted me to continue as his assistant on his next films, and proposed that I should accompany him back to America. He wasn't misty-eyed about it, though. He recognized that he needed me to sort out many problems with the large cast."[19]

Like many storytelling artists, Leone enjoyed embellishing his biography, so how close he became to Wise, based on the American's limited French, remains to be seen. But *Helen* was an epic, problem-riddled picture, and Leone greatly assisted in orchestrating an international cast and crew that also helped prepare the Italian for his later sprawling Westerns. Moreover, he was a fan of Wise's dark sagebrush sagas, with the Civil War prisoner of war sequences in the American's *Two Flags West* (1950) specifically influencing the same subject sequences in *The Good, the Bad, and the Ugly*.[20] An added *Helen* production bonus for Leone was that another noirish American director, Raoul Walsh, did uncredited second-unit work on the picture. Though Leone enjoyed working with both men, he felt their talents were being wasted upon cinema depictions of the ancient world. Paradoxically, Leone continued to dream of making movies about the Old West.

Blood was a critical and commercial success. While Wise's *Born to Kill* had been equally memorable, this noir Western gave viewers someone good with whom to identify—Mitchum. Though flawed, like most antiheroes of this genre (he had initially sided with his one-time friend, Preston), Mitchum ultimately does the right thing. (*Kill* had no one to root for.) Hitching a noir story to a Western was also an effective box-office ploy in 1948, given the phenomenal postwar success of the genre. Two of that year's top-grossing films were Howard Hawks's noirish horse opera, *Red River*, and Bob Hope's Western spoof, *Paleface*—the comedian's greatest ticket seller outside of the *Road* series with Bing Crosby.

Mitchum's burgeoning "beefcake" popularity contributed to *Blood*'s success, arguably Wise's first major star, other than Boris Karloff in *The Body Snatcher* (1945). Mitchum, Oscar-nominated for William

Wellman's *The Story of G. I. Joe* (1945, filtered through Burgess Meredith as war correspondent Ernie Pyle), had the perfect hooded eyes and minimalist persona for film noir. Indeed, he had already starred in three pivotal variations of the genre: Raoul Walsh's Western noir *Pursued*, Edward Dmytryk's mix of noir and the problem (anti-Semitism) film in *Crossfire*, and Jacques Tourneur's straight noir, *Out of the Past* (all 1947). Critic David Thomson, a great admirer of Mitchum, once defined the actor's noir appropriate mesmerizing listlessness by way of some *Out of the Past* dialogue.[21] A cab driver asks Mitchum's private eye, "You look like you're in trouble." When Mitchum asked why, the driver responded: "Because you don't look like it."

This exchange would not have been out of place in *Blood*, especially as the film opens. Mitchum's rain-soaked party of one camp is flattened by a midnight cattle stampede. So much for "home on the range." When this near-death experience is followed by another, cattle-driving cowboys pulling guns on him, Mitchum responds, "You make a fellow feel right at home, don't you?" Fittingly, the actor's gift for noir's ever so casual use of dark comedy seems to have been innate to the man. Shortly after the film opened, Mitchum was jailed for fifty days on a marijuana conviction. In that era, many feared the case would end a promising career. Instead, his cool demeanor only seemed enhanced, bolstered with the public by his comments upon leaving the lock-up: "I could have got out last night. They asked me if I wanted to. But I told 'em I didn't want to disturb my sleep. As jail goes, it was alright. A little like being in the army a few weeks without a pass. The food? Well, it was sort of like that box lunch the studios serve you on location. . . . I'm not enthusiastic about it [film]. But I've got to go to work. I'm broke. RKO didn't pay my salary while I was in the pokey."[22]

Wise was moving to A pictures at a time when the war-driven box-office boom was over, and studios were starting to lose control of both their finances and their film stars. But RKO, anticipating that maybe the public would be more forgiving of its bad boy sex symbol, had actually rushed *Blood* into release when Mitchum was arrested on a narcotics charge. The studio's gamble, that marijuana and Mitchum would actually help sell tickets, proved to be true. Still, RKO would now attempt to keep the actor under surveillance, for everyone's benefit.

For the record, Mitchum at work was the consummate professional, and Wise later directed him in *Two for the Seesaw* (1962). In fact, the only problem on that shoot was that Mitchum and costar Shirley MacLaine, in the midst of a long affair, were forever breaking each other up. "They were having such a good time trying to top each other that one of my biggest jobs as a director was to settle them down long enough to get them to do the scene," Wise remembered. "They were very funny; I was laughing as much as the crew. It got so bad that one day I called the crew back about twenty minutes early from lunch and had a little talk. I said, 'We have to stop being such a good audience for these two. They're so funny and amusing, I'm as guilty as you. But if we don't stop, we'll never get this picture done.' They did settle down and we got the picture done."[23]

Blood is a great movie. But Wise's next film, *The Set-Up*, could be called his *greatest* picture, as well as winning the director immediate international recognition by taking the Critic's Prize at the renowned Cannes Film Festival. *Set-Up* was also his last movie for RKO, a company Wise now desperately wanted to leave because of the increasing instability of Howard Hughes, who purchased the controlling interest of RKO in 1948. Martin Scorsese's much-admired epic biography of this multifaceted and ultimately reclusive corporate giant, *The Aviator* (2004, with Leonardo DiCaprio in the title role), wisely keyed upon Hughes's glory days (the 1920s through the 1940s). Sadly for Hughes and RKO, the proverbial "wheels on the bus" were starting to come off when Wise was trying to make *Set-Up*. Even before this production started, Wise had a bad feeling about Hughes's impact on the studio. Yet like a dancing with the devil noir character, Wise had an obsession. "I wanted very much to direct *The Set-Up*," said Wise, "yet at the same time I wanted to escape from my exclusive, seven-year contract with RKO. Howard Hughes had just bought the studio, and

I could see it going nowhere."[24] As always, Wise is forever diplomatic about negative behavior. One of Mitchum's biographers put it more bluntly: "Hughes [eventually] put RKO out of business."[25]

Set-Up might be subtitled *Noir Visits the Boxing Ring.* Ironically, this fight picture was loosely based upon a narrative *poem* by 1920s journalist Joseph Moncure March. Sportswriter Art Cohn's adaptation changed the main character from a black boxer controlled by crooked promoters to a white, over-the-hill journeyman prizefighter (Robert Ryan) whose long-shot victory results in tragic consequences. The subsequent movie, which some film aficionados, such as Martin Scorsese (*Raging Bull*, 1980), would call the best boxing picture ever made, is a showcase of three frequent Wise components.

First, Wise's own journalist background often had him thinking problem-film subtext. Appropriately, both he and Cohn wanted to create a new kind of boxing picture, "one that exposed the fight game for the cruel and exploitative Roman circus that it was."[26] Thus, just as Wise's *Mademoiselle Fifi* (1944) planted a message about French collaboration with the Nazis in a Maupassant period piece, or the director's *I Want to Live!* (1958) was a plea to end the death penalty, *Set-Up* was patently antiboxing. The degree to which Wise's movie was artistically successful in delivering this message can be found in the opening to Edwin Schallert's superlative *Los Angeles Times* review: "A few more pictures like 'The Set-Up' and someone will be instituting a bill to put an end to prizefighting."[27] Wise's groundbreaking perspective was so fresh that several similarly themed follow-up vehicles, such as television's award winning *Requiem for a Heavyweight* (1956, later a 1962 movie), and Humphrey Bogart's *The Harder They Fall* (1956), were still receiving praise for their whistle-blowing stances *years later.*

Second, Wise enjoyed nothing better than playing reporter/fact finder on a movie project. His preparation for *Set-Up* represented one of his most active involvements. "I spent night after night doing research at the arenas around town [the greater Los Angeles area]," he recalled. "There was a little crummy one down in Long Beach I went to several times on their fight night. I would get there early and go to the dressing rooms and watch the fighters, their managers, and handlers coming in from the street. I would watch a whole evening of their actions and activities, making notes, getting pictures and lots of ideas. On other nights, I would watch the fights and see how the handlers act in the corners, what went on between the rounds, watch the crowds, pick up little pieces of business."[28]

The "watch the crowd" portion of Wise's research also served as a natural bridge to a third theme common to the director's pictures—the less-than-populist nature of the common man. Wise's indictment of boxing is bolstered by a sort of grassroots damnation of an audience simply out for bloodletting. But this is not drawn from a preconceived agenda. Each frenzied fight fan depicted is based upon an actual character observed by Wise and/or screenwriter Cohn while preparing the film.[29] Given the director's gift for dark comedy, so much a part of noir, Wise establishes these types early and then satirically skewers them by periodically intercutting the figures with the ring action.

The crowd in The Set-Up *(1949), with Robert Ryan as the winning fighter (far right).*

These frightening fight aficionados include: a blind man whose angry "close the other eye" attitude is fueled by a companion describing each blow, a glutton whose nonstop eating is never deterred by the violence (reminiscent of James Cagney eating a sandwich while killing a guy in the noir classic *White Heat*, 1949), a weekend gladiator shadowboxing his way through the fight (attempting to anticipate the blows of both boxers), a cigar man so taken with the action that he can never quite get the stogie in his mouth, and a woman patron so over-the-top in her kill mentality that she might have been a model for the nihilistic movie mob of Nathanael West's darkly comic look at 1930s Hollywood in *The Day of the Locust.*

As Wise had done with *Blood*, however, *Set-Up* also gave the viewer someone to root for. Ryan, in arguably *the* performance of his career, plays a decent but past-his-prime fighter who still believes he is "only one punch away" from ring glory. In reality, his devoted wife (Audrey Totter) sees he is simply flirting with terminal palooka-land. Consequently, she refuses to attend what will ultimately be his last fight.

Appropriately for a director whose films frequently show a great sensitivity to the trials of being a woman, this acclaimed boxing picture is just as much about the angst of being a fighter's spouse. As the movie unwinds in real time, and Ryan attempts to win a bout his crooked handlers have already thrown (without telling him), his wife wanders the streets of this tank town (perversely named Paradise City) attempting to make sense of their lives. In a film full of memorable moments, the best one belongs to her. In a scene shot on location in Culver City, she stands on a high bridge and looks down at the nighttime trolley and bus traffic. Though she is not suicidal, the scene is immersed in that kind of quiet desperation. After Totter's prolonged gaze at this chaotic urban canyon, with Wise cutting back and forth between her stoical yet sad face and the metal-entombed commuters passing beneath her, she tears up her ticket to Ryan's fight. As the paper flutters down on the trolley car tracks below, this haunting protest against life might have been inspired by Carl Sandburg's poem, "Limited" (1916). Like Totter's character, Sandburg's narrator contemplates the transitory nature of life versus rushing commuters. And just as she has earlier failed to really communicate this fear to her husband, Sandburg's figure meets the same unthinking wall: "I ask a man in the [train's] smoker [car] where he is going [metaphorically] and he answers 'Omaha.'"[30]

Rare for a film-noir female lead, Totter is given a respite, of sorts, at the picture's close. Ryan fights valiantly throughout the bout, refusing to lie down when finally informed that a fix was on, and upsets the gangster-owned younger fighter. After the fight the mobster's men crush Ryan's right hand in an alley outside the arena. By this time Totter has returned to their nearby hotel and is anxiously watching for her husband at the window. When she sees him stagger out of the alley, Totter rushes to a collapsed Ryan. As he attempts to explain everything to her, two of his lines stand out: "I can't fight no more . . . I won tonight." She closes the picture with her moving summary response, "We both won tonight. [pause] We both won tonight." In a genre where darkness is all around, here is a twisted bit of hope. In noir one gives thanks for the most unusual things.

Wise's preparation for the boxing sequences in *Set-Up* sound rather like a man later associated with musicals. "I call it choreography," he said."At the old YMCA in Hollywood, they had a ring up there, and I would go in on a Saturday, before we started shooting . . . [and work with boxer John Indrisano on staging the fight sequences.] Gradually [we] build it that way. Then when we shot it, we would just do it in sections, with three cameras on . . . [the] fight: one camera to cover the whole ring, another one to be in tighter . . . and another one, for those little pieces, the spray [of sweat] flying and all that. [The latter wild handheld camera] was up close."[31]

Wise helped to choreograph boxing sequences in two other films, the biography picture of fighter Rocky Graziano, *Somebody Up There Likes Me* (1956, with Paul Newman), and the naval police-action picture, *The Sand Pebbles* (1966, with Steve McQueen). Keep in mind,

Wise was a lifelong sports fan; and a great athlete frequently moves with the grace of a dancer. If people had not noticed the parallels between the two prior to the 1960s, Muhammad Ali corrected that lapse. Ali's style even inspired a dance number by the era's musical genius Bob Fosse, "The Champion," included in his *Sweet Charity* (1969). Appropriately, this was the same decade Wise won Oscar acclaim for two musicals, *West Side Story* (1961) and *The Sound of Music* (1965). Paradoxically, if there is one minor flaw to *Set-Up,* former intercollegiate boxing champion Ryan is, at times, possibly more artful than the stereotypical veteran palooka. But it is a modest complaint.

In a genre in which despair often makes the characters look as if they have *under*slept, one wonders when Wise ever slept. In a letter from 1981, the director included *Set-Up* on a short list of pictures that had a "major influence" on how he conducted business. That is, besides representing his "most thorough research up to that time," *Set-Up* was "the first time I used continuity sketches in [production] preparation."[32] With each successive film, Wise found new ways to minimize errors by

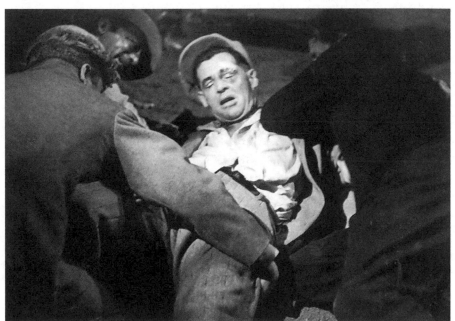

Mobsters working over Robert Ryan's (center) fighter after he refused to lose in The Set-Up.

an ever-increasing attention to detail. Not surprisingly, his realistic eye for everything in the film frame was fueled by a similar diligence behind the screen.

Wise's hard work was universally praised in newspaper reviews. The *New York Times* called *Set-Up* a "sizzling melodrama," and Wise's "roving, revealing camera paints an even blacker picture of the type of fight fan who revels in sheer brutality."[33] The *New York World Telegram*'s praise also underlined the movie's effectiveness as a problem film: "The fight itself is something very special in the staging of these orgies of pain and blood. . . . A few more pictures as graphic and dramatic and stirring and revolting as 'The Set-Up' could become a formidable menace to the whole fight business."[34]

Variety opined that the film should be placed in some pantheon "higher bracket," stating the picture's "values primarily lie in its unmerciless character studies. Under Robert Wise's skillful direction . . . the assorted ringside audience 'types' give an added luster of realism."[35] Eileen Creelman's *New York Sun* critique was of the same opinion: "Those stadium [crowd] scenes, the hideously excited spectators, the screaming woman, the fat man, the smiling gambler, these [segments] are the best of the film."[36] The *Hollywood Reporter* added, "Wise, with his direction, packs a hundred stories into the space of [a short film]."[37] Several publications, such as the *Los Angeles Times*, favorably compared the picture to the 1940s most admired national cinema, Italian neo-realism.[38] Like Scorsese's later championing of the picture, the *New York Daily News*' Wanda Hale might have been summarizing for critics past and present when she stated, "*The Set-Up* is terrific . . . the most persuasive, dramatic fight picture I have ever seen . . . a triumph."[39]

Ironically, while *Set-Up* went on to win the international prize at the Cannes Film Festival, the almost simultaneous release of United Artist's boxing movie *The Champion* (1949, with Kirk Douglas) stole some of Wise's thunder. The term "stole" is not applied casually. RKO won a copyright case against the United Artists movie, with which the newspapers had a punning field day, such as the *Hollywood Reporter* headline: "'Set-Up' Knocks Out 'Champ' As Court Orders UA Film Cut."[40]

Still, Champion's bigger-budget and more charismatic lead (Douglas, versus Ryan's journeyman pug), represented heavy competition at the box office. However, in later years, Set-Up was seen as the superior movie, as well as setting the bar for future fight films. For example, the Melbourne Film Festival (1995) drew parallels between Wise's work and John Huston's great boxing movie, Fat City (1972), crediting them both for being "about people who are beaten before they start but who never stop dreaming."41 In 2009, when Fat City had a special retrospective, the New York Times made a similar connection with Set-Up, crediting them both with being "on the short list of boxing movies . . . that linger in the mind."42 Wise's last RKO film could not have provided him with a better Hollywood launching pad.

Audrey Totter comforting her battered screen husband (Robert Ryan) at the close of The Set-Up.

Life after RKO: *The Day the Earth Stood Still* and Genre Diversity

"Your choice is simple: join us and live in peace, or pursue your present course and face obliteration. We shall be waiting for your answer. The decision rests with you."
ALIEN VISITOR KLAATU (MICHAEL RENNIE) DELIVERING
A WARNING IN *THE DAY THE EARTH STOOD STILL* (1951)

Since leaving Indiana for Hollywood during the Great Depression, Robert Wise's one goal was to reach the top. By way of the movies, he had met and married a lovely lady, Patricia Doyle Wise, and they had a son (Robert Allen) whom he adored. But his life revolved around pictures. The memorable movies he had been part of during the 1940s had now positioned him to be a major Hollywood player for the next two decades. Almost immediately he signed to do a film for Warner Brothers, *Three Secrets* (1950). The script's original punning title, "Rock Bottom," referred to both a *mountain* plane crash that left an adopted boy an endangered orphan in a remote area, and the *disturbed* mindset of three women (high-profile reporter Patricia Neal, bad girl Ruth Roman, and housewife Eleanor Parker) each convinced this was the baby she had given up years before. Why? A newspaper story had revealed the boy's age and foundling home, and it paralleled their backstories, with each woman now rethinking her decision.

The moving melodrama Wise fashioned from this property effectively juxtaposes the docudrama-like mountain rescue of the child with the sometimes noirish flashbacks of how each woman came to leave her baby. In other words, the picture allowed Wise to finesse his gifts for both realism and noir (particularly in the Roman tale), as well as showcase his feminist advocacy. And given that Neal's journalist walks away with the film, *Three Secrets* lets Wise once again become cinematically immersed in his first choice for a profession. Moreover, Neal's workaholic reporter has many parallels with Wise's obsession for film.

Two additional catalysts played into Wise making the movie. First, when he signed on for *Three Secrets*, his own son was just a year older than the script's orphaned boy. Second, though Wise's previous films had often had a feminist melodramatic tone, he had never made an overt example of the genre. Like Howard Hawks, one of his directing heroes, Wise wanted to direct an assortment of movie genres: "I realized *Three Secrets* was a soap opera but I liked the idea . . . and [I] was intrigued by working with [the] three actresses . . . particularly Patricia Neal."[1] But he was also excited about a compound genre effect—mixing a woman's picture with the realistic texture of the rescue portion of the movie. Indeed, Wise peopled the film's press conference with actual Sierra Club members doubling as the rescue team. This documentary-like staging also included real journalist Bill Welsh. "We had no set script on it [the press conference], just the general idea of what we wanted to be said," Wise noted. "I told Bill, 'You know what you're after. Just hold an interview with these [real rescue] people.' They knew the story, what they were there for, so I didn't give them any lines. What you see on the screen is an actual interview."[2]

With regard to Neal joining the cast, art was imitating life. She was involved in a long-term love affair with married film legend Gary Cooper. As with each of the *Three Secrets* characters, a Neal/Cooper pregnancy eventually complicated her life. But the Cooper footnote is relevant, because he was impressed with Wise's work. In Neal's memoir she added, "It [*Secrets*] had a very good director, Robert Wise. Gary [Cooper] thought I should grab it, and so did I."[3] Neal went on to star in two other Wise pictures: *The Day the Earth Stood Still* and *Something for the Birds* (1952). Besides enjoying each other's company, Wise and Neal shared the same liberal perspective on politics, which included bemoaning the inquisition-like communist witch-hunting of both the House Un-American Activities Committee, and U.S. Senator Joseph McCarthy, whose name became a label for an era, McCarthyism. As late as 1964 Wise passionately wrote to another of his liberal friends, actress Rita Moreno, an Oscar winner for the director's *West Side Story* (1961), about the still lingering impact of the blacklisting: "[It is] Maddening to think of the efforts of S.O.B. McCarthy still hanging on."[4] But sadly, many of Wise's future links to Neal would be tied to the tragedies that haunted her life, from a son's near-fatal accident when his baby carriage was struck by a cab, to her own flirtation with death from a massive stroke at thirty-nine. Thus, in a 1967 letter to Neal, Wise both accepted the performer's request to join her on a committee for the "Association for Brain Injured Children," and poignantly added: "Pat, I, along with all your many, many friends in Los Angeles, am so thrilled with your splendid recovery. It is such a tribute—not only to you but to your husband [British writer Roald Dahl] and family. I hope everything continues to go better and better for you all."[5]

In *Three Secrets* feminist Wise helps Neal orchestrate a landmark performance about gender double standards—she cannot exist in a marriage that does not allow her to also pursue a reporter's life. And not realizing she is pregnant until after the marriage is over, Neal's character opts for journalism over motherhood. While the plane crash five years later makes her briefly rethink this position, she ultimately chooses her career.

As a soap opera, however, *Three Secrets* also allows Wise to have it both ways—liberated woman and mother. That is, one of these "secret" mothers is, of course, allowed to reconnect with the now five-year-old child. But for maximum tear power, the new parent will *not* be the biological mother. That individual relinquishes the honor in the best interest of the child. To recycle an old Hollywood superlative for engaging soaps, "It was a three hankie picture." In addition to receiving respectable reviews, the movie did solid box office, fueled by high-profile serialization of the original novel. Margaret Lee Runbeck's book appeared in *Good Housekeeping*, with the initial cover story installment being pitched as the "Most Stunning Novel of the Year."[6] Overseas, the novel was serialized in Great Britain's top circulation magazine *Housewife*, coinciding with the English release of *Secrets*.[7] Consequently, while Wise's art had always been very sensitive to women, the commercial success of *Secrets* firmly established his family melodrama connection with both the public and the industry. Looking at Wise's filmography for the rest of the 1950s, one sees a natural progression to such monumental soaps as *So Big* (1953, from Edna Ferber's novel), *Until They Sail* (1957, from a James Michener story), and *I Want to Live!* (1958, based, in part, on Barbara Graham's letters). In fact, there is a line from the latter movie, spoken by a sympathetic nurse to a soon-to-be-executed Graham (Susan Hayward, in an Oscar-winning role), which could serve as a summary for the plight of many Wise screen women: "Divorced or separated—the way men are these days, that's about the only way you can live with them."

Wise made two pictures between *Secrets* and the iconic *Day the Earth Stood Still*: *Two Flags West* (1950) and the *House on Telegraph Hill* (1951). While both movies are now penciled in as being less inspired examples of his work, each film effectively profiles many of the director's values. The best of the two is the underrated *House on Telegraph Hill*, another variation upon a family melodrama, by way of standard Wise territory, film noir and horror. Leading lady Valentina Cortesa opens the picture in a German concentration camp during World War II. This horrible existence is only made easier by the friendship of a woman named Karin (Natasha Lytess), whose thoughts dwell upon a son (Gordon Gerbert) being cared for by a rich aunt off in San Francisco. When Karin dies and the camp is liberated by the Americans, Cortesa assumes her friend's identity. But by the time she reaches New York, the aunt has died, and the boy's new guardian has a name that reveals his real motives, Alan Spender (Richard Basehart).

Spender initially seems like a splendid chap (if one can get past Basehart's roles that often typecast him as a psychotic figure), and when

Cortesa marries him she simply appears to be following noir femme-fatale basics. But from this point on, as Cortesa clearly bonds with the boy, the film smoothly shifts into the haunted house domain of a witchy caretaker (the governess played by Fay Baker) and the slowly coming unglued master (Basehart, à la Charles Boyer in *Gaslight*, 1944). At the film's close Cortesa has thwarted Basehart's attempt to poison her and the boy. Her surprise ally is her husband's accomplice/lover (Baker), who could not condone killing the boy. Once again, mother love surfaces in an unlikely place, and men are the villainous gender. But an added titillation factor was later disclosed in the movie's casting. When the *Los Angeles Examiner* reviewed the film as having the "well-knit story-telling quality of Robert Wise's direction," it added: "TO GOSSIP FANS, in on the knowledge that Valentine Cortesa and Richard Basehart have just revealed their secret marriage two months

Valenta Cortesa (center), Richard Basehart, Fay Baker, and Gordon Gerbert (the child) in House on Telegraph Hill *(1951).*

ago in England, it may come as a shock to watch him trying to poison her most of the way through the 'House on Telegraph Hill.'"[8]

Given the familiarity of this material, one can understand why Wise only accepted the production as a favor to Twentieth Century Fox chief Darryl Zanuck. Yet, consummate professional Wise makes this an entertaining film. In addition to showcasing many genre themes and characters inherent to Wise's work, the director once again uses the spooky old house to maximum effect. I am reminded of the screenplay description of Hill House in Wise's later *The Haunting* (1963, with the italicized words being underlined by the director in his script: "*It is a monstrous building.* No one can say exactly what suggests evil in the face of a house, yet Hill House is overwhelmingly evil. *Enormous* and *dark,* it is so covered with decoration as to appear *diseased.*"[9]

The threat of evil acts in *Telegraph Hill* are often emblematic of the picture's foreboding dark house, a frequent motif in Wise's films, starting with the atmospherically creepy mansion in his first film as a director, *The Curse of the Cat People* (1944). Other Wise variations upon the haunted house syndrome would include the anatomy school in *The Body Snatcher* (1945), the psychotic killer's castle in *A Game of Death* (1945), Laury Palmer's (Isabel Jewell) murder site in *Born to Kill* (1947), and the seemingly empty but threatening mansion of *Mystery in Mexico* (1948). Wise's most inventive depiction of a setting as a bump-in-the-night character was the dark, closed boxing arena, devoid of people but ripe with potential danger, through which Robert Ryan's fighter attempts to escape in *The Set-Up.* The circular pattern created by the empty wooden seats in this temple of violence is reminiscent of a design for chaos, a perversely beautiful foreshadowing that Ryan will not escape.

While only with *Haunting* is the house actually responsible for the evil acts, Wise's talents as a filmmaker, utilizing his early training as both an editor of sight and sound, makes the viewer forever wonder if these other settings *might also be* collaborators in murderous mischief. Such Wise fright-night backdrops, even at their most innocent, seem like mausoleums for the dead, as suggested by this script description of the foreboding Victorian house interior in *Curse*: "The drawing room is cluttered with useless Victorian and Edwardian antiques."[10] Alfred Hitchcock later credited Edward Hopper's painting the *House by the Railroad* (1925) as the catalyst for the Victorian Bates home in *Psycho* (1960).[11] But clearly, Wise had been mining this area for over a decade *before* Hitchcock's landmark picture. And once again, as suggested by the opening of the previous chapter, Hopper and film noir go hand in hand. (This connection would have greatly pleased the artist so famous for his haunting freeze-frame depictions of urban loners; like Wise, he was a great film fan, too.)

Fittingly, the best transition to Wise's next memorable movie, *The Day the Earth Stood Still*, could be carried upon the director's use of atmospheric horror. When the benevolent alien Klaatu/Carpenter (Michael Rennie) first appears in a Washington, D.C., boardinghouse, after escaping from detention by the U.S. Army, his sudden shadowy presence at the edge of the film frame creates a frightening stir among the boarders. They have just been letting their imaginations run wild about the nature of this escaped alien, when suddenly there is a stranger among their midst whose appearance is initially obscured by darkness. Though his human features soon put them at ease, the viewer enjoys the darkly comic joke—their fears were correct; he is the alien, though they will not know this for some time.

The boarders' insensitive gossiping prattle here, and in other scenes, is consistent with Wise's frequent noirish mindset about the general populace—a mob mentality prone to negative behavior. Paradoxically, the monster these gossips are conjuring up might better describe themselves. I am reminded of Jean-Dominique Bouby's description of the ugly gossipers who mocked his "locked-in syndrome" paralysis: "that monster with a hundred mouths and a thousand ears, a monster that knows nothing but says everything, had written me off."[12] These real *Earth* monsters had "written off" Klaatu as something awful with no real facts. Many Wise films have a problem-film nature, such

as *Earth*'s push for world peace. But one could add a more generic
subtext problem-movie slant to his oeuvre—a challenge to humanity to
prove Charles Darwin wrong. The gossiping boarders and most other
everyman figures in *Earth* would not have been out of place among the
Mademoiselle Fifi (1944) coach passengers, or the fight fans of *Set-Up*.
Appropriately, however, this perspective is often a given in science-
fiction films, too. But what makes *Earth* unique is Wise's ability to graft
a populist message upon the movie, via Rennie's alien, who assumes a
Christlike role underlined by his assuming the cover name Carpenter.
To give such a "populist fantasy" some hope, there are a handful of
sympathetic human beings: boarders Helen Benson (Patricia Neal)
and her son Bobbie (Billy Gray), as well as the Albert Einstein-like
Professor Barnhardt (Sam Jaffe), who will assist "Carpenter" in getting
his message to a wider audience.

Unlike Wise's strictly-on-assignment status on *Telegraph Hill*, the
director was excited about putting a problem-film message across with
Earth. "It's very much of a forerunner in its warning about atomic
warfare, and it shows that we must all learn to get along together," Wise
observed. "I liked the fact that it was science-fiction but science-fiction
on Earth, not another trip to the moon, giving us the chance to address
some very important issues."[13]

By keeping this an earthbound tale, Wise could also minimize
the necessity for special effects, beyond the flying saucer's arrival in
Washington, D.C., and the occasional ray-gun disintegration of
weapons by Klaatu's giant robot/interplanetary policeman Gort (Lock
Martin, the seven-foot-tall doorman at Grauman's Chinese Theatre
in a metallic-looking costume). The greatest liability over time for
science-fiction special effects is that they can quickly move from state-
of-the-art work to laugh-out-loud high camp. For example, the George
Pal-produced *War of the Worlds* (1953, with story dominating Oscar-
winning special effects), now works more as a cultish campy picture
than a serious look at invasion from Mars. Whereas Wise's picture, or
Don Siegel's equally minimalist *Invasion of the Body Snatchers* (1956),

remain two contrastingly compelling variations upon what an alien world might mean to planet Earth. Both represent content over special effects. Moreover, Wise is yet again applying the realistic tone that was so often a part of the RKO film-noir legacy from which he came.

In contrast to Siegal's more traditional *Invasion* science-fiction scenario, *Earth* presents an enlightened species (as represented by Klaatu) offering permanent peace or "obliteration." At the height of the cold war, when money-grubbing capitalism and Godless Communism were constantly flirting with an apocalyptic dance of death, Klaatu makes a tough-love offer that seemed hard to refuse: "We have created a race of robots [such as Gort]. They have absolute power over us. At the first sign of violence, your Earth will be reduced to a burned-out cinder. Your choice—join us and live in peace or face obliteration." Obviously,

Klaatu/Carpenter (Michael Rennie) inside his flying saucer in The Day the Earth Stood Still *(1951).*

the picture then ends upon a tense note of hope. But in an earlier portion of Wise's script, when Klaatu escapes from army authorities, the director has written a telling note—"Connecticut Yankee business."[14]

What did the note mean? Wise was a huge fan of Mark Twain. One of Twain's greatest novels was the time-traveling satire *A Connecticut Yankee in King Arthur's Court* (1889), a brilliantly comedic attack on the underlying weakness of man, disguised as a children's adventure story. Twain's title character, like Wise's Klaatu, is an enlightened individual (a nineteenth-century Yankee in sixth-century England) who offers a better, civilized life to a primitive people. Now granted, the Connecticut Yankee attempts to implement change as a leader (reducing Merlin the Magician to being a weatherman!), and much of the novel comically skewers the days of Arthur's court. For example, baseball fan Twain, in a move that would have pleased sports enthusiast Wise, describes diamond activity in a suit of armor: "When a man was running, and threw himself on his stomach to slide to his base, it was like an ironclad [ship] coming into port. . . . The umpire's first decision was usually his last; they broke him in two with a bat, and his friends toted him home on a shutter . . . umpiring got to be unpopular. So I was obliged to appoint somebody whose rank and lofty position under the government would protect him."[15]

Ultimately the book becomes an attack upon the nineteenth century's love affair with utopian novels, where the future is always better. This might best be symbolized by Edward Bellamy's huge bestseller *Looking Backward* (1888), published the year before *Connecticut Yankee*. Bellamy's positive take on the twenty-first century so caught the public's imagination that "Bellamy Clubs" sprang up across America. In contrast, the bloodbath Armageddon finale of Twain's novel asks whether permanent progress is really possible and helps prepare the way for the twentieth century's obsession with *anti*-Utopian fiction, such as George Orwell's *1984* (1947), Ray Bradbury's *Fahrenheit 451* (1952), and Anthony Burgess's *A Clockwork Orange* (1962).

Wise's script description of a scene as "Connecticut Yankee business" was undoubtedly mere shorthand for "superior being among the boobs." But Twain's darkly comic cynicism would not be an inappropriate judgment upon what might have happened to Earth after Klaatu's exit. While Wise films, whatever the genre, usually include some figure(s) of hope, his general picture of humanity is often as damning as that of his favorite humorist.

Above: *Real-life giant Lock Martin exiting the spaceship in his Gort costume during* The Day the Earth Stood Still.
Right: Patricia Neal's The Day the Earth Stood Still *character is yet another Robert Wise woman involved with the wrong man (Hugh Marlowe).*

The alien (Michael Rennie) and the boy (Billy Gray) visit the flying saucer in The Day the Earth Stood Still.

Regardless, if earthlings cannot change for Klaatu, they do not really deserve a second chance. Film historian Peter Biskind said of the character and actor: "Soft-spoken, mild-mannered, cultured, Michael Rennie, more Milquetoast than Martian, is surely the best behaved, most polite alien who ever hopped across hyperspace."[16] And consistent with the Wise milieu, *Earth* also has a "women's picture" melodramatic component—Neal's character is a young widow struggling to raise her son, with a less-than-sympathetic suitor (Hugh Marlowe).

The original plan was to have English actor Claude Rains play Klaatu. Rains, whose film credits included Oscar nominations for Frank Capra's *Mr. Smith Goes to Washington* (1939) and Alfred Hitchcock's *Notorious* (1946), would have been fine in the part. Indeed, given Rains's Capra connection, his casting might have further accented *Earth*'s almost *Mr. Alien Goes to Washington* populist ambience. But when Rains was unavailable, Darryl F. Zanuck, head of Twentieth Century Fox, suggested Rennie, a younger English actor recently signed by the studio. Zanuck called him a "very good actor," with an "interesting look," and Wise quickly recognized another bonus: "[Using Rennie] was a big plus for us because here was a man . . . [largely unknown on the American screen]. That brought much more credibility to it [the role of an alien] than, for instance, if we'd had [famous] Claude Rains."[17]

Neal and Gray lent strong support to Rennie, with the youngster demonstrating the boyish charm that soon made him a television star on the hit show *Father Knows Best* (1954–60, with Gray playing the son of title character Robert Young). The pairing of Rennie and Gray is pivotal to the *Earth* storyline, since the boy acts as the alien's unofficial tour guide through American history à la various capital sites, including a stop at Arlington National Cemetery, where the child's father is buried. Among the many thousands of war dead at Arlington, Klaatu also sees a living human hero—the loyal, loving son. Wise, who so frequently chose properties that involved youngsters and antiwar themes, later credited Gray with being his favorite child actor.

As with Capra's *Mr. Smith*, the most memorable Washington,
D.C., stop is the Lincoln Memorial. Impressed by this great man's
innate wisdom and comparable mission for peace, Klaatu's connection
with Lincoln gives greater credibility to why the alien would show
such patience to a species that shot and wounded him when he exited
his space vehicle and later fatally guns him down. The latter incident,
of course, allows for the most obvious link to Christ—after some
mysterious assistance from Gort, Klaatu rises from the dead. The code
that begins this miracle process also doubles as *Earth*'s most iconic line,
Neal telling Gort: "Klaatu barada nikto!" Years later, Neal revealed a
funny footnote to this famous command, courtesy of costar Rennie.
The actress was still involved with Cooper, and the press followed her
everywhere, demanding information. The studio's publicity department
was now even providing replies for Neal. In her memoir she wrote:
"Dear Michael [Rennie], who was as exasperated as I was, thought I
should honor their rude questions with my favorite line from the film.
'Miss Neal, did you break up Gary Cooper's marriage?' 'Klaatu barada
nikto!'"[18]

As in a Wise movie, Cooper eventually disappointed her by
breaking off their lengthy relationship. Neal's subsequent marriage
(1953) to writer Roald Dahl, most famous for writing the children's
book upon which *Willy Wonka and the Chocolate Factory* (1971) is
based, also ended poorly. But such things were in the future; at the
time Neal struggled with the importance of the film. Sticking with
the material because of her great faith in Wise, she later confessed:
"I sometimes had a difficult time keeping a straight face. Michael
would patiently watch me bite my lips to avoid giggling and ask, with
true British reserve, 'Is that the way you intend to play it?'"[19] Wise,
ever the humorous gentleman, diplomatically described Neal's *Earth*
performance: "she could accomplish a lot without *doing* very much."[20]

Interestingly, at the same time anti-blacklist Wise was in
Washington, D.C., scouting locations for *Earth*, gifted director Leo
McCarey was shooting his unfortunate Communist melodrama *My*

Son John (1952).[21] While Wise was attempting to defuse cold war paranoia with some common sense, a commodity then seeming less and less common, McCarey's *John* represented dramatically overwrought red-baiting, yet both pictures doubled as excellent social histories to a troubled age.

Although *John* soon became an embarrassment on the McCarey filmography, *Earth* was the great Wise picture that never went away. By the director's "own reckoning, it had through the 1990s been shown on television more than all of his other films put together."[22] A revisionist (1992) *The New Yorker* examination of the film better puts its television popularity in perspective: "[*Earth*] shaped baby boomers' idea of classy sci-fi. A theatrical hit in 1951, it reached big new audiences in the early sixties via NBC's prime-time movie showcase, 'Saturday Night at the Movies.'"[23]

This success might have been predicted by the great attention Wise paid to every detail of the script, making the screenplay one of the most annotated in the director's private papers. For example, here are his abbreviated comments on the alien's initial screen appearance at the boardinghouse, where he will take up residence: "This is Klaatu's first contact with people out of his role as 'space man.' [I] Can play very easy concern on his part as to how he is carrying it [being accepted as a human] off. As I see it, this would be [the] only place in [the] story we could try to get this sense of [Klaatu's human-like anxiety]."[24]

Earth reviews were overwhelmingly positive and often acknowledged Wise's ability to incorporate moral or philosophical messages that do not get in the way of the movie's entertainment. For example, *Time* magazine stated, "It makes its points with all the tang and suspense of a good adventure yarn."[25] The *Los Angeles Times* added, "It's more than simply a thriller. It has a sociological and philosophic side, besides being vastly interesting and exciting."[26] The *Hollywood Reporter* praised Wise's ability to emphasize realism in this genre: "Wise's direction imbues the narrative with the compelling atmosphere of the documentary . . . an illusion of presenting the real thing rather than a fictional motion picture."[27] Fittingly, Klaatu's greatest demonstration of force—stopping all power sources for thirty minutes, "the day the earth stood still," in order to get the attention of world leaders—played into Wise's minimalist approach to special effects. This alien miracle simply required an unworldly stillness and quiet.

While Wise worked from an excellent Edmund H. North script (based on a story by Harry Bates), one cannot help thinking that the material might have reminded the director of his movie-obsessed childhood. Klaatu's ability to briefly freeze-frame the world is reminiscent of René Clair's *The Crazy Ray* (1924). And Gort is not unlike the Golem, the supernatural clay monster from a sixteenth-century Jewish folktale (a forerunner of Frankenstein), who inspired several silent films, such as *The Golem* (1920).

Regardless, Wise was deservedly at the center of the kudos for *Earth*, such as the *Los Angeles Daily News* noting, "Wise, one of the more talented of our younger Hollywood directors, steered this ship on its course, and we'd say his aim was true."[28] *New York Journal American* critic Rose Pelswick, in a review titled "Don't Miss This Thriller," said, "Robert Wise keeps the piece moving swiftly and engrossingly."[29] The critical hosannas sometimes even anticipated possible political attack from the conservative right, such as the *Los Angeles Times* reviewer warning, "Certain subversive elements might, of course, see fit to turn the [antiwar, antimilitary] philosophy of this picture to [some anti-American] account."[30] Prophetically, the film became more controversial in the years immediately following its release. Zanuck and Wise had had to fight the McCarthy element to keep the liberal Jaffe in the Einstein-like part. But he was subsequently blacklisted for much of the 1950s. Albert Einstein came under strong conservative criticism in 1953 when he "publicly urged [HUAC] witnesses . . . to refuse to testify. By making an Einstein figure [played by Jaffe] a hero . . . *Earth* was crawling far out on a very thin limb."[31]

Still, the movie's legacy has never been questioned. In 1998 the scholarly *Pacific Film Archive* called *Earth* "one of the most enduring and influential science fiction films ever made, and among the first produced by a major studio."[32] Editor Steven Jay Schneider's entertainingly seminal genre handbook *101 Sci-Fi Movies You Must See Before You Die* (2009) observes: "Science Fiction's power to generate and inject iconic images of great lasting power has never been more convincingly demonstrated than by Robert Wise's *The Day the Earth Stood Still*. Not only have the words 'Klaatu barada nikto' entered the vast murky pool of 20th century pop trivia (whatever they may actually mean), but the [movie's images] . . . have remained immediately recognizable long past the film's moment of historical urgency."[33]

The director's immediate follow-up films, though lacking the high-profile significance of *Earth*, further explore Wise's insatiable appetite for various genres, while demonstrating an ongoing thematic consistency. *The Captive City* (1952) was a low-budget independent film released through United Artists. As noted earlier in the book, a small-town newspaper editor (John Forsythe) is attempting to blow the whistle on an international crime organization. Thus, like *Earth*, there is a problem-film message to the movie that challenges the public to be aware of another potentially Armageddon-like scenario (a mobster-controlled world which, unlike Klaatu's crowd, would not be motivated by peace). As with so many Wise films, the public in *Captive City* is unmotivated to fight for right, because, to paraphrase an axiom from a popular period newspaper cartoon strip, "sophisticated cartoonist"/activist Walt Kelly's *Pogo*, "We have met the enemy and he is us."[34]

Wise's documentary-like slant continued by shooting *Captive City* on location in Nevada, with Reno doubling for a midwestern town. Like the real newscasters used in *Earth*, *Captive City* showcases U.S. Senator Estes Kefauver, whose committee investigating organized crime inspired the movie, in an effective addendum to the close. Despite this realism, the lengthy escape from town by Forsythe and his screen wife (Joan Camden) could have been a dress rehearsal for Siegel's fleeing couple in *Invasion of the Body Snatchers*. In both cases, the largely off-screen menace (two varieties of monsters) seems real, proving yet again

Val Lewton's basic rule that the viewer's imagination produces the most frightening imagery.

After *Captive City*, Wise shot his first overt comedy, the farcical problem film *Something for the Birds* (1952). This was a new genre for him but peppered with familiar Wise themes and characters. *Birds* has Neal playing a representative of the Society for the Preservation of the California Condor. She has traveled to Washington, D.C., to prevent an oil company from drilling in a condor sanctuary. Neal's character finds two unlikely allies in womanizing lobbyist Steve Bennett (Victor Mature), and retirement age printing shop specialist Johnny Adams (Edmund Gwenn).

Birds was an assignment piece for Twentieth Century Fox, but one Wise enjoyed making. He especially liked directing Gwenn, whose long career included an Academy Award for playing Santa Claus in *Miracle on 34th Street* (1947). For Wise, Gwenn "was a delightful old gentleman to work with."[35] And given the director's private papers at the University of Southern California, so full of issue-orientated correspondence on a litany of subjects, the film's subject matter would undoubtedly have been something he would have enjoyed spoofing.[36] Besides, as with *Earth*, he could satirize Washington leadership (or the lack thereof) and still use on-location footage.

Birds' farcical story could also be tied to Wise's editing days on screwball comedies such as *My Favorite Wife* (1940). But a more logical link to the director's work would be to bleed the comedy out and look at the basic narrative. Mature's character only helps Neal because he wants to bed her. This amoral lobbyist is initially even unaware that his organization represents the evil oil company in question. Gwenn's character is more sympathetic, but it soon comes out that he uses his engraving job as an entry into Washington high society. Invitations for tony engagements come to his printing company, and presto, Gwenn, pretending to be a retired admiral, includes himself on many elite guest lists. Consequently, *Birds* is yet another Wise excursion into the world of manipulative males and vulnerable women. But as a farce, the viewer trades melodrama for merriment, and *Birds* is often a funny film.

The entertainment factor gets a sizable boost from I. A. L. Diamond's script (with Boris Ingster), who later collaboraed with Billy Wilder on such screen masterpieces as *Some Like It Hot* (1959) and the multiple Academy Award–winning *The Apartment* (1960, including a script Oscar). Gwenn's "admiral" is the chief beneficiary of several still insightful Will Rogers-like witticisms, including, "There's so much confusion in Washington, that if you only seem to know what you're doing, you can get away with anything" and "You know how it is in Washington; the more you deny something the more people believe it." Given Diamond's now farcical-driven reputation, one cannot help thinking that the subtext for the title, *Something for the Birds*, was less about Neal's condors and more about Mature's "birds" (women).

Although some of the farce seems dated, like Mature defending his amoral lobbying/womanizing with lines such as, "A woman wearing a low-cut gown is lobbying," the picture scores revisionist political points today with its satirical jabs at U.S. Senate hearings during a period now labeled infamous for the Red Scare. While Wise's comedy avoids any sermonizing, when his senators bully Gwenn in a hearing, it would seem to encourage a more sympathetic period take on those allegedly subversive filmmakers being victimized by fearmongering legislators. Couple this position with *Earth*'s Washington-based open ridicule of trigger-happy soldiers and narrow-minded politicians, and two such seemingly diverse pictures suddenly have a lot more in common.

Melodrama in Various War Settings:
Run Silent, Run Deep as Metaphor

"My intelligence has given me to understand there is considerable friction between you two allies [British officers and Australian troops]."
GERMAN FIELD MARSHALL ERWIN ROMMEL (JAMES MASON) ADDRESSING
A BRITISH PRISONER OF WAR (RICHARD BURTON) IN *DESERT RATS* (1953)

Of the ten films Robert Wise directed after *Something for the Birds* (1952), five were war-related: *Destination Gobi, The Desert Rats* (both 1953), *Helen of Troy* (1955), *Until They Sail* (1957), and *Run Silent, Run Deep* (1958). But only *Desert* and *Deep* are conventional war films, and even these two might better be called "action melodramas," a genre description of more recent origin.[1] As will be fleshed out shortly, while violence has always had a subtext, Hollywood movies have often neglected to explore the inner angst.

Though these war-related films once again show Wise increasing his genre filmography, the movies continue to conform to the director's cinema world. That is, as with Wise's Prussian-occupation picture *Mademoiselle Fifi* (1944), the cold war setting of *The Day the Earth Stood Still* (1951), and the noir/horror foundation of so many Wise films, there is little jingoism or glamor in his conflict-connected films. Despite all but one of the movies involving World War II, what historians sometimes reference as the "Good War," (given that America knew who the enemy was and what they were fighting for), Wise often explores war's murky subtext.[2] And while much of what follows does not involve actual combat, even his depictions of battle scenes avoid Hollywood heroics. For example, *New York Herald Tribune* critic Otis L. Guernsey Jr. praises just such a sequence in *Desert Rats*: "He [Wise] prefers an atmosphere of noise, danger, and confusion to an atmosphere of heroism, and most of his staged scenes have a grainy, half-lit quality that matches the photography of the real things."[3]

Critic Richard C. Keenan suggested Wise was attracted to combat scenarios "because war films lend themselves so readily to the documentary style that is present in much of his best work."[4] Yet Keenan might couple this perspective with the idea that war heightens the propensity for a key Wise theme—the melodramatic stress of interpersonal relationships.

In each of these Wise war-related movies, the personal conflicts supplant any real battles. For example, *Run Silent, Run Deep* could be called a World War II variation of *Moby Dick* meets *Mutiny on the Bounty*. Clark Gable plays a submarine commander whose ship was sunk by the Japanese destroyer *Akikaze*. After a prolonged desk assignment, he orchestrates another submarine command—one that possibly should have gone to Burt Lancaster's character, who becomes Gable's first officer on the new sub. If that situation did not create enough underwater tension, the ship's crew is divided into separate Gable-Lancaster cliques. Now add Gable's obsession with sinking the *Akikaze*, and a nonsadistic yet martinet persistent practicing of an attack drill if the destroyer is found, and Lancaster is forever close to leading a mutiny. An actual revolt is avoided, in part, by an eventually fatal injury to Gable. But Lancaster and Gable manage a sort of unofficial joint command before the latter's death and poignant burial at sea.

Although the *Akikaze* is ultimately sunk, and the movie has the prerequisite white-knuckle submarine scene where depth charges are dropped on the potential coffin ship, Wise best plays melodrama with a touch of realism. Due to the confined space of a World War II submarine, most movie submarine sets cheat by expanding the dimensions for easier actor movement. But Wise re-created the actual submarine size, and this authentic violation of normal personal space, among characters already at a powder-keg state, makes all the melodramatic difference. His combustible coffin is even reminiscent of a phrase German sailors used for a submarine: "the Devil's shovel."[5]

Both *Destination Gobi* and *Desert Rats* also deal with officer-enlisted men conflicts, but *Gobi* generally avoids *Deep*'s melodrama. Instead, Wise's first desert war picture takes the stress factor in a different genre direction. *Gobi* is an action comedy, with a narrative that initially flirts with absurdity, though hardly in the sense of an Albert Camus novel. Richard Widmark is a by-the-book *navy* veteran more than a little upset at being assigned to command a team of meteorologists in a sea of sand. Given Widmark's frustration with his situation and his personnel, his charismatic character imbues *Gobi* with the make-do spirit that was the

Battlefield beneath the sea, Clark Gable (left) and Burt Lancaster in Run Silent, Run Deep *(1958).*

watchword of both Wise and his old studio, RKO. For film fan Wise, just as his greatest *Deep* pleasure was working with Gable, the brass ring for *Gobi* was megaphoning Widmark.[6]

Though *Desert* is Wise's most traditional war film, Richard Burton plays yet another harsh disciplinarian commander. The setting is World War II's North African theater, and Australian-British troops are battling a German army led by the famed Field Marshal Erwin Rommel (James Mason). But as with *Deep*, the friction is largely between Australian enlisted men and their British commander, a situation acerbated in *Desert* by a lingering Australian resentment of British superiority toward its former colony. There is even a near fragging (an officer shot by an enlisted man) of Burton's British captain early in the film, followed by his later sarcastic crack to another Australian soldier, "If you'd lowered your aim a bit you could have got me, too!" And in a variation of the awkward working arrangement of the Gable-Lancaster characters in *Deep*, Burton's second in command is someone he tried to court-martial.

Burton and Mason are very entertaining in this follow-up to the latter actor's popular title turn as *The Desert Fox: The Story of Rommel* (1951). *Fox* had been a critical and commercial hit, though the picture's reception by some veteran groups was stormy, given its heroic treatment of a former adversary—one who later died because he had supported an attempted coup against Adolf Hitler. Wise's movie mirrored the earlier picture's success, yet centers upon the underdog British-Australian operations in North Africa that eventually led to the defeat of Rommel's forces. Though Mason's part is hardly more than a cameo, there is an inspired darkly comic face-off with Burton, a melodramatic chance meeting of war. Wise's Rommel is still formidable but drained of any previous glory, and one could imagine Burton's figure thinking the same thoughts of a later character by British novelist Robert Harris, which also describes a once heroic figure: "Now I was closer to him, I could discern the younger man staring out from the older: age had blurred him."[7] Yet, Burton and Mason's sometimes darkly comic repartee (see the chapter's opening quote) suggests the British captain's upper-class demeanor has more in common with his aristocratic enemy than with the blue-collar Australian troops he leads. The situation is analogous to the equally ironic privileged-class connections between another German commandant (Erich von Stroheim) and a prisoner of war officer (Pierre Fresnay) in Jean Renoir's *Grande Illusion* (1937). Of course, there is no time in *Desert* for a comparable friendship to blossom. Indeed, Burton's character is often insolent (all the better to demonstrate Rommel's grace), yet the class parallels are there.

Despite Mason's minimal screen time, the actor's presence on the set was of great assistance to Wise with Burton, who even then had a reputation for hard living. "In between takes Burton and Mason would discuss books they had read," Wise recalled. "I think Burton envied Mason's grasp of screen acting, and I know that Mason gave him some tips. . . . Before Mason began work on the film, Burton was anxious and nervous and eager to do well but just so intense. Then he worked with Mason and he began to calm down. I'd expected Burton to be resistant to the kind of role he had . . . I thought [the classically trained

Richard Burton (right) and Robert Newton in Desert Rats *(1953).*

stage actor] Burton would have preferred a script with some lovely language. But he said to me, 'You know, I am really enjoying being an action star. It's tremendous fun.'"[8]

This assist from Mason was another variation on Wise's belief that directing was all about good casting. He also believed strongly in preproduction conferences with stars in which he could share his overview of the picture. At this stage Wise was happy to field input from his principal performers. But as a practical, efficient filmmaker, once shooting began Wise was not a fan of an overly analytical actor. The director was pleased to discover Burton was equally "professional": "if you ask him to make a [physical] move in a scene to accommodate the camera, [he] doesn't ask, 'Why? What is my motivation? He'd just do it."[9]

Wise's sense of "professionalism" also involved connecting with the consumer/viewer whatever the genre, whatever the subtext message: "The most important part of making a film is that the audience should be involved," said Wise.[10] This commitment to storytelling made Wise a huge fan of sneak previews. He later bemoaned the fact that a true preview was increasingly difficult by the 1960s. "I was raised in the generation of the real sneak previews. I love them," said Wise. "Nowadays everybody knows what's sneaking where and the audience is loaded with friends of everybody in the picture. [Real previews are important because] You see the dailies and the rough cuts and after a while it's difficult to keep your perspective. You miss things that ought to be perfectly obvious. . . . Sitting in the [preview] audience tells you everything. The [viewer's evaluation] cards afterward usually confirm it but the coughing, the restlessness, the wrong laughs have said it all before."[11]

Melodrama was an especially popular genre with 1950s audiences, and while *Gobi*, *Desert*, and *Deep* all addressed this phenomenon among the warriors, *Helen of Troy* and *Until They Sail* gave the woman's perspective, too. There is also a foreshadowing of this feminist slant on war-related melodrama in Wise's *Three Secrets* (1950), where two of the three broken relationships are shown, via flashbacks, to have been born of hasty World War II romances. *Until They Sail*, from a James Michener story, keys on the same sort of scenario, only the focus is four New Zealand sisters. For many women in their country, World War II has turned relationships helter-skelter. Their able-bodied men have departed, and American servicemen have filled the void, "until they sail" on service assignments.

The Leslie sisters have lost a father and a brother to the war. Pure Barbara (Jean Simmons), the movie's lead, is quickly widowed. Spinster Anne (Joan Fontaine) initially resists any romantic involvement. Reluctantly, she falls for a courtly American captain (Charles Drake), only to lose him to yet another Pacific theater battle. The good/bad news is the relationship produces a child but no wedding ring. The well-named Delia (Piper Laurie) impulsively marries a ne'er-do-well native son (Wally Cassell), only to bed countless American servicemen after he ships out. Teenage Evelyn (Sandra Dee) has the potential to follow in Delia's footsteps, but her youth and the fact that she is still living at home keeps her faithful to an in-uniform New Zealand boyfriend.

As with *Three Secrets*, a cross-section of weepy scenarios are presented. And besides the baby out-of-wedlock link, both movies add murder to the melodrama. In *Secrets*, Ruth Roman's character gives birth in prison, where she is serving time for killing the child's despicable father. *Until They Sail* reverses the scenario; the low-life cuckold of a husband murders Delia. As noted in an earlier chapter, the violent dysfunctional family settings for Wise's film-noir picture (*Born to Kill*, 1947), sometimes surface in his dysfunctional family melodramas. And while murder is never an acceptable option, the viewer's sympathy in both *Sail* and *Secrets*, as in most Wise films, is with the women. Roman's act of violence is against a man who has casually cast her aside, without any thought of marriage or of their unborn child. Laurie's adulterous party girl is far from admirable, but her behavior is little different than that of many male servicemen in these

Wise war-related melodramas. One would now be tempted to recycle a line from Quentin Lee's *The People I've Slept With* (2010), "A slut is just a woman with the morals of a man."

Paradoxically, macho male sports have countless phrases metamorphically applicable to melodrama, or life in general. When an injured athlete is "playing through the pain" of an injury, he qualifies as "one of the walking wounded," with his status as "day to day." Who has not felt, at some point, like one of these word pictures; those psychological wounds are the focus of melodrama. But I am not suggesting that Wise, a lifelong sports fan, was consciously making a link between two activities synonymous with each gender. Still, in addition to the many strong women this book has already chronicled in Wise's life, the director's fascination with that nail-biting activity called sports might have made him more sensitive to the multiplicity of pain in melodrama, a genre to which he was equally drawn.

The catalyst for these sports-melodrama musings involves the casting of Paul Newman in *Sails*, fresh from a breakout performance in Wise's biography film of boxer Rocky Graziano *Somebody Up There Likes Me* (1956, to be addressed in the next chapter). Though Newman's Rocky has his own internalized demons, the actor's character from *Sails* (Captain Jack Harding) is a greater example of the "walking wounded," not unlike the Leslies. But this is no tangential figure to the narrative-driving sisters. Harding, though his sensitivity makes the name ironic, becomes intertwined with the soaper stories in several ways. First, just as the war will cause them to question the concept of love and relationships, his military position guarantees a diffusion of romance. Newman's character, like the male advice columnist of novelist Nathanael West's *Miss Lonelyhearts* (1933), becomes too deeply involved in his relationship-oriented job—investigating the legitimacy of petitions for marriage between American marines and New Zealand civilians. Already the victim of a war-related divorce himself, Harding's ulterior motives and/or simply the fear he finds behind many wannabe war marriages increases his depression. To guard against further hurt to himself or others, he confesses to Simmons's Barbara that alcohol is his escape: "This [bottle] is what I spend the night with . . . [resulting in a] hangover but nobody gets hurt."

Second, again like West's title character, Newman's Harding provides periodic insight about these troubled relationships, from a forgiving overview, "Most of the involved [couples are] just lonely," to the more self-incriminating, "I loved her [my ex-wife] but I didn't like her." Newman's multifaceted character is even reminiscent of a description once made of West himself: "This tall slim young man with the warm handclasp . . . had composure . . . quick repartee . . . [yet] his sudden silences, resounding like a pebble dropped into a well, suggested the complexities, the contraries to be found in . . . [his] work."[12] (Interestingly, an excellent adaptation of West's novella was made the year after *Sail. Lonelyhearts*, 1958, starred a method actor who influenced Newman, Montgomery Clift.)

Third, given Wise's interest in journalism, Newman's Harding represents a figure whose position is not unlike a reporter researching ever-changing stories. When Wise is not giving viewers journalist characters, such as Patricia Neal's reporter in *Secrets* and John Forsythe's *The Captive City* editor, or casting news people in cameos, such as *The Day the Earth Stood Still* and *Secrets*, the director often gravitates to surrogate journalists. Though Harding's reports are not normally published, his research on Delia becomes part of the public record via *Sail*'s murder trial framing device. Like many film noirs, *Sail* opens at the close and is told in flashback. While Newman's character has an impact upon each of the Leslie sisters, the connection to Delia's trial is the most explosive.

Newman meets Simmons's Barbara early in the film, but nothing happens romantically until after her husband's death—killed a mere month after their wedding. Both Newman and Simmons proceed slowly, even reluctantly, given the history of his job and her family. But just after he has demonstrated ongoing loyalty to her, survived being one of the messengers of death (concerning the demise of

Anne's lover), and remained a positive male figure for the young and potentially Delia-like Evelyn, the narrative returns the viewer to the trial that briefly opened the picture. That initial courtroom scene is a tease, with little disclosed, other than that Newman is a witness. The defense for Delia's murderer is attempting to soften the verdict and/ or sentencing by documenting the breadth of her unfaithfulness. Since the victim had planned to marry a marine once she could divorce her husband, a plan delayed by her spouse's incarceration in a prisoner-of-war camp, Newman's Harding had an unflattering file on her. Given that Newman's figure was now romantically involved with Delia's sister, his testimony jeopardizes their relationship. Though Harding had few options, Simmons's character initially makes it appear any negative comments about Delia would be a deal breaker. But in this nuanced weepy, Newman and Simmons ultimately allow *Sail* viewers to exit on a positive note.

Like so many of Wise's cinema reporters and quasi-journalists, the director did a great deal of research on the subject, including interviews with many New Zealand women whose lives paralleled the events of the movie. Again, this documented Wise's attention to detail, since he thought "*Sail* was a warm and human story . . . [which] touched me when I read it in Michener's book."[13] Though this Metro-Goldwyn-Mayer film was shot on the studio's back lot, Wise exercised his love of travel to visit New Zealand, both for those aforementioned interviews and to scout background shots for his second-unit crew.

In addition to being moved by the material, Wise was pleased to have Newman as *Sail*'s male lead. Always the diplomatic director throughout his long career, Wise forever avoided playing favorites publicly. But in a much later letter (1982) to a film fan, he privately confessed, "I would say that Julie Andrews is the most talented actress I've worked with, [and] Paul Newman would be the best actor."[14] Newman had accepted the part because he appreciated Wise having taken a chance on him for *Somebody*. Newman biographer Shawn Levy later called Wise "an ideal director for Newman," and shared the filmmaker's thoughts on their *Somebody* collaboration, which were then replicated on *Sail*. "Paul would get an idea for something [during rehearsal], a little switch or a change, something he wanted to do—and on the surface I would say, 'No, I don't think that's right, Paul. Forget it.' And we'd go on," Wise recalled. "But I learned very quickly that he couldn't forget it—it was stuck in his craw. So I found it was simpler with him to let him try it and then prove to himself that it was not good."[15] Unlike his later friend and costar Robert Redford, Newman loved to endlessly analyze his movie parts. Their director on both *Butch Cassidy and the Sundance Kit* (1969) and *The Sting* (1973), George Roy Hill, had a similar challenge with the actor: "Newman will talk a scene to death . . . Redford would just stand there and squirm during all the intellectualizing."[16]

Critics liked *Sail*, including the *New York Journal American*'s Rose Pelswick, whose review was titled, "Stirring Tale of Girls Who Wait on War." Her descriptive phrase, "a war film without battle scenes," is a poetic summation of any home front during an armed conflict.[17] *Variety* championed the picture via its auteur: "Under Wise's deft and sensitive direction, [Robert] Anderson's screenplay takes explosive form in following love affairs of four sisters. Clandestine romance is subtly handled. And in touching on loneliness of love-starred years plot builds dramatic punch. Top flight cast generates often poignant unfoldments."[18]

All of these Wise war films, with or "without battle scenes," were well received by the public and the press. This acclaim was especially true for *Deep*, which the *New York Times* claimed, "A better film about war beneath the ocean and about guys in the 'silent service' has not been made."[19] But just as the title of this chapter suggests, the moniker *Run Silent, Run Deep* represents an excellent metaphor for war films "without battle scenes," reviews for this picture could also double for Wise's general melodrama sensitivity, regardless of setting and/or genre. For example, critic Alton Cook of the *New York World Telegram and Sun* said *Deep* is "a very good picture, a seething brew of suspense. . . .

Robert Wise has directed for maximum nervous strain."[20] The positive *Toronto Global Mail* critique of *Deep* stated: "Fortunately, director Robert Wise has kept a tight rein on all this [conflict] and has kept it from slipping into the ranks of sloppy melodrama while keeping tension building to a gradual crescendo."[21] Again, such wording might have been equally at home if applied to *Sail,* or the other at-war melodramas examined thus far.

The chapter's final highlighted picture, *Helen of Troy*, might be labeled the only creative failure in this film grouping. Paradoxically, as often happens with an artistic misfire, its basic components, in this case another look at the inherent melodrama of a society at war, stand out all the more. Though not without its champions, even *Variety's* kudos reveal read-between-the-lines problems for a film aspiring to greatness: "The word 'spectacular' achieves its true meaning when applied to Warner Bros.' 'Troy.' The retelling of the Homeric legend, filmed in its entirety in Italy, makes lavish use of the CinemaScope screen."[22]

During the 1950s, when competition from early television encouraged Hollywood to embrace both a quasi-genre (the epic) and techniques (such as widescreen color) impossible to emulate on that era's tiny, twelve-inch, black-and-white television screens, movie narrative sometimes became lost in a quest for spectacle. *Newsweek's* review of an epic fittingly titled *Giant* (1956) called it "the time of the mastodon movie, visually immense."[23] Though *Helen* was a critical and commercial disappointment, and *Giant* was an Oscar-winning box-office success, *both* movies now seem like slow-moving "mastodons." Such is often the fate of prodigious pictures.

While the period produced several quality epics, such as Cecil B. DeMille's *The Ten Commandments* (1956) and David Lean's *Bridge on the River Kwai* (1957), the majority of these cinematic exercises in elephantiasis now seem like "much ado about nothing." Unlike "an art object without the energy or courage to be a work of art," epics often fail precisely because the work expends too much energy trying to be a work of art.[24] Regardless, the melodramatic war story at the heart of so many Wise pictures surfaces again in *Helen*, with heartland publications satirizing the title character long before the film was even finished. For example, the *Chicago Tribune* suggested christening the movie *Miss Universe of 1200 B.C.*, and the *Des Moines Register* summarized: "[Helen] married one man, ran away with another, after he died, married his brother, betrayed him to her original husband, who took her back. Hollywood, naturally, isn't going to let a chick like that go unnoticed."[25] One might bookend *Helen*'s prerelease susceptibility to satire with the film's almost simultaneous opening against one of cinema's greatest parodies—the historical epic-skewering *Court Jester* (1956, starring Danny Kaye).

Of course, as with most traditional renderings of Homer's story, the revised title should be *Melodramas Concerning the Woman Who Caused the Trojan War*, since even Christopher Marlowe's famous acknowledgement of her beauty, "Was this the face that launched a thousand ships?" referred to Greek *war* ships.[26] In short, the Trojan king sends his son Paris on a peace mission to Sparta to avoid war with the Greek city states. Instead, Paris causes a conflict by falling in love with Helen, the wife of Sparta's king, making Paris arguably history's worst peace envoy. However, as in all melodramas, there are extenuating circumstances: Helen was in an unhappy marriage, Paris did not ask any questions, and passion trumps wisdom. Consequently, short of *Helen*'s epic scope, one could be discussing Wise's lovely loose Delia from *Sail*. In both these films about warriors on ships, unfaithfulness leads to violent consequences.

The more interesting "melodrama" concerning Wise's *Helen* involved the making of the picture. The Warner Brothers Archives at the University of Southern California provide a blow-by-blow account of the studio's often troubled *Helen* production.[27] Much of this documentation involves letters and telegrams between studio chief Jack Warner (in Hollywood) and production watchdog T. C. "Tenny" Wright on location (based out of Rome). Interestingly, another great multiple-genre auteur, Howard Hawks, was also being monitored by

Wright. Hawks was in Egypt making the Warner epic, *Land of the Pharaohs* (1955). Like *Helen*, Hawks stumbled on *Pharaohs*, too, though as his definitive biographer later noted, head to head Wise wins: "[In 1959 *Pharaohs* was] reissued on the bottom of a [long] double bill with *Helen of Troy*."[28]

Before briefly examining the melodrama behind the melodrama that was *Helen*, one should recognize that most major movie productions involve a great deal of compromise. In Francois Truffaut's *Day for Night* (1973, an Oscar-winning film about filmmaking), Truffaut also doubles as the wise but overwhelmed director in the movie within the movie. His character's simile on directing is dead-on: "Shooting a movie is like a stagecoach ride in the Old West. At first you hope for a nice trip. Soon you just hope to reach your destination." As always, Wise liked to challenge himself, feeling it was "time to get myself into that mainstream of big-size picture-making. . . . I was [not] mad about the material . . . [yet] I wanted to see if I could do it."[29] But as film historian Richard C. Keenan noted, "it was almost more than Wise could handle."[30]

In defense of Wise's *Helen*, one could almost argue the gods were against him, from the movie mogul variety (Warner) to the star of Michelangelo's Sistine Chapel. For example, early in the production a fire destroyed 80 percent of Wise's sets at the Cinecittà Studios in Rome. This nightmare guaranteed *Helen* would both go over budget and come under closer studio financial scrutiny. Throw in Tower of Babel communication problems (with a cast and crew composed of Americans, English, Italians, and French), add the most mediocre of scripts, top it off with two beautiful but wooden leads, and a flawed film outcome is hardly surprising.

Worldwide publicity was generated when Italian actress Rossanna Podestà (Helen) and French actor Jacques Sernas (Paris) were chosen among many to star in the film. While the cinema couple appeared in European films both before and after *Helen*, including Serna's memorable supporting role as a faded star in Frederico Fellini's later *La*

Dolce Vita (1960), here the pair's histrionics recalls Dorothy Parker's satirical review of an early Katharine Hepburn stage role, "She ran the gamut of emotion from A to B."[31] Neither Podestà nor Sernas had ever been asked to carry so much artistic weight, and like Wise, they were handicapped by the script. Still, the good and/or comfortable actor is able to physicalize things either implied by the writing and/or even improve upon it. For example, in John Hillcoat's adaptation of Cormac McCarthy's *The Road* (2009), when the boy (Kodi Smit-McPhee) has to deal with the coughs of a dying father (Viggo Mortensen), he instinctively puts a hand to his parent's lips and improvises "Stop."[32] These poignant additions were in neither the novel nor the script. For whatever reason, Podestà and Sernas were unable to elevate their *Helen* roles. Certainly this would have weighed upon Wise as much as his performers, especially since the director felt the strength of a movie was so dependent upon casting. (Today, one is tempted to ponder how Bridgette Bardot, who had a supporting role in *Helen,* might have worked as the title character. The following year her appearance in *And God Created Woman,* 1956, made her an international star and a new kind of sex symbol—a "sex kitten." Using Bardot in this child-of-nature persona, or even Podestá, a Helen simply responding to the call of sensuality might have sexually energized the picture and better explained Paris's weakness.)

Sergio Leone, now famous for his own brand of epic filmmaking ("spaghetti westerns"), was a *Helen* production assistant concerned about the stress on his new friend Wise. As Leone biographer Christopher Frayling shares, "Wise was never at ease during his many months in another town [Rome], and his main concern was to minimize the amount of time spent standing around."[33]

For a movie that was not released until late 1955, Wise's long-distance stress from Hollywood began two years earlier. In December 1953 the director received the following telegram from Warner: "Tenny Wright coming [to] Rome [to] take charge [of the] production immediately after Christmas. [I] feel picture so important [I] want [my]

top man [to] give you all aid you need."[34] A defensive Wise wired back,
"Wright excellent but [I] feel badly you having [to] do without him.
Burbank are you sure you can spare him? [The] situation [at Rome's]
Cinecitta very good. *Helen* big job but can be well handled . . . [without
Tenny]."[35]

As one sifts through the mounds of correspondence between
Warner and Wright, one senses a Uriah Heep-like sandbagging of Wise
by Wright. Thus, a May 1, 1954, Wright letter to Warner states, "Bob
Wise is working hard and judging from your cable, the stuff [early
Helen footage] is excellent but . . . [I am] trying hard to keep him
on schedule but he is behind."[36] Three days later Wright's faint praise
of Wise is again more about sowing concern: "Everything is going
along but slowly. Bob Wise working hard but taking plenty of time. I
am anxiously awaiting your . . . reaction to the continuity that Wise
rewrote on the beach and fire ditch [scenes]."[37] Consequently, it comes
as no surprise that by early June Wright is congratulating Warner, "You
were very wise and fortunate in having [director Raoul] Walsh come [to
Italy and assist in orchestrating second unit action sequences]."[38] Uriah
Heep indeed! If Dickens had lived long enough to create cinema-related
characters, he would have been hard pressed to improve upon Wright.

Though Wright's initial usurping of Wise's autonomy was not a
shock, given studio politics, the stature of this second-unit director
was. Walsh was cinema history incarnate, starting out as an actor and
assistant director to no less than D. W. Griffith. He even played John
Wilkes Booth in Griffith's landmark movie *Birth of a Nation* (1915).
But Walsh soon focused on directing, and this strong auteur's forte
quickly became the virile action adventure, laced with a streak of heroic
vulnerability. His long list of classics stretched from *The Thief of Bagdad*
(1924, starring Douglas Fairbanks, Sr.) to *High Sierra* (1941, with
Humphrey Bogart), *White Heat* (1949, starring James Cagney), and *The
Tall Men* (1955, with Clark Gable, the same year *Helen* was released).

The stun factor for Wise, moreover, would have been multiplied
threefold. First, while it is standard fare to have a second-unit action

director on a picture, Wise *already* had a great one on *Helen*, legendary
stuntman/director Yakima Canutt, whose honorary Oscar awarded in
1966 read, "For creating the profession of stuntman as it exists today
and for the development of many safety devices used by stuntmen
everywhere."[39] Most singularly, Canutt's choreography of the Indian
attack *and* his stunt work in John Ford's watershed *Stagecoach* (1939),
including spectacular leaps from and onto galloping horses as a double
for John Wayne and various Native Americans (in effect, fighting
himself), are signature action scenes in world cinema. So memorable is
the sequence that Steven Spielberg essentially replicated much of it in
Raiders of the Lost Ark (1981), in which Indiana Jones (Harrison Ford)
fights Nazi soldiers in, on, and under a speeding troop truck.

Second, Wise had to be amazed that the man who directed his
favorite boyhood movie star, Douglas Fairbanks Sr., in arguably the
iconic swashbuckler's best film, was now *one* of the Hoosier's second-
unit directors.

Third, the myriad of Walsh-related emotions Wise would have been
feeling three decades later (1954) then splintered into further surprise
and anger when the older director overstepped his position regarding
the selection of locations for *Helen*. For instance, the two men differed
on where the invading Greek army should have their camps. Walsh
wanted to economize by having the second Greek camp, from which
the army lays lengthy siege to Troy, also double as the initial beach
camp landing site. What follows is yet another biased Wright letter to
Warner from June 1954:

> Wise seems to forget that this is Warner Bros. money, not his,
> and his only reason for wanting to get on the beach [to] re-cre-
> ate the Greek camp] is that he says it is a more interesting shot
> . . . [Wise said] "I will shoot it myself if Walsh won't." [But]
> That would mean a couple of [production] days longer for Mr.
> Wise.[40]

The hypocritical irony of Wright's diatribe is that Wise was simply
attempting to fulfill a basic artistic request made earlier by Warner.

Douglas Fairbanks Sr. (circa 1925), a favorite of Robert Wise's boyhood, had been directed by Raoul Walsh.

Though USC's production files on *Helen* do not reveal whether Wright ever shared the following correspondence excerpt with Wise, over two months before the Greek camp conflict Warner wrote to Wright:

> [Encourage Wise to] take some chances in getting unusual shots instead of straight on photography. Get some tricky [camera] angles, à la [Michael] Curtis [1888–1962, director of such Warner masterpieces as *Casablanca*, 1943, and *Mildred Pierce*, 1945], with good composition . . . this picture must be right.[41]

Walsh makes no mention of these events in his memoir, which is hardly a surprise, given that on *Helen* his lucrative second-unit work went unacknowledged by request. But his autobiography suggests, like the previous correspondence from Warner to Wright, that the studio chief was as much concerned with quality as penny-pinching.[42] And one is not limited to reading between the lines on the subject. Another *Helen*-related Warner to Wright letter clearly and entertainingly paints the assistant as a whiner:

> [I] am leaving it up to you, Tenny [Wright], to stop asking for everything from here. Go back to the days when you and I made pictures with what we had. They were damn good and the business was prosperous and everyone was happy.[43]

Wise received a more direct endorsement from Warner later that year (1954) when the studio mogul attempted to re-sign the director. But Wise got the last laugh, given that he also had an ongoing working relationship with MGM. Yet, his polite, no "burning of bridges" reply displays both the Hollywood clout and diplomacy he had achieved by the age of forty, even in the midst of a lesser work:

> So far as re-signing with Warners is concerned, I'm afraid that will have to be out [of the question] for the time being. However, I appreciate your interest and desire to have me remain at Warners, and realize that there are possibly several advantages that would make it well worth while. So let's leave the door open for future discussion on this [offer] at the time I finish the Metro [MGM] deal.[44]

Helen might have been one of those epics where "some critics line up to point out that they think the big vessel is a little on the empty side," but Wise's ability to soldier through on this most difficult of projects demonstrated his perseverance when *everything* about the movie stripped away his comfort zones.[45] Flawed cinema can sometimes tell the film student more about an artist than a triumph. Such is the case here.

10

"Portraits" and Biographies Doubling as Melodramas and/or Noirs

"Everybody who is young is promising.
The world should sue the young for breach of promise."
BENNY (JOSEPH BULOFF) IN *SOMEBODY UP THERE LIKES ME* (1956)

Robert Wise directed nearly half of his forty films during the 1950s. Such a concentration of work better allows a biographer to note auteur patterns in an artist's work. Before diving into those important constants in his cinema, defining Rosetta Stone elements inexplicably missed in previous studies, one should pause on that eventual forty-film work ethic. It comes out of an earlier "seize the day" American mentality. The decade following Wise's artful industriousness he received the industry's greatest acclaim with directing and producing Oscars for both *West Side Story* (1961) and *The Sound of Music* (1965).

To put this "seize" philosophy in period perspective, briefly consider some parallels with a Hoosier contemporary of Wise, University of California at Los Angeles basketball coach John Wooden. Born four years before the director, Wooden led his Martinsville High School to three consecutive state finals (winning in 1927), just a few miles from Franklin College, where Wise was a freshman in 1932. That same year Wooden led Purdue University to the Helms Foundation's unofficial national basketball championship, and was named America's player of the year. For Hoosier Hysteria fanatics, a club that definitely included a young Wise, Wooden was something special long before he began piling up national championships at UCLA. Yet, like Wise, Wooden's validation in his field also came after relocating to Los Angeles, paying his dues during the 1950s, topped off with monster success in the 1960s. More significantly, both men had parents who instilled these core values. Indeed, Wooden always carried a scrap of paper on which his father had imparted living guidelines that would not have been out of place in Wise's pocket: "Be true to yourself. Make each day a masterpiece. Help others. Drink deeply from good books. Make friendship a fine art. Build a shelter against a rainy day."[1]

The previous chapter addressed Wise's propensity to explore melodrama in various war settings. This tendency will be further examined here in a series of portrait and biography films, often with noir flourishes, a genre that goes back to his 1940s emergence as a gifted editor turned director. But first, a note of explanation concerning the phrase "portrait film." This description was used by critic and later celebrated French New Wave director Francois Truffaut in his positive critique of Wise's *Executive Suite* (1954), one of this chapter's focus films.[2] A "portrait" picture is a close biography-like look at a fictional character whose roots often have a basis in reality. Biographer/critic Paul Murray Kendall's study of the genre's various permutations actually prefers the phrase "fictionalized biography" over the term portrait.[3] Regardless, Wise's *Executive* picture is a sketch of an absent/invisible central figure drawn from the reactions of several characters once close to this person.

Naturally, the Wise aficionado will immediately think of *the* portrait film, Orson Welles's *Citizen Kane* (1941), with a production team that included Wise as editor and John Houseman as producer—a role Houseman repeated on *Executive*. But unlike *Kane*'s flashback approach, Wise's *Executive* always stays in the present. The absentee centerpiece is the constantly discussed driving force of the film, but he remains unseen.

Several previously examined Wise films have already demonstrated this portrait-film phenomenon. For example, his character study of a patriotic prostitute in *Mademoiselle Fifi* (1944) is a sympathetic nonstop dissection of a singular figure from French literature. By the conclusion of *The Body Snatcher* (1945), the insights shared by several characters, particularly John Gray (Boris Karloff), make the true villain (Henry Daniell's Doctor MacFarlane) a borderline tragic figure. The stylized realism and effective ploy of shooting *The Set-Up* (1949) in real time often makes this noir masterpiece seem like a documentary portrait of an everyman palooka desperately fighting for a break. Both *The Captive City* (1952) and *Destination Gobi* (1953) open with the implication that what follows is a true tale, with the camera zooming in on government files. Moreover, John Forsythe's portrayal of a crusading journalist in *Captive* is similar to Gary Cooper's iconic character in *High Noon* (1952, released shortly *after* the Wise film). Both films are about a crisis of conscience in communities sorely lacking in that trait. And while each picture pastes its realistically shot story around an equally realistic character—a flawed, less-than-monolithic man, working through fear to do the right thing—these then timely portraits (made during the paranoia of the McCarthy Era) suggests such figures were almost extinct.

The *Desert Rats* (1953) and *Helen of Troy* (1955) deal with historic figures (World War II's Rommel and the ancient world beauty Helen) metamorphosized into myth. *Run Silent, Run Deep* (1958) was adapted from Captain Edward L. Beach's novel, but period reviews suggested the military man turned author was drawing from a composite of real World War II stories.[4] And even when a "war film tells a fictional story [it is] within a context of actual events," which fuels that sense of "fictionalized biography."[5]

That being said, Wise's key "portraits" and biographies of the 1950s are: *So Big* (1953) *Executive Suite, Tribute to a Bad Man* (1956), *Somebody up There Likes Me* (1956), and *I Want to Live!* (1958). Wise's *So Big* was the third screen adaptation of Edna Ferber's Pulitzer Prize–winning novel (1924); the first appeared as a silent film (1925, with Colleen Moore), and the second version surfaced early in the sound era (1932, with Barbara Stanwyck).

As previously noted, Wise, like many great directors, was not fond
of remaking a movie. But that being said, the Ferber material could
not have been more appropriate for Wise, given both his background
and filmmaking tendencies. This Dickensesque melodrama is a
"fictionalized biography" of Selina DeJong (Jane Wyman), tracing
her roller-coaster life, starting as an 1890s debutante, only to struggle
as a bored small-town teacher, "graduating" to overworked farm
wife and when widowed, success as both a single parent and a 1920s
businesswoman creating and operating a profitable truck farm. The
story's thirty-year arc is largely anchored in New Holland, a community
of Dutch Farmers southwest of Chicago.

Wise was covering a heartland story very close in time and space
to his own Indiana childhood. Plus, for an artist so sympathetic to
feminist themes along family melodrama lines, Selina soldiered through
an assortment of male-related angst. Her father mismanages his
fortune and dies unexpectedly, without providing for her. She marries a
seemingly sensitive man of the soil (Sterling Hayden), only to have him
quickly transition, in the words of the *New York Times*, into a "solemn,
stupid [husband]."[6] And most disappointing of all, her only child, Dirk
(Steve Forrest), falls short of expectations. Yet, Selina somehow manages
to "Make each day a masterpiece." Her constant reframing of anything
negative is best capsulated by the story's younger version of Selina, the
artist Dallas O'Mara (Nancy Olson), who observes to the materialistic
Dirk, "What I don't have, I don't need." This spirit parallels the kind of
Indiana Great Depression youth from which Wise sprang, or the overly
frugal production limitations he creatively cut his teeth on at RKO.

Selina's greatest accomplishment is her upbeat resiliency, the ability
to weather disappointment, as *Variety* stated, "serenely, philosophically
and with dignity."[7] But she has an unexpected joy, her prodigy and
surrogate son, Roelf Pool (Richard Beymer as a boy, Walter Coy
as an adult). Selina's enthusiastic tutoring of the boy gives him the
foundation to become a famous composer. Years later he tells her she
has had a "fine life." Surprised by this comment, Selina responds in
modest George Bailey-like (*It's a Wonderful Life*, 1946) fashion: "I've

been here for years, just where you [Roelf] left me when you were a little boy. I've been nowhere, done nothing, and seen nothing. But when I think of the things I was going to see, the places I was going to go." But Roelf affectionately corrects her, just as George celebrated his high-achieving younger brother, whose many accomplishments were made possible by Stewart's everyman: "You [Selina], why you've been everywhere in the world, you've seen all the places of great light and beauty from right here."

Beyond this "wonderful life" legacy that so resonated with Wise, there is a more specific auteur link with the director. In the scene in which the Selina-like Dallas rejects Dirk's marriage proposal, and he sarcastically asks if it is because he is not arty enough, she replies, "[No] it'll be the [hardworking] hands that'll win me . . . I like them scarred. There's something about a man that's fought for it . . . there's scars." These lines are reminiscent of a Val Lewton quote fondly remembered by Wise: "Man should have hands that dig in the soil . . . to work, to build things."[8] So strong was their shared belief, that even a manicure was tantamount to blasphemy for Lewton and Wise.

These work-related aspirations bring the viewer full circle to Selina's perspective on productive people. Learned from her father, there are two camps. The "wheat" people create life's basic necessities, such as Selina's truck farm. The "emerald" people feed the human soul with their gift for making artistic beauty, such as Roelf's music. While rare would be the director not flattered by Selina's "emerald" designation for the artistic, the fact that Wise's mother was supportively similar to Wyman's character undoubtedly contributed to his receiving positive notices such as, "Robert Wise has directed with knowhow."[9] (The business failure of Selina's father, which only surfaced with his death, was also not unlike the financial setbacks suffered by Wise's dad. In both cases, a young person's privileged game plan is radically changed.)

As with many Wise pictures, *So Big* showcases the untold sacrifices women—as mothers, daughters, wives, single parents, entrepreneurs in a male world—undertake with little or no recognition. Without being mawkish, it is reminiscent of the Ma Joad (Jane Darwell) lines with which John Ford chooses to end his 1940 adaptation of John Steinbeck's *Grapes of Wrath*: "We're the people that live. They can't wipe us out. They can't lick us. We'll go on forever, Pa, 'cause we're the people."

So Big also serves as a neglected but very important precursor to *The Sound of Music*. That is, the latter movie is sometimes used as an anti-auteur argument against Wise. *Music*'s huge grassroots popularity, despite the fact many major critics found the picture overly sentimental, was falsely alleged to fly in the face of a select few earlier noirish Wise works. Yet, the vast majority of his movies, be they cynical or defiantly hopeful, are peppered with the melodramatic paradoxes of life. For example, when the *Music*-like *So Big* showcases Selina's ongoing struggles as a woman truck farmer, such as fighting the gentleman's agreement that a woman was not supposed to take her produce to a public market, the only supportive people are the area prostitutes, who help make it happen. Suddenly, one is in the world of *Mademoiselle Fifi*, the whore with a heart of gold. Selina and these sisters of the street are working women in a male-dominated chauvinistic environment. Helpful harlots, cynicism, and sentimentality—all facets of life coexist in Wise's cinema.

All this is not to argue that the melodramatic angst of *So Big* and *Music* are to be embraced as art, though such a case can and should be made. No, the point here is that *Music* was not some aberration in the Wise canon, and the critical response by national publications to *So Big* often sounds like what happened to the director's biographical musical of the Von Trapp family. For example, *Newsweek* described *So Big* as "one of those regrettable affairs," while *Time* punned that the farm-related film was "pretty well cropped-over by now."[10]

Naturally, *So Big* did receive endorsements from many metropolitan dailies, including the *Los Angeles Herald Express*'s left-handed praise: "Robert Wise . . . [has] avoided most of the pitfalls of sentimentality . . . . 'So Big' is a tear jerker but a superior one."[11] Yet, the movie was more appreciated by the middle-market publications, including the *Denver Rocky Mountain News*: "Robert Wise has given the picture highly sensitive directing which brings out every ounce of emotion but stops short of being maudlin. This is a great dramatic film, both for women and men."[12]

Anticipating the heartland market stretching between bicoastal America, Warners held a Midwest premiere of *So Big* at Indianapolis's Circle Theater. Consistent with the nurturing spirit of Selina's character, the city's Police Athletic League Clubs participated in the opening, using the gala as a recruiting event: "[The PAL Clubs] teach boys of 8 to 18 the principles of clean fun and sportsmanship, responsibility and cooperation, respect for decision of their elders, and elements of good citizenship."[13] Similar civic-related *So Big* tie-ins occurred in other areas of the country, with reviews often championing the spirit of the story more than the movie. For example, under the headline, "'So Big' Is Bigger Because of Message," the *Indianapolis News* critic wrote: "The idea behind 'So Big' . . . is more important than the fable itself. The theme is that nothing in life has any real value unless the individual finds his self-fulfillment in creating beauty with hands guided by his brains."[14] Appropriately, Hoosier-born film historian Conrad Lane, who was a young adult when Wise's *So Big* opened, continues to have only the highest praise for the picture.[15]

So Big's period response at the box office was equally strong and foreshadowed the family values allegiance later generated by *Music*. To illustrate, the Warner Brothers files at the University of Southern California are full of passionate fan letters praising *So Big*. The letters also provide insightful asides about a Hollywood then in crisis. A letter from Mrs. Robert F. Iott, of Deerfield, Michigan, is typical of the *So Big* correspondence: "If all movies were of this caliber, I'm sure your industry would have nothing to fear from [the new] television [craze]. To say we enjoyed the picture is a masterpiece of under-statement. We literally ate it up."[16]

The picture's popularity was such that its release, in late 1953, contributed to Wyman making the annual top ten box office list for 1954. She came in at number eight, just behind Bing Crosby but ahead of Marlon Brando, whose work for 1954 included *On the Waterfront*.[17]

This was the first and only time Wyman, a Best Actress Oscar winner for *Johnny Belinda* (1948, as a deaf-mute rape victim) made Hollywood's most powerful list.

Wyman, the second wife of Ronald Reagan, was the same age as Wise (both were born in 1914), but she enjoyed how *So Big* necessitated her playing Selina's life over thirty years. Wyman would joke about this with Wise: "Nowadays, I have to check with . . .

Above: *Jane Wyman and Sterling Hayden share a rare mutually happy moment in* So Big *(1953).* **Left:** *James Cagney (center) with Robert Wise on location for* Tribute to a Bad Man *(1956).*

[you] each morning to find out how old I am instead of looking at a calendar."[18] Wise acknowledged this playfulness in his comments about working with Wyman: "As a director who believes that a pleasant and 'up' atmosphere on a set is terribly conducive to better results, it's always a plus to have leading actors who do have a sense of humor and can help in keeping the atmosphere from getting too heavy. This was one of the strongest attributes that Jane brought to the making of the picture, apart, of course, from her fine talents as an actress."[19]

Wyman's real-life daughter, author/actress Maureen Reagan, later suggested her strong-willed mother's belief in teaching self-reliance made her close to the Selina character. Maureen recalled her mother's favorite parenting line was, "'If I get hit by a Mack truck tomorrow, you're going to have to take care of yourself."[20] Though Wise also saw Wyman as an independent woman, she was a team player. "She has a definite approach to the role from her own standpoint but was always most receptive to suggestions and help from me as the director. . . . She never resented direction nor became temperamental at any point. She is a very talented, highly intelligent, 'fun' kind of person to work with," said Wise.[21]

While the *So Big* wheat/emerald collaboration of Wise and Wyman might now seem idealistically anchored to an earlier Norman Rockwell time, the film's universal values still resonate today. A recent *New York Times* "Book Review" section critiqued poet Paul Guest's *One More Theory about Happiness: A Memoir*. Paralyzed since youth from a childhood biking accident, Guest was saved by what he later wryly called "an accident of the mind"—writing.[22] And as critic/author Christopher R. Beha praises Guest's book, and the remarkable life journey it represents, his comments could just as easily come from Selina's lips: "Guest's work . . . cannot redeem his brokenness or ours but makes something beautiful of it. And that is enough, almost."[23]

The Warner/USC files on *So Big* also provide a fascinating studio slant on the genre that touches so much of Wise's work—melodrama. Given that Ferber's 1920s best seller went through several reprintings during the succeeding decades, Warner Brothers considered various

movie remake ideas in the decade prior to Wise's adaptation. One
radical reworking from 1943 would have started the story on a World
War II troop train as a segue from Roelf the soldier to an extended
flashback of Selina the great teacher.[24] Certainly, with this as an opening
premise, the studio might have done something like MGM's later
White Cliffs of Dover (1944), in which another resilient widow has lost a
husband to World War I and a son to World War II.

Another potential twist on the work, this time from 1945, involved
changing the title to a stereotypical soap opera moniker. Instead of
So Big, a reference to Selina's son as a little boy, the studio considered
the title *Selina Peake* [her maiden name]: "There is nothing more
interesting on the marquee than a title which suggests an interesting
woman—witness 'Mrs. Miniver' [1942, English mother holding World
War II family together] and 'Stella Dallas' [much adapted "soaper" of
a mother who sacrifices everything for her daughter]."[25] Naturally, a
person's name would also further enhance the "portrait" fictionalized
biography references with which this chapter opened.

Wise's next profile picture, after *So Big*, was *Executive*, which
chronicles a big-business power struggle following the death of a
dominant leader, Avery Bullard. As with the ties to *Citizen Kane*,
Executive might better have been titled *Citizen Bullard*. However, since
Wise does not go Welles's flashback mode in re-creating a life, the
director effectively recycles a classic horror device to begin *Executive*.
The film's opening is shot from Bullard's perspective as he leaves his
New York City high rise "executive suite" office for Tredway Enterprises
(a major furniture manufacturer), takes an elevator to the street level,
and dies of a heart attack preparing to catch a cab. We never see his
face, even in death. Moreover, just as horror does not respect the
dead, à la Wise's own *The Body Snatcher* (1945), Bullard is a victim
of a pickpocket as he expires on the pavement. This plot device, an
unidentified body, advances the narrative in both a macabre manner
(characters carry on as if Bullard were still alive), as well as drawing
upon Wise's noir/mystery background.

Other than their portrait parallels, the feel-good sentimentality of *So Big* might seem miles away from the cynicism of *Executive*. Yet, both are essentially family melodramas. Despite his corporation's size, Bullard is a patriarchal company president, whose identity is so closely attached to the product one might be discussing Henry Ford and automobiles. Imagine the film as *So Big* plus a few years. Selina's truck farm business has grown huge, and she has suddenly died. Who will replace her? This is the scenario for *Executive*. The various metaphorical sons not worthy and/or willing to replace Bullard include his close associate Frederick Y. Alderson (Walter Pidgeon), production guru Jesse Grimm (Dean Jagger), super salesman Josiah Walter Dudley (Paul Douglas), and comptroller Loren Shaw (Fredric March). But as pop-culture film historian Peter Biskind later observed: "Finally, there is Don Walling, a design engineer and dark horse. As soon as we see that he is played by William Holden, we know he's the right man for the job."[26]

In the parlance of Selina's *So Big*, Holden is both a wheat and emerald person. As a design engineer, he is an artist who creates something (furniture) potentially beautiful, yet a necessary basic of life. Holden's screen wife, Mary (June Allyson), attempts to protect his creative dreams and fights her husband's plan to become corporation chief. Like Selina's disappointment in a son who has not pursued his architectural training, the mother-like Mary fears the top spot will kill Don's emerald side: "Bullard made you a promise. Plan what you want, design what you want, develop new ideas. But it's over [with his death]."

Yet, if Holden's character does not become the boss, March's comptroller, the least sympathetic candidate for Bullard's position, will take over. Already, March's profit-first philosophy has led to an inferior line of chairs, which only cheapens the Tredway tradition. As in Clint Eastwood's trainer in *Million Dollar Baby* (2004), Holden must take an action he thinks is right, even if it is not right for him. His victory would guarantee the continued excellence of a cherished family business grown large. Thus, Holden's figure embraces a pivotal component of melodrama—sacrifice. Even before assuming Bullard's position, Holden's McDonald misses some memorable moments in his son Mike's (Tim Considine) young life. But McDonald is playing a good surrogate son to the corporate "father," Bullard.

Executive strikes a melodramatic balance between Holden's feelings for his mother-like wife and son, and his emotional links to his iconic boss/father figure. Consequently, one can "read" the movie along traditional melodramatic lines à la *So Big* and *Mildred Pierce* (1945), in which a matriarch figure is disappointed by the child figure (Allyson to Holden). Or, *Executive* could be critiqued as modern melodrama: the parent, not the child figure, is at fault, as in Wise's *The Curse of the Cat People* (1944) and *Audrey Rose* (1977). That is, Bullard had started to let his standards slip by allowing March's penny-pinching accountant to compromise the product integrity of Tredway, and now the son-like Holden needs to restore the balance.

Regardless of one's take on the subject, *Executive* is definitely a melodrama hiding under a corporation cover. While some period critics flirted with pigeonholing the film in a new genre, such as the *New York World Telegram and Sun* comment, "This . . . dramatic study of modern business warfare should keep rapturous audiences at the Radio City Music Hall for some weeks to come," sometimes it is more informative to draw from the past.[27] *Executive* has more to do with a middle ground between Sinclair Lewis's *Dodsworth* (particularly William Wyler's 1936 adaptation), and Booth Tarkington's *The Magnificent Ambersons* (the Orson Welles-Wise adaptation, 1942). In both cases, a melodramatic "profile" novel from the 1920s serves as a bridge between an idealized past and a seemingly valueless present, and yet each film concludes with a sense of hope. Wise brings this same multifaceted reality to *Executive*.

In *So Big* and *Executive*, both battling mothers are given some movie-ending balm for their sacrifice. Selina's son returns to her wheat/emerald fold once his lover finds him philosophically shallow. And Allyson's Mary somehow finds an inner peace, like a Buddhist monk about to achieve nirvana, after her son/husband's decision. Today's viewer might question these positive sign-offs, but they are consistent with the modicum of hope with which Wise can touch the most somber endings, starting with the Val Lewton-influenced *Body Snatcher*.

The naysayer of hope might find a warning in two other *Executive* characters—Barbara Stanwyck's Julia Tredway (daughter of the furniture founder) and Nina Foch's Erica Martin (Bullard's loyal secretary). Julia had been Bullard's companion, and from the neurotic nuances of Stanwyck's performance, one assumes that Bullard the workaholic neglected her and killed himself through overwork. Will this be the fate of the Holden-Allyson marriage? And for all the greatness attached to Bullard's entrepreneur reputation, by the picture's conclusion, viewers just might assume that Foch's anonymous figure was an equal power behind the throne—a common scenario in many boss-private secretary relationships. This sacrificial woman is also consistent with the focus of so many Wise films.

In the Metro-Goldwyn-Mayer tradition of such all-star productions as *Grand Hotel* (1932), the studio picked *Executive* to represent its thirtieth anniversary in motion pictures. The film's critical and commercial success produced more kudos for its director. *Variety* said: "Under Robert Wise's direction, the film's movement never becomes heavy and he deftly avoids the pitfalls that could have resulted in making this a ponderous show."[28] The *New York Herald Tribune* observed: "'Executive Suite' is an extraordinarily direct and uncluttered film. Director Robert Wise swiftly establishes his sense of importance and his symbolism, and he allows for few distractions. His work is as competent as that of his illustrious cast."[29]

Wise received Best Director nominations from the Motion Picture Academy, the Venice Film Festival and the Director's Guild of America. The British Academy of Film and Television Arts nominated *Executive* for Best Film, and the Venice Festival also awarded the movie a Special Jury Prize for excellence. As with Wise's *Set-Up*, he received greater critical acclaim overseas. This would come as no surprise to the England-educated *Executive* producer John Houseman, whose confessional backstory reveals a great deal about Hollywood: "I wanted Robert Wise to direct 'Executive Suite,' and I felt fairly certain that I could get him eventually. But first I had to think of sound logical reasons for rejecting every director on the [MGM] lot that the studio offered me. It isn't that I wanted to be difficult or unreasonable. It's just that I have learned through bitter experience that once you agree to take someone you *don't* want, even though you take him as a favor . . . he becomes your responsibility. . . . And if he doesn't deliver, that's your responsibility, too. The graves of Hollywood are filled with producers who tried to do their studios a good turn."[30]

The why behind Houseman's passionate desire to collaborate with Wise further links *Executive* to *Kane*. In addition to the "portrait" parallels between the two pictures, defining a "fictionalized biography" subject through the perspectives of various characters, Houseman was impressed by Wise's Oscar-nominated editing on *Kane*. The producer wanted the same gift for tempo and cutting that Wise had brought to *Kane*'s similar story structure of small incidents jigsawed together into an inspired whole. Film historian Arthur Knight even suggested the movie's pacing improved upon the best-selling book: "But where Mr. [Cameron] Hawley cluttered his story [novel] with irrelevant incidents and personnel . . . the film sweeps along with incredible skill and certainty."[31]

Wise had yet another melodrama subtext in his noirish "portrait" Western, *Tribute to a Bad Man*, which was originally titled *Jeremy Rodock*. A tongue-in-cheek story synopsis can be drawn from the opening to the positive *New York World Telegram and Sun* review: "James Cagney brawls around the Palace [theater] screen as a half crippled old codger with a mania for blood in 'Tribute.' But he still has enough gumption to take the girl away from a couple of his handsome juniors."[32] But before decoding these comments, one has to begin with the real melodrama behind the scenes. As noted earlier, Wise was looking forward to working with screen legend Spencer Tracy in the part eventually played by Cagney.

As Wise later observed, "[While] Tracy always came on the screen like the Rock of Gibralter . . . he was actually the reverse of his screen image."[33] Though Wise had been warned about the actor's insecurities, he had no idea of their scope. For example, the day after a preproduction meeting with Tracy, in which the performer had enthusiastically encouraged Wise to select a shooting location high in the Rocky Mountains, the director received the following phone call from Tracy: "'Bobby, do you think we're doing the right thing? Do you think this picture has a chance? Do you think it's any good?' I was amazed because just the day before he had practically been selling *me* on the film, he was so excited about it."[34]

Naturally, Wise had worked with insecure actors before. But it was disconcerting, given both his admiration for Tracy and the actor's capable, fatherly screen image. Still, in an industry where the iconoclastic axiom is, "How tall is King Kong? [Answer: The giant was created with a three-foot tall model]," Hollywood veterans become used to disillusionment. Besides, Wise was busy with selecting a high-altitude location, as suggested by Tracy. The director settled upon a beautiful pristine area near Montrose, Colorado, roughly 250 miles southwest of Denver, and a nine-building horse ranch was constructed on location, consistent with the movie's 1875 setting.

Things began to unravel when it was time to shoot the movie. Tracy had promised to arrive early, in order to acclimate himself to the 8,000-foot altitude. Instead, he came a week late and then immediately disappeared for a week. Tracy was an alcoholic, and in periods of stress, especially when his longtime companion, Katharine Hepburn, was not available to play nursemaid, Tracy would binge drink. His routine was to check into a hotel with a suitcase full of alcohol and arrange his bottles around the bathtub. He would then disrobe and spend several days drinking in the tub, which eliminated the mess of soiling his clothes during a lengthy drunken stupor. When the bender had run its course, or the liquor was gone, he simply washed the excrement away and returned to reality.

During Tracy's absence, Wise managed to shoot around the missing actor, covering several scenes with his costars, particularly his much younger love interest (Greek actress Irene Pappas's Jocasta), and a surrogate son (Robert Francis's Steve Miller). But when Tracy returned, he was diva-like, from complaining about the difficulty of working at the high altitude he had requested (and wanting a new lower-altitude set constructed), to not taking direction. Finally, as one of Hepburn's biographers observed, "The patient, considerate director [Wise] did his best to be supportive, but it was useless."[35] Paradoxically, in Christopher Anderson's best-selling dual-biography of Tracy and Hepburn, the author chronicles how the director ultimately had to play social worker even after the actor was released: "Wise had had enough. With [MGM head] Dore Schary's backing, Tracy was fired from the picture [and the studio]. Back in his motel room Tracy collapsed in tears. 'It's the end of my career,' he sobbed to Wise. 'I'm finished. It's never happened to me before.'"[36] Wise confessed to another Tracy biographer: "As angry as I was, I was moved by Tracy's emotion. . . . This was the first time they [the studio] had not taken his side and not backed him up. Even I found myself reassuring him that his career was not over."[37]

Tracy's unprofessional behavior merited sacking, and Wise's action was consistent with his attempt to salvage *The Magnificent Ambersons* (1942) when Welles was less than professional on that project. But to put the Tracy firing in perspective, television had so hurt Hollywood at the box office that prestige studios such as MGM had already begun to release major stars. They could no longer afford to keep them on a year-round salary. Tracy's actions had merely quickened an inevitable fate.

MGM boss Schary was an honest and honorable man who had championed Wise at RKO, when the director was in danger of losing *Set-Up* (1949) as an assignment. (Both men left RKO when Howard Hughes bought that studio.) But given Schary's long history with Tracy, from making his Broadway acting debut in Tracy's star-making *The Last Mile* (1930) to sharing an Original Story Oscar (with Eleanore Griffin) for *Boys Town* (1938, for which Tracy won his second Best Actor

Academy Award), one has to assume Schary's backing of Wise's hard line on *Tribute* was not an action taken lightly. Sadly, the melodrama concerning Tracy did not end with his exit. Cagney, the actor's equally iconic replacement, was not immediately available, and while the production was shut down, Francis was killed in a plane crash. All the Francis-Pappas footage that Wise had conscientiously shot during Tracy's two absences had to be scrapped. Once Francis's part was recast (Dan Dubbins), the production essentially started over. Cagney was the consummate professional and *Tribute* had no more ego delays. But because of all the personal drama, Wise forever lost his taste for Westerns and avoided the genre for the rest of his career. Years later in Cagney's memoir he shared his love of Westerns and some thoughts on Tracy: "Spence's problem was a slightly unsettled personality. He was a most amusing guy, a good companion who told great stories beautifully—but there was always the tension that was tangible. You can *feel* the tension in such people."[38]

The synopsis cited earlier suggests Cagney's character wins a romantic victory for Pappas's against two male rivals, Dubbins's tenderfoot and Stephen McNally's tough foreman. While both men were taken with Pappas's former saloon girl/prostitute, neither was any real competition for Cagney. The only threat to their May-December relationship was his sense of vigilante justice—hanging anyone who threatens his life and/or livelihood: "I'm the only law I got."

Cagney is very good in the part, and while his persona is still closely associated with gangster and film-noir pictures, *Tribute* is like Wise's *Blood on the Moon* (1948)—a noir Western. That is, besides his "hangin' fever," as described by Cagney's mistress, this "bad man" is equally noir-like in his sadistic forced march of rustlers over hot, rocky terrain—barefoot. Cagney's Jeremy Rodock would have been right at home with the actor's celebrated psychopathic Cody Jarrett in the watershed noir *White Heat* (1949), with its frequent Western overtones. Patrick McGilligan, Cagney's definitive biographer, both praised Wise's direction, and said the title, *Tribute to a Bad Man*, would also "suit

Cagney well . . . [and was] perhaps a suitable metaphor for Cagney's entire career, which took on the form of a grudging salute to an aging, surly but likeable 'tough.'"[39]

The melodramatic *White Heat* had Cagney's only true ally be his mother, and in *Tribute* the much younger Pappas essentially revisits that role in her relationship with Cagney's appropriately named Rodock. She tames him of his violent ways, while also mothering their surrogate son, Dubbins, suggesting he leave the tough West: "This is not your kind of life . . . In ten years you'll be like them [the bunk house-hardened wranglers], a nomad on a horse . . . with bad teeth, broken bones, double hernia and lice." When the boy/man persists in his attention toward Pappas, she tells him she is not a woman to marry: "I'm a child of war. [Coming to America from Europe, I turned to prostitution.] I had a reason. It was the easiest thing to do." Consequently, she is like so many other melodramatic Wise women victimized by war, including the prostitute of *Mademoiselle Fifi* (1944), Linda Darnell's war widow

Irene Pappas acting as a caretaker to James Cagney in Tribute to a Bad Man *(1956).*

in *Two Flags West* (1950), the women who give their babies up for
adoption in *Three Secrets* (1950), Valentina Cortesa's concentration
camp victim from the *House on Telegraph Hill* (1951), Patricia Neal's
widow/mother from *The Day the Earth Stood Still* (1951), the title
character of *Helen of Troy* (1955), and all the New Zealand women
victimized by war in *Until They Sail* (1957).

With *Somebody Up There Likes Me*, the "portrait" artist Wise
embraced a straight-up biography of boxer Rocky Graziano. This time
around Wise's signature brush strokes of melodrama and noir could be
realistically attached to an unbelievably longshot true success story. As
Cue magazine noted: "[Graziano's childhood] teachers were punks and
prostitutes, petty hoodlums and crooks, gunmen, drunks, heisters and
hopheads. His father was a third-rate ex-pug ["Fighting Nick Bob"]
who drowned his frustrations in a bottle. . . . . [Graziano found success
when] he stopped fighting society, and set out to conquer himself."[40]

Also, as previously cited, Wise's sensitivity to problem-film issues
found fertile ground in a picture the *Saturday Review* described
as demonstrating a "splendid awareness of what makes a juvenile
delinquent."[41] Graziano's friend and fellow middleweight champion
Jake LaMotta, the subject of Martin Scorsese's biography picture *Raging
Bull* (1980), described his tough early years with Graziano: "We were
the original juvenile delinquents. Always in fights. Stealing stuff. In
fact, we both ended up in reform school in Coxsackie, New York, at the
same time. I remember Rocky was in quarantine, so I'd set him up with
comic books and candy and cigarettes."[42]

Somebody's troubled-youth ambiance is further strengthened by the
casting of Sal Mineo as Graziano's pal from the boxer's wayward early
years. During the 1950s Mineo made a career of playing the angst-
ridden teenager, most memorably as James Dean's sidekick in *Rebel
Without a Cause* (1955).

Wise's anti-boxing problem film *The Set-Up* (1949), which had so
influenced Scorsese, also resonates throughout *Somebody*. Paradoxically,
while Graziano ultimately used the fight game to better his life,
Somebody vividly depicts the sport's dark side, from a broken fighter of

a father to Graziano being pressured by racketeers to throw a match—
mirror reflections of *Set-Up*. Moreover, this subject was a natural for
Wise's penchant for realism, with many of the early exteriors being
shot on location where Graziano grew up on the Lower East Side of
Manhattan. Plus, both Wise and Paul Newman, who portrays Graziano
in the picture, spent a great deal of preproduction time with the boxer,
to better re-create this rough-edged funny man/child of New York's
"mean streets." Naturally, this "study" period had a major influence
upon Newman's method acting preparation. But it equally impacted
Wise's style. "I wanted the picture to really . . . express the restlessness
of Graziano himself," said Wise. "I kept pushing Paul. I'd say, 'Let's pick
it up a little bit more. . . . Let's force the temp[o] just a bit and see if
by forcing it, the scene won't be better.' I [also] did a very mechanical
thing on that picture because I wanted it really to move. I tried not to
have a single dissolve or fade-in to it. . . . When I'd end a sequence, I
started the next scene with a close-up of Paul. . . . In order to give that
on-rushing kind of feeling, I started the dialogue for the incoming
scene ten or twelve [film] frames ahead of the actual cut to give us a
[sound cut] thrust into the scene."[43]

Graziano's flair for appreciating the human comedy gave his life a
second act as a character performer once his boxing career was over.
Graziano the raconteur often had fun with his challenging childhood.
"I quit school in the sixth grade because of pneumonia," he noted. "Not
because I had it but because I couldn't spell it. We stole everything
that began with an 'a'—a piece of fruit, a bicycle, a watch, anything
that was not nailed down."[44] Both Wise and Newman enjoyed
their "research" sessions with Graziano. But on the boxer's turf, the
filmmakers' methods sometimes comically backfired. "He [Graziano]
didn't want to talk about his family," Newman recalled. "So one night
at the Embers [bar/restaurant], Bob Wise . . . and I tried to get Rocky
stoned [drunk] so that he'd loosen up and talk about himself. The fact
is that Rocky loosened *us* up. We told him *our* life stories. He poured us
into two taxicabs."[45]

Wise's overview of Graziano's attitude, taken from the director's early notes on his personal copy of the *Somebody* script, basically captures the essence of the movie itself, including the boxer's ultimate unlikely success: "The way he [Graziano] runs, ducks, hugs walls, the look on his face as well as the nature of the shots will picture a boy in some kind of trouble—on the lam from something or somebody. Although wary and cautious, he is at the same time excited and terribly pleased with himself that he managed to break out of the protector— he thumbed his nose, once again, at authority."[46]

Wise's pocket definition, "picture a boy in some kind of trouble," plays directly into the director's fascination with vulnerable young protagonists. Though more often associated with girls and/or childlike

Sal Mineo (left) and James Dean in Rebel Without a Cause *(1955).*

women, the director's filmography has its fair share of boys and/or man/child characters in crisis, from rudderless little Billy Gray in *The Day the Earth Stood Still* (1951), and the talented youngster (Richard Beymer) starving for cultural attention in *Big*, to Steve McQueen's boy/adult in *The Sand Pebbles* (1966). Fittingly, McQueen's first screen appearance, as an unbilled juvenile delinquent, occurs in *Somebody*.

This Wise child component is a natural transition to the director's affinity to the melodramatic women's picture. Graziano's wife and surrogate mother figure (played by Pier Angeli) is pivotal to the story. For example, the *New York Times* suggested the "lovely Pier Angeli . . . does as much for the hero—and for the picture—as does 'somebody up there.'"[47] *Variety* also struck a heavenly note in its praise of Angeli's calming, supportive presence, "she must have the agent for the guy upstairs looking after Graziano, because the swing from the sordid to the good starts with her appearance."[48] Her character's greatest challenge was helping maintain his moral compass when "gangster blackmailers tried to use his old sins to confound him in his new life."[49] Such mobster involvement recalls Wise's *Set-Up* and *The Captive City* (1952).

Pier's Jewish character also represents another basic element in the Wise canon—the rainbow coalition of races sympathetically intertwined in his stories, which reflects the director's fierce aversion to racism and sexism. While *Somebody* simply replicates reality, with both Graziano's wife, Norma, and his father-like manager, Irving Cohen (Everett Stone), being Jewish, this positive showcasing of minorities is consistent with so many other Wise pictures, at a time when colorblindness was not the norm. For example, his early RKO producer Lewton reinforced casting people of color in dignified congenial parts in Wise's first picture as a director, *The Curse of the Cat People* (1944); using black actor and fellow Hoosier James Edwards in a prominent part in *Set-Up*; depicting racist behavior against Native Americans in *Two Flags West* (1950); having a concentration camp survivor be the heroine of *The House on Telegraph Hill* (1951), and making the two most compassionately sensible adults in *The Day the Earth Stood Still* (1951) be an alien from another solar system and a Jewish scientist.

Paul Newman as Rocky Graziano in Somebody Up There Likes Me *(1956, with Pier Angeli).*

Among Wise's post-*Somebody* films, minority issues surface most significantly in *Odds Against Tomorrow* (1959, in which racism derails a noir heist team), and *The Sand Pebbles'* (1966) pivotal biracial couple.

Wise's reviews for *Somebody* were outstanding, with the kudos often echoing the critical praise for pacing and authenticity that had been a critique norm since *Set-Up* and *Captive City*. The *New York Times* reported, "Wise's direction is fast, aggressive and bright, and the picture is edited to give it a tremendous crispness and pace."[50] *Variety* opined: "[Wise's] direction builds a picture that, for revealing frankness, will be hard to match, as will the handling of the considerable talents of the cast."[51] The *Christian Science Monitor* said, "[Wise's] candor, rather than alienating the spectator, sharply impresses him with the enormous obstacles facing the ex-hoodlum before he could reform."[52] The *New York Herald Tribune* added, "Wise's direction is taut—it has the same nervous energy as the hero's life"—the precise tone for which Wise was striving![53]

Interestingly, Hoosier-born James Dean was originally set to play Graziano. But his death in a car accident (September 30, 1955) set in motion a series of events that eventually resulted in Newman getting the part. Most important, Wise saw Newman in a live television broadcast of "The Battler" (October 1955), an Ernest Hemingway story about an aging ex-boxing champion—a part originally meant for Dean. Wise, who normally avoided the commercial-plagued world of 1950s television, was impressed by the performance, which also showcased the character as a young fighter. Despite the legend that has now grown around Dean, Wise forever maintained Newman was a better fit for *Somebody*: "I always had in my mind that maybe Dean was not physically a middleweight [boxer size]. . . . And Paul did one of his best characterizations in it; he really caught that man [Graziano]."[54]

Wise's perspective on Dean's size is well-taken, given that the slender actor weighed in at approximately thirty pounds under the middleweight's standard of 160 pounds.[55] Wise was not simply putting a positive spin on a tragic situation, he had real reservations about Dean playing the part *before* the actor's death. Regardless, for today's movie

Richard Attenborough (right) and Marayat Andriane as a biracial couple in The Sand Pebbles *(1966, with Steve McQueen).*

fan, given Newman's now inspired body of work, one of the joys of rescreening *Somebody* is seeing a performer, as warmly familiar as an old friend, in a defining early part. (Wise and Newman remained close long after *Somebody*. Years later, when the award-show recluse Newman won a Best Actor Oscar for Martin Scorsese's *The Color of Money*, 1986, he had his friend Wise stand in for him at the ceremony.)

Just as *Somebody* made Newman a star, Wise's next biography, *I Want to Live!*, was the director's own personal moon shot. His biography of convicted killer Barbara Graham (Susan Hayward) was an effectively strong anti-capital punishment problem film. (Graham was also only the fourth woman ever to be executed in California and the first female gassed at San Quentin.) While Wise had had many critical and/or commercial hits since becoming a director in the mid-1940s, *Live* resulted in his first Academy Award nomination in that category. Responding to Schary's congratulatory telegram, Wise wrote, "Many thanks for the wire. It's my first [experience] with a director's nomination and I find it very exciting."[56] The honor also turned out to be an RKO reunion, since one of Wise's fellow nominees was his friend and colleague from the 1930s, Mark Robson, nominated for directing *The Inn of the Sixth Happiness* (1958, with Ingrid Bergman as a Chinese missionary). The other nominees included Stanley Kramer for *The Defiant Ones*, Richard Brooks for *Cat on a Hot Tin Roof*, and Vincente Minnelli for *Gigi* (all 1958). Ironically, Minnelli won for directing the only nonissue/problem film among the nominees—the musical comedy *Gigi*. And, as if taking a cue from Minnelli, Wise's four future Oscar nominations (all wins) were for both directing and producing two Best Picture musicals, *West Side Story* and *The Sound of Music*.

While the alleged guilt or innocence of Graham remains unresolved, Wise's passion to tell her story was tied to his strong views against capital punishment. These feelings were further pumped up by his workaholic attention to detail. Wise later confessed to being "more emotionally involved in that film [*Live*] than any other because of the nature of the story and the fact that I did talk to so many people about Barbara Graham."[57]

One could argue that *Live* showcased more of Wise's basic cinema components than any other film. Genrewise, *Live* is a biographical account of a true film-noir life, chronicling the story of a strong but ultimately victimized woman in a real melodrama. Marry the tale to Wise's penchant for an often documentary style, and it is no surprise that the director always referenced *Live* as one of his pivotal works. Wise's drive for realism proved even more painful than the director's "researching" ugly fight crowds on *Set-Up*. For example, Wise later shared, "I felt like a ghoul, asking to see . . . [an execution but] I wanted to be able to say to anybody commenting on the film that this is the way it is."[58] Graham's incarceration/execution also necessitated that the second half of *Live* explore yet another genre, the prison film, which would have further inspired Wise, given his interest in "essaying" new-to-him film formats. In fact, Wise wrote to writer/director/producer Joe Mankiewicz (whose nephew, Don, coscripted *Live*): "I very strongly feel that our best values lie in staying as much as possible with Barbara and the gas chamber during all this [portion of the film]. If we do it properly, the accumulation of pressure on her, as well as everybody else around [her], will be almost unbearable."[59] Genrewise, since the story chronicles thirty-three-year-old Graham's long history of petty crimes, one could also file the film, as *New York Journal American* critic Rose Pelswick did, under a label fitting for Wise's well-established interest in struggling young people—an "adult delinquent" story.[60]

Given the film's ability to document how easily newspapers could inflame or manipulate public opinion, with Graham characterized as "Bloody Babs, the Tiger Woman," one is reminded of a litany of movies Wise worked on, starting with *Kane* (1941), in which journalists are seminal to the story. Moreover, if the Wise film focus is simply the mob mentality, *Live* is even more emblematic of the director's canon, with a public screaming for the death of "Bloody Babs" sounding very much like the crowd in *Set-Up* crying for the blood of Robert Ryan's vulnerable boxer.

Since Wise's Indiana childhood, his life had been shaped by the movies and an energized can-do attitude. One can hear that enthusiastic youngster in another letter to Mankiewicz, written shortly before production began on *Live*: "There are a lot of headaches and sweat ahead of us out here [in California] but I'm sure everything will eventually pull together—and I'm more and more excited at our prospects for an excellent picture."[61] A few years later, in a revealing letter to Walter Schmidt, Wise's excitement about the movie was still unabated: "The thing that intrigued me about *I Want to Live!* was the tremendous last act, her night and morning in the death cell, which the original material had."[62]

Even in the midst of crafting such a moving message movie, Wise, the former high school humor columnist, sometimes utilized a comic touch to obtain serious results. For example, at a point in the story when Hayward's Graham must be especially tough, Wise has satirically scribbled the following directions for his sometimes rebellious lead actress, "*Don't forget the star attitude.*"[63]

As this composite picture demonstrates, Susan Hayward (right) bore a striking resemblance to the convicted killer (Barbara Graham) she played in I Want to Live!

In addition to providing pithy directing tips, Wise sometimes tweaked the script with neglected details that heightened the poignancy of the picture. For example, late in the original script the warden tells Graham, "Barbara, I'm very sorry, but this is it. Goodbye and God bless you." "*Barb gulps and smiles weakly,* 'I have to go to the bathroom.'" Wise scratched out her reply and added the dramatic but true response, "I want a mask"[64] While one normally associates a mask with violence and horror, here is the other side of the nightmare—a mask providing protection/privacy from a real horror story, the prying eyes of the gas chamber crowd. Once again, Wise plays with the ironies of a victim as entertainment for an audience. (But the official executioners display a sort of helpless compassion over the task they must perform, including a matron guard who provides her own sleeping mask upon Graham's request.) Plus, given Wise's early association with the horror genre, his paradoxical use of a mask in *Live* is a special gift to the film fan. Or, as art critic Roberta Smith once observed of another artist (Matisse), "Attention paid is profusely and profoundly rewarded."[65]

Among the congratulatory letters received by Wise and/or *Live* producer Walter Wanger, metaphorical references to horror also occurred. To illustrate, journalist turned screenwriter Dudley Nichols (a frequent collaborator with director John Ford, including an Oscar for his *Informer* script, 1935), wrote: "This is the only real, actual, down-to-earth horror film I've ever seen. . . . My hat (if I had one) would sweep the floor for you, for Bob Wise, for [Susan] Hayward . . . [and] the writers."[66] Along similar lines, celebrated actor James Mason wrote to Wanger: "I believe that 'I Want to Live!' is going to affect the [anti-capital punishment] thinking of those who see it more deeply and to better purpose than any single film in motion picture history."[67]

Though attention to detail can sometimes feel like riding a bike into a sand pit at full speed, Wise's successfully creative macromanagement of *Live* did not stop with simply making the movie. The director's influence was especially sensitive when addressing how the picture should be released. In a letter to United Artists executive Arthur Krim,

Wise advised against an early *Live* opening in Los Angeles, given that Graham's controversial execution had occurred in California only five years before, in 1953: "[There are potential] political problems we can have with the local officials. The picture is a hot potato in Los Angeles and . . . the problems and pressures can be greatly diminished by the highest [critical and commercial] level acceptance elsewhere—in New York and even abroad."[68]

Wise's suggestion was followed by United Artists; the *Live* reviews from New York were superlative, and the picture's delayed West Coast release was bolstered by this policy. The *New York Times* called *Live* a "sensational new drama," adding that the death row portion was "by far the most harsh and devastating—and, indeed, most original—phase of it. . . . Robert Wise has shown here a stunning mastery of the staccato realistic style . . . *Live!* is a picture to shake you—and give you pause."[69] The *New York World Telegram and Sun* labeled *Live* "emotional and explosive," going on to state: "Robert Wise has crammed his picture with graphic details that tax the nerves and stomach. But judging from the opening day swarm at the Victoria [theater], Broadway is full of sturdy patrons."[70] The *New York Herald Tribune* said, "the film vindicates Miss Graham" and "imparts a documentary point of view, an indictment not only of capital punishment but of the form of it [the sadistic psychological horror of the death-row prisoner] in our society. . . . [*Live*] is calculated to leave one a bit shaken, and I think it accomplishes its purpose."[71]

Coming out in late 1958, *Live* went on to be one of the top-grossing pictures of 1959, topping such box-office hits as *Separate Tables* (which showcased both the year's Oscar-winning actor, David Niven, and the supporting actress, Wendy Hiller) and the *Big Circus* (both 1958).[72] In addition to Wise's Academy Award nomination for Best Director, *Live* was nominated in three additional Oscar categories: Best Actress (Hayward), Best Screenplay from another medium (Nelson Gidding and Don Mankiewicz), and Best (black-and-white) Cinematography (Lionel Lindon). Hayward was the only one to take a statuette home, and her victory supported the Wise axiom, borrowed from Leo McCarey, about good directing being closely tied to good casting. That is, the actress bore a striking physical resemblance to her character, and Hayward was being asked to play a variation of what she did best on screen—the fallen woman valiantly trying for a comeback. And Graham's prostitute background also tapped into an long list of sympathetic hookers, or hooker-like women, in Wise pictures.

For Wise's 1950s work, *Live* was the capstone biography/"portrait" picture. *Live* also elevated him from being a respected artist within the Hollywood community to achieving a broader public profile. This was no small accomplishment for a scandal-free director with a blue-collar work ethic. Wise's self-image as a filmmaker was essentially that of a man with a lunch pail. But to paraphrase writer Richard Stern's provocative thoughts on the links between novelists and death (which also beautifully describes a biographer), Wise often "assembles the contacts and associations one has had with a person and then makes some sense out of what had been more or less incidental encounters."[73] Or, to recycle a colloquial expression of praise favored by early Wise disciple Martin Scorsese, "[Wise] gives you the goods."

11

Wise's Brass-Ring Decade: The 1960s

"You hoodlums don't own these streets, and I've had all the roughhouse I'm gonna put up with around here. If you want to kill each other, kill each other, but you ain't gonna do it on my beat."
LIEUTENANT SCHRANK (SIMON OAKLAND) TO THE JETS AND
THE SHARKS (STREET GANGS) IN *WEST SIDE STORY* (1961).

During a turbulent time in New York Yankees history, infielder Graig Nettles summarized his "Bronx Zoo" experience: "When I was a little boy, I wanted to be a baseball player and join the circus. With the Yankees, I have accomplished both."[1] The same analogy could be applied to Robert Wise, if one simply substituted Hollywood for the Yankees. Young Wise was obsessed with the movies, and as a Hoosier youngster born during the lifetime of Indiana's nationally beloved poet James Whitcomb Riley, whose signature verse included "The Circus-Day Parade" poem, the future filmmaker was also a fan of the circus. But as this biography has documented, Wise's adventures in cinema were often like being in the circus, too. Comparable "Bronx Zoo" incidents for him would range from the grief he suffered over attempting to salvage *The Magnificent Ambersons* (1942) to the litany of headaches chronicled in the previous chapter, including Spencer Tracy's meltdown on *Tribute to a Bad Man* (1956) and the host of problems that derailed *Helen of Troy* (1955). The good news, however, related to Wise's cinema/circus scenario, was that he both continued to produce uniformly solid pictures, and that the great critical and commercial success of *I Want to Live!* (1958) gave him additional insurance against Hollywood craziness.

The 1960s promised to be an even more memorable decade for Wise—an opportunity he fully embraced. His personal life was in an equally good place. In 1962 Robert and Patricia Wise celebrated their twentieth wedding anniversary. His marriage to Irene Dunne's former stand-in had been as rock steady as the director's drive to succeed. Like June Allyson's wife to the equally workaholic William Holden of Wise's *Executive Suite* (1954), Patricia had a husband obsessed by his career. But once his growing 1950s success allowed him to build travel into his preparation schedule, the couple managed to incorporate many working holidays into their life together. Sometimes these trips involved background research for a given picture, such as a preproduction jaunt to New Zealand for *Until They Sail* (1957). More frequently, though, the couple enjoyed regular trips to New York to scout Broadway plays Wise might want to adapt, not to mention rekindling Patricia's memories of being a vaudeville dancer. Stage productions the music-loving director later brought to the screen included *West Side Story*, *The Sound of Music* (1965), and *Two for the Seesaw* (1962). Still, in a long (1964) letter to some old friends, Wise struck a wistful note: "Change is in the air here at home. [Our son Robert Allen] Rob went into the Navy about three weeks ago. . . . It feels kind of like the finish of an era in our life to Pat and me, and we feel it's time to make a change. You know we've been thinking about moving from 702 [Ocean Front Avenue, Santa Monica, California] for a couple of years. . . . Traffic and the crowds get worse each season, and we're getting pretty fed up with it. Now, with Rob being away, it does seem to be the time to make the change. We're excited about the prospect of building a house—a brand-new contemporary one with all the latest in design, materials, colors, furniture, etc., etc. Of course, we still want to live on the ocean, but that becomes a problem because beach lots are more scarce than the proverbial hen's teeth these days."[2]

Hen's teeth or not, within two years the Wises had relocated to another oceanfront property on the Pacific Coast Highway in Malibu, at a time when the area was not nearly as commercialized as today. They would move into a nearby "brand-new" dream house of their own design the following year (1967). Located on the beach in Trancas, California, a little beyond Malibu, it had a small-town atmosphere of what Steve McQueen, a later resident, called "real people."[3] In fact, based upon Wise's long history with McQueen—giving the actor his first screen appearance in *Somebody Up There Likes Me* (1956), casting McQueen's first wife, Neile Adams, in *This Could Be the Night* (1957), and directing the actor to his only Oscar-nominated performance in *The Sand Pebbles* (1966)—Wise was probably a factor in McQueen's relocation to Trancas. Regardless, the Wises loved the area, though the director enjoyed kidding about its remoteness from Los Angeles. In a later letter to Christopher Plummer, Wise punned Trancas's Outer Mongolia distance from the film capital by describing it as "outer Malibu."[4]

Between Wise's intense focus on filmmaking (including the ever-increasing time he spent in pre- and post-production), and his becoming a major director at the same time (1950s) Hollywood was losing much of its audience to television, he was never a small-screen fan. Wise revealed his thoughts on the subject in a 1961 letter to a New York film revival house operator after plans to show the director's *The Set-Up* (1949) had been sabotaged by a recent television broadcast of the movie: "So television has reared its ugly head again. I certainly can understand your position and the impossibility of showing *The Set-Up*. . . . However, it's always disturbing to realize how constantly and diligently people do look at old movies on TV. How in the world do they stand those endless and idiotic commercials?"[5]

Wise's 1960s thoughts on the "boob tube" were not uncommon among Hollywood veterans. That same year Stan Laurel expressed genuine anger over what television commercials do to rebroadcast movies: "That's why I hardly watch our [Laurel and Hardy] pictures anymore. It upsets me so damned much to see how they turn the plot of our pictures into a hash. We worked so carefully to get the sequence of action just right in the editing process, and then some idiotic fool comes along and cuts the film up in big chunks just to squeeze in a mess of advertising. . . . The pictures just don't make sense on television."[6]

So how did a driven director such as Wise unwind, besides work-related travel? He and his wife frequently entertained, welcoming everyone from casual friends dating back to the Val Lewton RKO days (his widow now lived nearby) to maintaining ties with many of his actors when they were in the Los Angeles area, such as Rita Moreno, Patricia Neal, Robert Ryan, Joan Camden (*The Captive City*, 1952), and, after *The Sound of Music*, Christopher Plummer, Julie Andrews, and her husband, director Blake Edwards. Moreover, the former movie-crazed youngster, who had regularly seen three films a week during his childhood, continued to watch sixteen-millimeter prints of pictures he had been unable to attend. In the pre-videotape, digital video disc era, this often involved borrowing copies from friends and colleagues. Wise's private papers are peppered with correspondence, such as the following thank you to Rock Hudson: "Many thanks for the use of your print of SECONDS [1966]. Somehow I missed it when the film was first released [the underrated thriller was an off-beat role for Hudson and never found a broad audience] and had always wanted to catch up with it. The word was that you had given an outstanding performance in SECONDS. Certainly the word-of-mouth was not exaggerated. Warmest congratulations on a really fine dramatic characterization."[7]

Wise also remained a major sports fan, from continuing to follow Indiana basketball to being a longtime fan of the National Football League's Los Angeles Rams. He and Patricia often attended home games with songwriter Saul Chaplin and his wife. Chaplin later won his third Oscar for scoring Wise's *West Side Story*. (His previous wins were for *An American in Paris*, 1951, and *Seven Brides for Seven Brothers*, 1954). Wise later recalled: "Both Solly [Saul Chaplin] and I have been

RAMS fans since the time they moved here [1946] from Cleveland, lo these many years ago. We started attending the games together with our wives, around 1960, when we started working together for the first time on WEST SIDE STORY. We have been . . . [four-some] regulars ever since."[8]

In Wise's long life he remained remarkably healthy. But like many people, he forever had to fight putting on weight during periods of stress. Such a time was the early 1960s, during the preproduction of the film that soon topped all box-office records. Writing to dancer Rita Moreno, whom he had recently directed to a Best Supporting Actress Oscar in *West Side Story*, he confessed: "[I] am so aggravated at trying

Robert Wise, Julie Andrews, and Saul Chaplain in the late 1960s.

to cast the kids in SOUND OF MUSIC that the old compulsive eating bit is on me [again]. Not that I'm gaining but I sure as hell am not dropping any weight."[9]

Pounds or not, the politically progressive Wise continued to be a strong advocate for positive change in the activist 1960s. The letter to Moreno also addressed a blacklisted artist, and in Wise's correspondence to the Screen Extras' Guild from just a few weeks before (December 1963), the director lobbied for a minority candidate in a Hollywood guild: "In view of the industry's drive to use more Negroes in films and to properly reflect the Negroes' place in society, it would seem to me that people such as Mr. [Paul] Lewis would be a real asset to the Screen Extras' Guild."[10] Lewis had appeared in Wise's *Two for the Seesaw* the previous year, and was typical of the director's rainbow-casting tradition that dated back to his films of the 1940s. In fact, Harry Belafonte specifically courted Wise to direct and produce *Odds Against Tomorrow* (1959, a noir caper movie about racism). The film later received a Golden Globe nomination as the "Best Film Promoting International Understanding."

Odds was one of Wise's 1950s films that often slips under the radar, like his romantic comedy *This Could Be the Night* (1957, with Paul Douglas stealing the show as a small-time nightclub owner). But *Odds* is a neglected noir classic, and an unconventional segue to *West Side Story*. Done for Belafonte's HarBel Productions (released through United Artists), William P. McGivern's novel was adapted by blacklisted writer/director Abraham Polonsky, with black novelist John O. Killens acting as a "front." (In 1996 Polonsky officially received credit for the screenplay.) The opening paragraph of *Variety*'s review provides an excellent summation: "On one level, 'Odds' . . . is a taut crime melodrama. On another, it is an allegory about racism, greed and man's propensity for self-destruction . . . directed by Robert Wise with an alert eye and ear to sooty realism . . . [*Odds*] is an absorbing, disquieting film that should draw [a] good response."[11] As the same critique baldy suggests, "the odds against tomorrow coming at all are very long unless

Robert Wise and Harry Belafonte making like bank robbers on the set of noir bank heist picture Odds Against Tomorrow *(1959).*

there is some understanding and tolerance today."[12] Though Belafonte bought the original property, this *Odds* overview could serve as the axiom attached to countless Wise films. The picture also meshes three of the director's preferred genres—noir, melodrama, and the problem film, as well as reuniting Wise with his noir *Set-Up* star, Robert Ryan. But unlike that film's sympathetic down-and-out boxer, Ryan's character in *Odds* is a psychopathic racist, not unlike his killer in *Crossfire* (1947), or Lawrence Tierney's male lead in Wise's watershed noir *Born to Kill* (1947).

Award-winning actor Ed Begley plays a crooked retired cop who masterminds a bank robbery in upstate New York. He recruits two "associates" for the job: Belafonte is a nightclub performer whose gambling addiction has ruined his marriage and put his family at risk from possible mob reprisals; Ryan's angry southern ex-con is fighting a born-to-be-unimportant mentality that never acknowledges his self-destructive tendencies. While this represents *Odds'* noir and problem-film components, the melodrama concerns the women in Belafonte and Ryan's lives. Belafonte and his ex-wife are still deeply in love, which is made obvious when he visits his young daughter. The split is over his gambling problem. Belafonte's share of the robbery money would be yet another "gamble" to both keep the mobsters at bay, and maybe buy him a second chance with his wife. In contrast to the rare for that era depiction of a normal middle-class African American home, maintained by Belafonte's ex-wife (Carmen DeLavallade), Ryan's girlfriend (Shelley Winters) is yet another of Wise's hookers with a heart of gold. But Ryan feels the only way to keep her is with a big score. Moreover, with the picture's robbery being planned with the detail of a military operation, the story's narrative unwinds with the desperate intensity of a ticking clock (see Chapter 9).

Odds received uniformly solid reviews, though its violence and language sometimes created press coverage reminiscent of Wise's provocative *Born to Kill*. For example, the *New York World Telegram and Sun* critique was entitled, "Shocker Opens at Victoria."[13] Given Wise's predisposition to on-location shooting when possible, the tone of the

New York Times' review was typical of the critical praise the picture received: "Under the tight and strong direction of the realist, Robert Wise, whose last similar achievement was . . . 'I Want to Live!,' the drama accumulates tensely, with fast, easy clarity, and the whole thing has an intensely sharp, true pictorial quality."[14]

Ironically, though *Odds'* reviews were generally positive, there was sometimes a subtext tentativeness about mixing a positive racial theme with money.[15] Granted, there are more idealistic ways to sell the importance of racial solidarity, such as the tragic love story Wise tackled with *West Side Story*. But in the context of late 1950s America, progress was frequently measured by the *color of money*. For example, when Jackie Robinson was on the verge of integrating Major League Baseball with the Brooklyn Dodgers (1947), their swaggeringly profane manager Leo Durocher broke up a possible mutiny by southern Dodger players with a combination of moxie and money. Telling the racists he would play an elephant if it would help the Dodgers win, and that this talented great athlete was no elephant but rather someone who "can make us rich. And if . . . you can't use the money, I'll see that you're traded."[16] He then sarcastically added: "Boys, I hear . . . some of you have drawn up a petition [not to play with Robinson]. Well, boys, you know what you can use that petition for. Yeah, you know. You're not that fucking dumb. Take the petition and, you know, wipe your ass."[17]

While Wise is one of those "nice guys" Durocher was famous for claiming always "finish last," both men were pragmatists about society's dark side.[18] Wise's large filmography usually gives viewers someone for whom to root for (such as Belafonte's *Odds* character), but the director also peppers his films with enough realistically depicted bottom-feeders (such as Ryan's racist) to suggest even modest victories are a long shot. Wise's journalistic tendencies for truth in storytelling linked him philosophically with historian Tony Judt, who noted: "The historian's task is not to disrupt for the sake of it [a cause] but it is to tell what is almost always an uncomfortable story and explain why the discomfort is part of the truth we need to live well and live properly. A well-organized society is one in which we know the truth about ourselves

Natalie Wood and Richard Beymer as the updated Romeo and Juliet in West Side Story *(1961).*

collectively, not one in which we tell pleasing lies about ourselves."[19] One is also reminded of Napoleon's provocative dictum that history is the "agreed-upon myth."[20]

From *Odds'* bleakly paradoxical equality ending, where Belafonte's and Ryan's charred bodies are both burned beyond recognition in a failed getaway, Wise next produced and codirected the screen adaptation of *West Side Story*. Much more than Belafonte's company on *Odds*, Wise was joining a creative juggernaut on *Story*, including such theater icons as Leonard Bernstein, Stephen Sondheim, Jerome Robbins, and Arthur Laurents. Pencil in Chaplin, and *Story* already having redefined the Broadway musical, and one obviously does not have a traditional case for an auteur, in which a personal vision often reshapes original material. Here Wise was adopting a preexisting classic from another medium. *But* just as the populist John Ford was the perfect fit to bring John Steinbeck's novel *The Grapes of Wrath* (1940) to the screen, Wise was *the* director for *Story*.

Consider briefly the basics of *Story* against what by then one had come to expect from a Wise film. First, this musical updating of *Romeo and Juliet* is essentially a relationship melodrama set against gang *war*. The Jets and the Sharks have "war councils" before battle. A gang member says Maria (Natalie Wood) is an "excuse for World War III." Doc (Ned Glass), the wise old candy store owner, where the Jets frequently hang out, admonishes them for killing "all for a piece of land [neighborhood turf]," and later asks, "Why do you kids live like there's a war on?" When the Jets cut through an alley on the way to the fatal rumble, the "warehouse" wording on the building directly behind them is initially obscured to read "war."

Given that Maria/Juliet lives in this telling, the melodrama with a war backdrop is even more like the woman's perspective norm so often seen in Wise movies. Life is lived in short bursts of passion between bouts of horrific fear that the warriors will not return. When the worst scenario occurs, the women have to pick up the pieces and soldier on. Ironically, with Tony/Romeo's (Richard Beymer) tragic failure to play peacemaker at the rumble (where the couple each loses a brother figure, the updated Mercutio and Tybolt characters), one is reminded of Wise's adaptation of an ancient star-crossed lovers set against war, *Helen of Troy* (1955), in which Paris's peace mission is a disaster that guarantees more suffering.

A second *Story* narrative strand that coincides with Wise's canon is his problem-film tendencies, which are most attentive to issues of race and/or childlike protagonists. With *Story*, both components are well represented. Natalie Wood plays a Puerto Rican teenager trying to keep her biracial relationship with native-born Tony a secret in the most volatile of New York ghettoes. Though Beymer's suicide-like murder closes the picture (he courts death from a Shark gang member after he thinks Maria is dead), Wood's character forces some understanding between the rival groups by an impassioned plea for tolerance. This is then symbolized visually by members from both gangs lifting and carrying Tony's body off the street, and a Jet delinquent putting Maria's black scarf back on her head. Though such demonstrative pleas are now sometimes "read" as passé, this ending is not unlike the conclusion of such Wise films as *Set-Up*, in which staggering sadness also offers a faint chance for positive change, if what the "Psalms" describe as "tender mercies" are allowed to grow.[21] For all Wise's noirish realism, this is not a stone tossed from inside a glass house. Strange things, like hope, can sprout from despair, too. But when Wise includes it, he avoids overselling the concept, because unlike Ford's celebrated *Stagecoach* (1939), the cavalry never rides to the rescue in any problem-film saga.

Maria's plea for peace is a substitution for Shakespeare's Prince of Verona's concluding speech upon the wages of hate, once Romeo and Juliet's double suicide is first known. While the death of both partners makes for a more tragic love story, the fact that *Story*'s Maria must continue on alone is consistent with Wise's preference for melodramatic narratives that highlight the angst of long-suffering women. Maria is not unlike one of Wise's cinema war widows railing against the ongoing absurdity of nations battling nations.

A third *Story* link with Wise's previous work is the director's ability to blend and/or move from on-location realism to a stylized psychological realism, such as he had done so often since *Born to Kill* (1947) and *Set-Up*. But the degree of difficulty on *Story* was maximized, given that this brand of "realism" involved street characters singing and dancing. "The very unreality of parts of *Story* becomes something that needs very special handling in order that it not be embarrassing to watch," Wise noted. "It could not be done in any way that could be called 'documentary.'"[22]

One example of some creative realism Wise applied to *Story* from an earlier work involved *Odds*. In the latter picture he had briefly employed a high-angle aerial shot of Ryan and Begley exiting New York. By miniaturizing them against a Gotham City backdrop, the shot fatalistically underlined bad things to come. In an expanded variation of this shot—Wise's much heralded four-minute opening aerial shot for *Story*—the director's goal was a more ambitious musical genre wake-up call for viewers. Still, a cubist-like dissection of a New York scene also suggests tragic tones that will have little in common with the top hat and tails Empire State City of Fred Astaire and Ginger Rogers. Wise later described his goal for this opening: "What I wanted to do was to show a New York that people hadn't seen, a different look of the city, almost an abstract one. I wanted to put the audience in a frame of mind to accept the kids dancing in the streets without feeling that twinge of embarrassment."[23]

Wise's comments are reminiscent of Pablo Picasso's dark comedy take on cubism, in which traditional perspective and illusion are abandoned in favor of subject analysis from all perspectives simultaneously. Wise, also a fan of dark comedy stretching back to his Robert Benchley-influenced high school humorist days, realized a dramatic stylized realism was the only way to open this revisionist musical. The director also intuitively applied another cubist basic to this inspired *Story* opening: "[cubism] can be done only with more or less familiar forms. Those who look at the pictures must know what a violin looks like to be able to relate the various fragments in . . . [Picasso's "Violin and Grapes," 1912] picture to each other. That is the reason why the Cubists painters usually chose familiar motifs."[24] Wise's self-described "abstract" *Story* opening works, in part, because he has chosen the "familiar motif" of New York.

In spite of *Story*'s great success on Broadway, adapting the play to the screen would be no easy task, and the challenge fascinated Wise. Moreover, he was forever drawn to directing different genres. While he had not yet directed a musical, his RKO effects-editing beginnings included two Astaire and Rogers pictures (*Gay Divorce*, 1934, and *Top Hat*, 1935), and since his nightclub comedy, *This Could Be the Night*, Wise was increasingly interested in the genre. The latter picture had effectively included the sexy song and dance skills of Neile Adams. The added significance of music had also surfaced in the integral part jazz scores played in both *I Want to Live!* and *Odds Against Tomorrow*.

Not since *Tribute to a Bad Man*, however, would Wise face so much real-life melodrama in making a movie. Paradoxically, the reason for the greatest conflict on the movie (the cost overruns of codirector Jerome Robbins) is precisely how Wise came aboard the production! The company bankrolling the production (Mirisch-B+P Enterprises, releasing through United Artist) did not want a novice, despite Robbins's breathtaking choreography and direction of *Story*'s original stage show, as solo director on such a big-budget movie. Mirisch and Wise were a mutual admiration society. The director very much wanted to do the picture; Mirisch was impressed with his critical and commercial successes in multiple genres *and* his reputation for staying on budget, which stretched back to the 1940s. The compromise was to have the men codirect, with Robbins keying upon choreography and the songs, and Wise in charge of the traditional story elements, but both were free to give the other suggestions.

Unfortunately, by the halfway point on *Story*, Wise found himself affected by Hollywood's version of original sin, or an Orson Welles flashback from *The Magnificent Ambersons* (1942). That is, Robbins's creative perfectionism on the choreography had put the movie seriously over budget and Mirisch/Wise had him fired—though Robbins' editing rights on what he had completed kept him on the project for two more weeks. (The numbers yet to be filmed were shot according to Robbins's design, but without his costly revisionist tendencies.) Later, when *all* shooting ended, Wise showed an early *Story* rough cut to Robbins, welcoming any suggestions. After what Wise described as an "uncomfortable, emotional, and difficult time for everybody, and certainly for Jerry [Jerome Robbins]," the *Story* closing interaction went smoothly. "He [Robbins] saw the cut, liked the picture in general, had some criticisms and comments," said Wise. "I [Wise] accepted many of them . . . the film turned out well and certainly Jerry's contribution to it is enormous, from every standpoint."[25]

The oddness of the firing/ongoing cooperation was compounded at Oscar time (April 9, 1962), when Wise and Robbins became the first duo to share an Academy Award for directing—an accomplishment since repeated by the Coen Brothers (Joel and Ethan) for *No Country for Old Men* (2007). Still, the 1962 joint directing win by Wise and Robbins played out awkwardly on stage, as chronicled by Oscar historians Mason Wiley and Damien Bona: "Neither winner mentioned or thanked the other."[26] Earlier that evening Robbins had also been

Robert Wise (right) and Jerome Robbins early during the production of West Side Story.

given an honorary Oscar "for his brilliant achievements in the art of
choreography on film," clearly Hollywood's way of salving the firing
wound, since there is no guarantee a nomination will produce a win.[27]
But as if fated to be forever deadlocked that evening, producer Wise
also received a second statuette when *Story* was named the Best Picture.

Wise's theory on the difficulties of going from Broadway to
Hollywood (à la Robbins and *Story*) was that the theater directing
experience encourages wholesale tinkering until opening night, whereas
the scope of a picture necessitates completing (and filming) an endless
series of sequences that must all fit together by an equally unforgiving
release date. Given the Welles/Robbins parallels in Wise's career, the
director might have been reminded of several lines from T. S. Eliot's
Four Quartets: "We shall not cease from exploration / And the end of all
our exploring / Will be to arrive where we started."[28] Regardless of one's
take on the theater/film dichotomy, Wise's *Story* ability to blend art and
fiscal responsibility resulted in a watershed work that *Box Office Hits*
historian Susan Sackett described in the following manner: "William
Shakespeare, Leonard Bernstein, Robert Wise. An unlikely trio to
produce a Broadway/motion picture hit? Certainly, the Bard would
have been delighted to see what had become of his . . . [play] in
modern times."[29]

Story did huge box-office numbers, after opening in the all-
important New York market during October 1961. The picture then
demonstrated what the industry calls "legs" by drawing large audiences
throughout the year. In fact, *Story* ended up being second to only
Spartacus as the top-grossing movie of 1962.[30] Plus, when one does the
cumulative box office for all pictures released in 1961, *Story* is second to
only Disney's original animated feature, *101 Dalmatians* (1961).[31]

Impressively, the reviews matched the grosses—hardly a given in
pop-culture entertainment, as will be examined shortly with Wise's
Sound of Music. The *New York Times* called *Story* "nothing short of a
cinema masterpiece."[32] *Variety* stated: "'Story' is a beautifully-mounted,
impressive, emotion-ridden and violent musical which, in its stark

approach to a raging social problem and realism of unfoldment, may set a pattern for future musical presentations."[33]

Positive reviews followed these seminal bookend publication hosannas, such as the opening to the *Hollywood Reporter*'s critique, "'Story' is a magnificent show, a milestone in movie musicals, a box office smash. It is so good that superlatives are superfluous."[34] The *New York Herald Tribune* added, "The American genius for movie musicals has been excitingly reasserted with 'West Side Story.'"[35] Thirty-three years after *Story*'s release, *Entertainment Weekly*'s book-length guide to cinema's greatest films, genre by genre, puts *Story* number one on its top 100 musicals list.[36] It seems that winning ten of the eleven Oscars for which it was nominated was no fluke: Best Picture, Director, Supporting Actor (George Chakiris), Supporting Actress (Rita Moreno), Cinematography (color, Daniel L. Fapp), Art

Rita Moreno (center) and George Chakiris (left) in West Side Story.

Direction/Set Decoration (color, Boris Levens, Victor A. Gangelin),
Sound (Fred Hynes, Gordon E. Sawyer), Scoring of a Musical Picture
(Saul Chaplin, Johnny Green, Sid Ramin, and Irwin Kostel), Editing
(Thomas Stanford), and Costume Design (color, Irene Sharaff). *Story's*
one miss came in the category of screenplay based upon material from
another medium. Ernest Lehman, who had also worked with Wise on
Executive Suit (1954) and *Somebody Up There Likes Me* (1956), lost to
Abby Mann's adaptation of *Judgment at Nuremberg* (1961).

A year after *Story's* high-flying screen success (first in limited, higher
priced road-show engagements), Wise's next picture, *Two for the Seesaw*,
struggled to get off the ground. As with *Story*, the director and his wife

*As the picture in the background suggests, a relationship "dance" can turn into a battle of
the sexes, Shirley MacLaine and Robert Mitchum in* Two for the Seesaw *(1962).*

had enjoyed seeing the William Gibson play on Broadway (1958). The minimal plot involves a Nebraska lawyer (Robert Mitchum) who comes to New York as his divorce from an overly possessive wife is being finalized. Naturally, he meets a free-spirited kook (Shirley MacLaine) in Greenwich Village, and a mercurial relationship ensues. The bittersweet conclusion finds them both wiser friends but with him heading back to his ex-wife. The title to Rose Pelswick's *New York Journal American* review might have best pinpointed the problem: "An Interesting but Talky Film."[37] And Paul V. Beckley's *New York Herald Tribune* critique opening for *Two* both notes another possible liability while inadvertently nailing what probably most attracted Wise, the ardent feminist, to the property: "'Two' on stage was essentially a one-woman play; on film its population has been increased but it still remains a one-woman picture [the ex-wife is never seen], belonging for better or worse to Shirley MacLaine. Yet warm and deeply felt as her performance is, too much has been asked of her."[38]

Variety's review of *Two* best encapsulates a subtext criticism found in the New York-based critiques: "The multitudes who haven't yet seen William Gibson's 'Two' figure to respond as favorably to the screen version as playgoers did for stage version"[39] The play presented a more befuddled male (Henry Fonda) and a beatnik (Anne Bancroft, in a Tony-winning performance) with attitude. The story is still a stumbling romantic comedy, but Wise has done what any auteur does—tweaked the story in a direction more consistent with his canon. Thus, MacLaine is a more vulnerable heroine as victim than Bancroft's award-winning portrayal of the Bronx gypsy, Gittel Mosca. Consistent with this Wise melodrama tendency, Mitchum's mate sometimes comes across, according to the *New York Times*, as a "supercilious brute."[40] Part of this is Mitchum being Mitchum, just as MacLaine's woman/child screen persona was a poignant mix of sexuality and innocence years before *Two*.

MacLaine's performance is more winsome than Mitchum's because she nails yet again that sacrificial melodramatic gamin (making him realize he still loves his ex-wife) viewers had come to expect after

Some Came Running (1959) and *The Apartment* (1960). In contrast, despite making Mitchum's male tougher than Fonda's stage version, the character's inherent indecision is totally alien to what moviegoers had come to expect from the nonchalantly rugged actor, such as the Wise-directed *Blood on the Moon* (1948). For example, in *Two*'s Greenwich Village party scene, having his straight-arrow character feel out of place just does not mesh with an actor whose career was anchored to an "I-don't-care" cool attitude, which was the real man, too. MacLaine, who was his longtime lover at the time, later wrote of Mitchum: "I never really knew what he wanted. Anything was okay. He was like that with his work too. He never asked for anything. Not even good parts. He'd take 'B' pictures because he said, 'Better me than some other poor fool.'"[41] Both Wise and Mitchum initially balked at casting the actor against type. But *Two* producer Walter Mirisch finally prevailed.[42]

The *Two* production was such a cozy shoot that Wise sometimes felt like a homeroom teacher trying to keep the affectionately bantering leads on topic. "Our director, Robert Wise, who was a lovely man and a fine director, witnessed our chemistry early on," recalled MacLaine. "Mitchum and I kidded around a lot, so much so that Wise took us aside and pleaded with us to take a little time and be serious before each take."[43]

Ironically, while Mitchum and MacLaine were a couple (though their open marriages to other people necessitated keeping the relationship secret), the "chemistry" does not come across in the movie. But this is a fairly common problem in pictures. For example, Warren Beatty and Annette Bening sizzle in the movie that launched their real-life romance, *Bugsy* (1991), while there is little sexual spark between them in Beatty's otherwise solid remake of the durable romantic comedy/melodrama *Love Affair* (1994, filmed previously in 1939 and 1957, the latter as *An Affair to Remember*). Though Mitchum had initially felt he should avoid playing a character so indecisive, the actor expressed rare rage over the negative New York reviews. While one of his biographers, Alvin H. Marill, felt what follows was Mitchum venting about just his notices, today it reads more as a defense of the company and/or close friend MacLaine: "The toughest chore in show business is trying to please them [reviewers] when an actor appears in a film or a stage play. No matter what you do, it's wrong as a sow's ear in a silk purse factory, especially to New York critics, who are guilty of intellectual snobbery. With them nothing can be done in Hollywood, or anywhere else, as well as in their town."[44]

In Mitchum's defense, the early West Coast reviews, which in that presaturation booking era, predated *Two*'s New York opening, were decidedly more positive, such as the *Hollywood Reporter*'s critique headline: "'Two for [the] Seesaw' Rated One of the Year's Best Pix [Pictures]."[45] The same review went on to describe *Two* as "A true love story . . . directed for the screen by Robert Wise with humanity and delicacy, [it] is a man's picture, a woman's picture, a couple's picture."[46] How the critics might have responded to the original plans to cast Paul Newman and Elizabeth Taylor in the leads is anyone's guess.

Given Wise's passionate views against censorship, *Two* also allowed the director creatively to examine an adult relationship in a period moving toward a movie rating system. *Variety* ended its *Two* review by applauding the movie's frank attitude towards sex, "such as who sleeps where, when, and with whom. . . . This is honest, not obnoxious. It shouldn't and won't bother anybody except those who aren't satisfied unless they are bothered."[47] Moreover, despite Wise's propensity for the melodramatic in assorted genres, any relationship picture that concludes with a couple going their separate ways reinforces the director's inherent slice-of-life tendencies.

With the musical *Story* and the realistic romantic comedy *Two*, Wise had essentially completed his goal of directing all the mainstream genres. Therefore, the time seemed right to revisit his horror-film roots by tackling an adaptation of a novel considered to be one of the twentieth century's pivotal works of horror, Shirley Jackson's *The Haunting of Hill House*, in the process turning it into an unofficial tribute to mentor Val Lewton. In addition to the book's psychological

Julie Harris's (right) childlike heroine in The Haunting *(1963, with Claire Bloom).*

horror foundation being fertile ground for a homage to the subtextual terror of Lewton, Jackson's work taps into a popular component in many Wise pictures—the spooky old house as a metaphor. Fittingly, the director's great pleasure in simply reading the novel was undoubtedly further embellished by the fact that "Houses loomed large in her [Jackson's] imagination [and work], as places that promise but never quite deliver some respite from everyday terrors."[48] And just as this novel is Jackson's best example of a house as a depository for evil, Wise's adaptation holds a comparable cinematic place among his films.

Film historian William K. Everson has praised the psychological horror picture, or what might simply be labeled an "intelligently scary—non-gore movie," as "nothing that the camera can show can possibly be as horrible as what the mind can imagine; it suggests nothing, and suggests all."[49] While this wonderfully describes the Lewton/Wise approach to horror, the quote can also have a subtextual meaning. That is, just as the viewer's imagination can be more frightening than on-screen special effects, watching the meltdown of a child or childlike horror film heroine, be it young Ann Carter in Wise's *The Curse of the Cat People* (1944) or Julie Harris's naïve recluse in *Haunting*, takes the audience's horror musings to a disturbing second tier. One is not just imagining the cause of that movie bump in the night. There is now a disturbing concern for whatever is going on in the mind of the picture's vulnerable core character—an innocent civilian who has not paid money, à la the horror aficionado, for what Alfred Hitchcock claimed was the genre's "beneficial shocks."[50] Thus, while Christopher Nolan's *Inception* (2010) reveals disturbing dreams within dreams, *Haunting* encourages scary imagining about another's imagination.

For the casual fan, however, the downside of intelligent horror is that, to paraphrase critic/author Jeff VanderMeer, the film requires the viewer to "collaborate with the artist, to fill in the gaps."[51] Paradoxically, as much as Wise admired the novel, he sometimes struggled with Jackson's purpose. At its most basic, the tale is about an anthropologist who brings together three people for "an experiment

Julie Harris's symbolic envelopment by the "twisted" staircase is a subtext to what the man-sion is doing to her in The Haunting *(with Richard Johnson).*

in psychic research." The setting is Hill House, a spooky old New England Victorian mansion (Ettingen Hall, near Stratford-on-Avon in England, doubled for Hill House), which may or may not be haunted. The academic is Doctor John Markway (Richard Johnson), and the subjects include Eleanor Lance (Julie Harris), who had a poltergeist experience as a child; Theodora (Claire Bloom), a Greenwich Village free spirit with extrasensory perception powers; and Luke Sanderson (Russ Tamblyn), a nephew watchdog for the mansion's absentee owner. Ultimately, Harris's character is the house's only victim, but there is no overt act. Instead, Hill House's seemingly supernaturally possessed nature, from its spiritual world cold spots to the animalistic noises and deafening poundings on interior doors, seems to be taking over Eleanor's mind, just as her controlling invalid mother had done during the daughter's trying time as a caretaker. But Wise later wrote a fan that during preproduction he and his screenwriter (Nelson Gidding) went back East to discuss Eleanor's plight with Jackson, since the author generally avoided interviews/explanations about her writing. "At one point, she [Jackson] said that everybody needed a home and since there was no home for Eleanor . . . anyplace else [after her mother's death], she . . . [went] to Hill House," Wise said. "Reasons why she succumbed and others didn't were explained the way you have put it [the others had someone]. I know the picture caused confusion among quite a number of people who saw it. I could only wish that they had gotten the point as clearly and succinctly as you did."[52]

Wise's comments were possibly influenced by mixed reviews from *Variety* and the *New York Times*.[53] Sadly, Richard C. Keenan's often insightful book, *The Films of Robert Wise*, suggests the film met with "little enthusiasm by the reviewers of the day."[54] Keenan seems to base that perspective on only the *Variety* and *Times* reviews. A more thorough examination of period critiques finds *Haunting* and Wise heavily praised. Indeed, even the majority of New York City newspapers, publications that had so nitpicked *Two*, were full of praise for *Haunting*. The *New York World-Telegram*'s William Peper wrote: "'The Haunting' is a movie that believes in ghosts and before it's over, it should have audiences believing in them, too, for it is a genuinely spooky film. . . . At creating a mood of unseen terror, Wise is a thumping success."[55] Rose Pelswick's *New York Journal American* critique, "Bang-Up Thriller Full of Suspense," closed with the following good-humored praise for the chilling tale: "If this one had been released during the summer months, the theatres wouldn't have had to turn on their cold air units."[56] Critic Judith Crist was even more superlative in her *New York Herald Tribune* review, serving up sagely pluralist perspectives on the film's meaning, indicating that the film was "a thoroughly satisfying ghost story for grown-ups done with a style and professionalism that has long been denied spook-story addicts. . . . Is it the story of a haunted house, a study of the effects of fear upon an already neurotic mind, an allegory of a nervous breakdown? Play with it as you will . . . and have a delicious wallow in the horror of 'The Haunting.'"[57]

The brilliance of Jackson's novel, and Wise's adaptation, regardless of one's interpretation of the story's meaning (one could also apply critic Roland Barthes's constant theme of "the instability of [any] meaning"[58]), involves the ultimate act of betrayal in which the home is *not* a sanctuary. Like the desertion of one's friends/family in film noir, another genre that shaped Wise, this kind of hurt stung the most. Yet, just as an abused child and/or spouse will often cling to the oppressor because that is all she/he has, Harris's Eleanor ultimately seems to succumb to the house because that is all she has.

As a final footnote to the power of *Haunting*, beyond the horror genre, the work can also be seen as a tongue-in-cheek metaphor for any abode where creative types work their magic. Critic Terrence Rafferty once wrote of another Jackson literary home, "In a way . . . [this] crazy house is where writers go when they write, that quiet spot where nothing is ever as peaceful as it seems."[59] Imagine the imagery swirling around in the mind of Stephen King as he writes his novels in yet another New England Victorian mansion.

While *Haunting* was tightly budgeted, Wise's next film, a screen adaptation of Richard Rogers and Oscar Hammerstein's musical *The Sound of Music*, was an expensive, opera-like epic that was, for a time, history's top-grossing movie. (*Music* still comes in at number three, behind *Gone With the Wind*, 1939, and *Star Wars*, 1977, as the all-time, inflation-adjusted box-office hit.[60]) William Wyler, winner of three Best Director Oscars, was originally slated to direct *Music*. But after starting preproduction he left the project to direct *The Collector* (1965). Prior to Wyler, several prominent filmmakers, including Stanley Donen, Gene Kelly, George Roy Hill, and Wise himself, had turned down *Music*. When Twentieth Century-Fox chief Darrel F. Zanuck and his son, Richard, vice president in charge of production, approached Wise a second time, circumstances had changed for the director. While Wise still found *Music* overly sentimental, the extensive preproduction work on the director's dream project, an adaptation of *The Sand Pebbles*, had delayed shooting for at least a year. Worse yet, the Mirisch Company, which had bankrolled both *West Side Story* and *Two for the Seesaw*, had suddenly withdrawn from *Sand Pebbles* over budget concerns. Consequently, Wise and the Zanucks came to an understanding; he would direct *Music* (with what turned out to be a lucrative profit-sharing arrangement, 10 percent of the net profit, or roughly $10 million), and their studio would finance *Sand Pebbles*.

As with *So Big* (1953), where Wise was also slow to warm to the project, the production "marriage" proved fortuitous. Wise excelled at screen biographies and fictionalized profile pictures. *Music* falls somewhere in-between, and was drawn from Maria von Trapp's autobiography, *The Trapp Family Singers* (1949). Wise had a talent for directing children and championing tales of victimized and/or vulnerable childlike women. *Music's* saga chronicles just such a life in Maria (Julie Andrews). This musical melodrama entertainingly careens from one life crisis to another: will she stay with her religious studies and become a nun? As a governess, can she bring joy into the home of widowed military man Captain von Trapp (Christopher Plummer)?

What about falling in love with the captain, and all its complications (starting with potential wife number two, Eleanor Parker, waiting in the wings)?

Wise's career was anchored in the human evil of two genres—film noir and horror. What better personification of evil ever existed than Nazi Germany, *Music*'s group villain? Although Wise the director came late to the musical, the genre had fascinated him since his Connersville High School days. Plus, with his award-winning adaptation of another musical seeped in danger, the New York gang wars of *West Side Story*, Wise was a logical choice for the Zanucks.

Given Wise's early concerns about the "saccharine" nature of the *Music* material, he attempted to reframe the experience by creating a "different kind of musical . . . one that could entertain all kinds of people."[61] Thus, Wise and star Andrews's first order of business was, to quote a question she immediately asked of him, "How are we going to cut down all the sweetness that's in this piece?"[62] Years later she summarized what happened: "What can you do with nuns, seven children and Austria [and not be "saccharine"]? But Bob Wise decided to get rid of the sugar—no filigree [folksy cute material], no carved wood, no Swiss chalets, and he stuck to his guns. We all felt the same way. It helped that it was a motion picture [versus a stage production] because they could do such sweeping things visually."[63]

Some secondary songs were also cut, and new dialogue (from Wise's favorite screenwriter Ernest Lehman) leading into numbers helped minimize the awkward transitions of someone suddenly bursting into song. Andrews was also a great help in attempting to de-sweeten *Music*. "Maria *couldn't* be sweetness and light with seven kids on her hands all the time . . . so I tried once in a while to show that I might be slightly exhausted by them," Andrews remembered. "On the bed [before the "My Favorite Things" number], when they ask me to do this or that and say, 'What kind of things do you mean?' just before I go into . . . [the song], I thought, 'Oh my God! Children always do ask questions like that.'"[64]

Christopher Plummer's captain shocks Julie Andrews by the militaristic manner in which he runs his Sound of Music *(1965) household.*

Ironically, for all Andrews eventually brought to Maria (Wyler had favored Audrey Hepburn, and the studio wanted Doris Day, which Wise very much opposed), there were questions about Andrews carrying a movie, in that her first two films as an adult, *Mary Poppins* (1964, for which she would win a Best Actress Oscar) and *The Americanization of Emily* (1964, arguably her best straight dramatic part), had yet to be released. But both Lehman and Wise were high on her, and when Disney let them see an early print of *Poppins*, there were no doubts. Conversely, Andrews's concerns about the "too sweet" *Music* material were greatly diminished just knowing who would direct: "[when] I found out that Robert Wise was directing, well, let's just say I changed my tune."[65]

Several actors were in the mix to play the brusque captain, including Bing Crosby, Yul Brynner, Peter Finch, and cinema's best James Bond, Sean Connery. From a musical standpoint, Crosby or Brynner made the most sense, since the ultimate winner's (Plummer) singing voice would be dubbed. But Wise and his wife, Patricia, greatly admired a Shakespearean stage actor they had seen on Broadway during one of their annual trips East scouting both talent and cultural fun. Wise later confessed casting Plummer "was my wife's idea . . . [and] I think he was marvelous in the role. He gave a kind of dark edge to it, which I felt was very helpful [for this stern military figure]."[66] One wonders if Patricia was partly bowled over by Plummer's striking handsomeness. No less a personage than Maria von Trapp exclaimed, upon meeting the actor, "My God, darling, I wish my husband had looked as good as you."[67]

Although Plummer's involvement eventually proved a plus for the picture and for his budding film career, he was more than prickly during *Music*'s production. Decades later Plummer wrote in his memoir: "I'll admit it, I was also a pampered, arrogant young bastard, spoiled by too many great theatre roles. Ludicrous though it may seem, I still harbored the old-fashioned stage actor's snobbism toward moviemaking. . . . I was determined to present myself [during the production] as a victim of circumstance—that I was doing the picture under duress. . . . My behavior was unconscionable."[68]

Laced throughout the autobiography, however, is constant praise for Wise's patience. For instance, "Wise was kindness itself," or in another passage, "Wise, true to his name, was tolerance itself."[69] The two men somehow connected, and based upon Wise's collected correspondence at the University of Southern California, became lifelong friends. Nearly a decade after *Music*, Wise wrote a long letter to the actor in response to an invitation to visit Plummer's French estate: "Pat and I were delighted to get your warm and newsy letter. We were really sick about not having the chance to see you in [a stage production of] *Cyrano*. . . . I made a picture last year [*Two People*, 1973] in France and Morocco which unfortunately, didn't fare too well with the critics or the public. . . . [If a new European production develops] we'll have an opportunity to visit you on your new farm in the South of France. It sounds like a lovely idea."[70]

There is also an irony hidden in the letter's reference to *Cyrano*. One of the reasons Plummer consented to do *Music*, after much courting from Wise (including the director flying to London to lobby his case), was the role would help prepare the actor for a musical version of *Cyrano*. Consequently, Plummer had another meltdown when it became apparent that his *Music* songs would be dubbed.

One should keep in mind, of course, that Plummer's generally arrogant attitude going into *Music*, which he rechristened *The Sound of Mucus* (an experience he also satirically described as "S&M"), was hardly limited to snobby theater folks. When Fred Astaire's only rival as the screen's greatest dancer, Kelly, turned down a chance to direct *Music*, he used a four-letter word to describe the material; when Lehman told his Oscar-winning friend, Burt Lancaster, that he was adapting the musical, the actor said, "Jesus, you must need the money."[71] And another Lehman friend, the inspired writer/director Billy Wilder, who was himself in the habit of making precedent-breaking hit movies, such as *Some Like It Hot* (1959, a dark comedy triggered by the mass murdering mobsters of the Saint Valentine's Day Massacre), lectured, "My dear boy, no musical with a swastika in it can ever be successful."[72] Maybe this general attitude, even in Hollywood, was why Wyler's early take on the picture was to showcase much more of a Nazi military presence. Though Wise's version did not play this card, which undoubtedly contributed to it becoming a commercial juggernaut, the reviews (to be addressed shortly) often struck a note not unlike the comments by Kelly and Lancaster.

Paradoxically, the stoical Wise later became exasperated *not* by criticism of his "spoonful of sugar" musical, but rather by the constant attempts to unravel the puzzle of its amazing appeal for the general public. "I wasn't trying to say a damned thing in *The Sound of Music*," said Wise. "That's as good a face as I can put on it. People just feel good when they see it; there's a sense of warmth, of well-being, of happiness and joy."[73]

How strange that the most pacifistic of directors unraveled when asked for the umpteenth time his cinema secret in making the most popular movie in the industry's first seventy years. Maybe the best single description of Wise's sensitivity as a director, both on *Music* and/or any other production, amplifies the frustration he must have felt for a long unique career suddenly swallowed by *Music's* success. Charmian Carr, who played Liesel, the oldest von Trapp child, is the source of this Wise anecdote. Having won the part from a litany of memorable talents, including Patty Duke, Mia Farrow, Teri Garr, and Geraldine Chaplin, Carr was struggling in her first scene. She was supposed to come through a window after climbing up a trellis during a thunderstorm. Soaked, chilled, and unable to hear her cue through multiple takes, Carr feared her film career would end before it started. "Rather than make me feel like an amateur or that I was ruining the scene or upsetting his star," Carr later wrote, "Bob Wise took the time to help me become an actress. His attitude always was, if there was a problem, there was a solution. 'Julie [Andrews], let's have you say that one [cue] line loud. *Really* loud.'"[74]

"If there was a problem, there was a solution." But what if your solutions to concrete problems so successfully tap into intangible artistic universals that one creates an unprecedented phenomenon, with no defining Rosebud/sled/lost childhood epiphany? Wise's insightful "joy" factor about *Music* should be enough for critics, but it seems to pass through them like light through glass. One could simply equate this jubilation factor to Woody Allen's much praised opening to *Manhattan* (1980), where he also provides his own take on "My Favorite Things," such as the magic of watching Willie Mays play baseball. Instinctual artists, such as Wise, are not always able to fully define their accomplishments.

Later attempts to articulate just why the movie so moved the masses could not have been predicted after reading the blistering opening reviews from some tony critics. The *New York Herald Tribune's* Crist, who had so artfully praised multiple-meanings inherent in *The Haunting*, was in attack mode when she wrote "let me tell you that there is nothing like a super-sized screen to convert seven darling little kids in no time at all into all that W. C. Fields indicated darling little kids are . . . pure loathsome."[75] Stanley Kauffmann's *New Republic* critique was equally sarcastic: "Is there a special heaven for film critics? I feel confident of it, after enduring all of *The Sound of Music*."[76] *Redbook's* Pauline Kael titled it *The Sound of Money*, and complained the movie "makes it even more difficult to try anything worth doing, anything relevant to the modern world, anything inventive or expressive."[77] (Her loathing of *Music* so offended the *Redbook* editorial staff that Kael moved to *The New Yorker*.) Bosley Crowther's *New York Times* notice complained that Andrews brings a "'Mary Poppins' logic and authority to this role, which is always in peril of collapsing under its weight and romantic nonsense and sentiment."[78]

The critical ambush of *Music* was surprisingly broad but it was overstated, such as Robert Windeler's Andrews biography claiming "Every major national film critic in America hated *The Sound of Music*.[79] In contrast, the entertainment bible, *Variety*, praised the picture, beginning with its opening paragraph: "The music and charm of the. . . 1959 stage hit are sharply blended in this filmic translation which emerges as one of the top musicals to reach the screen. The Robert Wise production is a warmly-pulsating, captivating drama set to the most imaginative use of the lilting R-H [Rodgers and Hammerstein] tunes."[80] Even the title of the *Hollywood Reporter*'s review cheerleaded: "'Sound of Music' Restores Faith in the Art of Motion Pictures."[81]

Most of the sophisticated New York City dailies, other than the prickly *New York Times*, praised the picture. The *New York World Telegram and Sun*'s Alton Cook wrote: "The film's charm grows and sentiment becomes unabashed and naively sweet but never cloying . . . Director Robert Wise has insisted on keeping his people substantial and credible with none of the coy tricks that are likely to creep into an idyllic rhapsody such as this, particularly when small children are involved."[82] The *New York Journal American*'s Rose Pelswick added: "The picture opened last night at the Rivoli [theater] . . . a big, beautifully made adaptation. . . . As produced and directed by Robert Wise . . . it adds up to that rarity these days, a delightful screen entertainment for the entire family."[83]

The Wise/Lehman ability to open up the material might best be demonstrated by the "Do-Re-Mi" montage. On stage the song was frozen in the von Trapp living room. But no "canned theater" for the adaptation. The screen montage transitions through time and space to highlight varied Austrian landscapes and costumes, while forever demonstrating Maria's growing closeness to the children. With a former film editor as director, and an equally sensitive- to-cutting screenwriter, William Reynold's Oscar for editing *Music* seemed the most natural of wins. The film also won Academy Awards for Best Picture, Director, Sound, and Scoring of Music for an adaptation. As the *Los Angeles Times*' Philip K. Scheuer summarized in his review: "They have taken this sweet, sometimes slight story . . . and transformed it into close to three hours of visual and vocal brilliance."[84]

Andrews received an Oscar nomination as Best Actress, but her much-praised performance was undoubtedly hurt among Academy voters by the fact she had won the award the previous year for *Mary Poppins*. (The Best Actress Oscar winner for 1965 was Julie Christie in *Darling*.) The centrality of Andrews's *Music* part and performance might best be defined by the title given the film in Argentina, *The Rebellious Novice*.[85]

In closing, an offbeat assessment on why *Music* was so popular could also be culled from Jackson, the author of the novel *The Haunting of Hill House*. In her short story, "Colloquy," a young woman asks a doctor how to tell if you're going crazy. He attempts an explanation: "In a period of international crisis, when you find . . . cultural patterns rapidly disintegrating," but she cuts him off, and goes into a *disintegrating* monologue of her own topped by the comically disquieting crack, "Is everyone really crazy but me?"[86] Analogous to *Music*, one could argue that the musical was *so* embraced by the masses

Julie Andrews leading The Sound of Music *children against that breathtaking backdrop.*

because it opened at a time of "international crisis," and for at least three hours, the picture restored some of the "disintegrating cultural patterns." Along similar lines, the unprecedented popularity of the Beatles during this same period (1964–65), following the Cuban Missile Crisis (October 1962) and the assassination of President John F. Kennedy (November 22, 1963), is now often explained, in part, as America looking for something to be happy about again. For example, in Philip Norman's biography of John Lennon, he wrote that the Beatles phenomenon "signaled the end of mourning for J.F.K., through an event as hugely harmless as the November 22 had been hugely horrible."[87] And keep in mind, while the Beatles are now deservedly honored as watershed poets of music, their early hits, such as "I Want to Hold Your Hand" and "Love Me Do" expressed the same sentimentally comforting mind candy of *Music*, à la "Sixteen Going on Seventeen," "Do-Re-Mi," and so on.

Conversely, one could suggest Wise's adaptation of *Haunting of Hill House* (which also metaphorically embraces the "disintegrating cultural patterns" of life) was not a box-office hit because the work doubles as a frightening parable about the instability of the modern world and the dark underside of humanity. And it is fitting the film did not initially find a large audience. Jackson's work, though invariably praised by critics, has often upset and/or angered the general public, such as her best known and most frequently anthologized short story, "The Lottery" (1948). Jackson's oeuvre, like Wise's, often suggests the masses are less than stable and often sinister. Appropriately, the careers of both these artists were largely bracketed by the concentration camps of World War II, and cold war fears over the atomic bomb. But unlike Jackson, Wise's core characters are more likely to try and do the right thing/attempt to make a difference, even if a negative outcome cannot be avoided—they fight against their destiny.

Not surprisingly, Stephen King is a huge fan of both Jackson's novel and Wise's adaptation. In King's nonfiction book on horror, *Dance Macabre*, he calls Jackson's work one of "only two great novels of the supernatural [joining Henry James's *The Turn of the Screw*] in the last hundred years . . . [and] I recognize terror as the finest emotion (used to almost quintessential effect in Robert Wise's film *The Haunting*, where, as in 'The Monkey's Paw,' we are never allowed to see what is behind the door)."[88]

King is sometimes considered a Jackson student, but his close to *Dance Macabre* draws upon a metaphor from the writing of James Dickey. It posits him rather like the Wise perspective just noted—trying in a lost cause. Using a Dickey poem about falling to one's death, King sees the image as "a metaphor for the life of the rational being, who must grapple as best he/she can with the fact of his/her own mortality. We fall from womb to tomb, from one blackness and towards another, remembering little of the one and knowing nothing of the other. . . . That we retain our sanity in the face of these . . . blinding mysteries is nearly divine. That we may turn the powerful intuition of our imagination upon them [life's horrors] and regard them in this glass of dreams [the arts]. . . well, it's magic, isn't it?[89] Wise's "magic" is again inspiringly employed in his next project—an antiwar film about a *Heart of Darkness* kind of horror.

The Beatles in a scene from their hit movie musical A Hard Day's Night *(1964).*

12

Filmmaking: "A Terribly Expensive Paint Box"[1]

*"I'm an anti-militerist and was very
much against the the Vietnam War."* [2]
ROBERT WISE

Robert Wise's adaptation of Richard McKenna's novel *The Sand Pebbles* (1966) was a parable about the Vietnam War, set in China during 1926, when that country was hemorrhaging through both a civil war and imperialist intervention by Western powers, such as the United States. Though *Sand Pebbles* would be critically acclaimed, the movie was, to borrow a line from Orson Welles, "a terribly expensive paint box," which was a box-office disappointment—especially following the then unprecedented financial success of *The Sound of Music* (1965). Sadly, and ironically, given Wise's early talent for frugal filmmaking (previously contrasted with Welles's RKO spendthrift ways), Wise's last films included several more large commercial failures, often without the balancing tradeoff of critical acclaim.

It should come as no surprise that Wise, a lifelong liberal, should neither be a fan of the military nor the Vietnam War. Plus, an antiwar parable involving a U.S. Navy gunboat in the Far East takes on further resonance when one factors in the concerns of parents whose son was then in the navy—the Wises' only child, Robert Allen (Rob), entered the service in 1964.

Throughout Wise's film career he consistently and persistently demonstrated how the military (during war or warlike situations, such as *The Day the Earth Stood Still,* 1951), often produced less-than-ideal behavior by people in and out of uniform. And though several of his movies dealt with what later historians called the "Good War" (World War II [3]), Wise still realistically demonstrated there was *nothing romantic* about *any* armed conflict. During that very war he had chosen a film career over military service, yet produced one of the most metaphorically searing indictments of Nazi-French collaboration, via a picture ostensibly set during the Franco-Prussian War (1872), *Mademoiselle Fifi* (1944).

The difference, however, between Wise's early years as a director on *Fifi* (with producer Val Lewton), and Wise's helming of *Sand Pebbles*, was that the director had become an acknowledged Hollywood artist. As novelist Herman Melville once wrote, figures of history "are parts of the times; they themselves are the times, and possess a correspondent coloring."[4] While the significance of *Fifi* was sometimes obscured by being a low-budget RKO picture from a young director, Wise's *Sand Pebbles* was very much of "the times" and contributed to the increasing antiwar "coloring" of the late 1960s.

If life is a series of paradoxes best summarized by the first line of Charles Dickens's *A Tale of Two Cities* (1859): "It was the best of times, it was the worst of times," *Sand Pebbles* was a production wrought with ironies. This elaborately constructed epic had an antiwar director/ message, yet starred an iconic former U.S. Marine (Steve McQueen), who was initially a devout hawk on Vietnam. Though the picture was ultimately a flawed masterpiece, which generated McQueen's only Best Actor Oscar nomination and was the catalyst for Wise being given the prestigious Irving G. Thalberg Award (for consistent production achievement by a producer), the public was indifferent to *Sand Pebbles*. The movie finished out of 1966's moneymaking top twenty in a mind-candy year dominated by James Bond, with *Thunderball* trouncing the number two box-office picture (*Doctor Zhivago*), and two other top ten moneymakers being Bond-influenced parodies, *The Silencers* and *Our Man Flint* (all 1966).[5] *Sand Pebbles*' late 1966 release might have had it surfacing in the moneymaking top twenty of 1967, but it was a no show there, too. Though *Sand Pebbles* did *not* fail at the box office, expenses over its long shoot minimized profits.

These inherent paradoxes bled over into other high-profile Wise/McQueen pictures. The director was so passionate about making this dream project, he signed on to direct another picture first, *The Sound of Music*, in order to obtain funding for *Sand Pebbles*. Conversely, since *Sand Pebbles* was a film with major water scenes, bad weather so expanded the on-location shooting schedule (to eight and a half months) that McQueen had to drastically delay his own dream film—a racing movie tentatively titled *Day of the Champion* but completed years later as *Le Mans* (1971). Calling racing a "professional blood sport," McQueen's character in *Le Mans* states in a Hemingwayesque manner: "A lot of people go through life doing things badly. Racing is important to men who do it well. When you're racing—that's life; anything that happens before or after is just waiting."

The sea weather guaranteed there would be a lot of *waiting* on *Sand Pebbles*. Candice Bergen, one of McQueen's costars, later entertainingly described the strain this placed on the actor and his blue-collar "Rat Pack": "[He] arrived in Taiwan with a commando unit of six stunt men. . . . They were like his personal honor guard, and when he moved, they jumped. Hard-drinking, hard-fighting—as time on the island ticked by McQueen and his gang grew increasingly restless and often spent nights on the prowl, roaming the little city [Taipei, Taiwan]."[6]

By the time McQueen's flawed *Le Mans* was made, the actor's racing thunder had also been stolen by two similarly themed pictures, starring two of his self-appointed friendly rivals—James Garner in *Grand Prix* (1967) and Paul Newman in *Winning* (1969), making it all the more difficult for the insecure McQueen.[7] Sometimes when one wants things in the worst way (McQueen and *Le Mans*), that is the way they turn out.

As was often the case with temperamental stars and strong-willed directors, the McQueen-Wise teaming was not without fireworks. The director later eloquently described the actor's emotional volatility with the comment, "[McQueen] always seemed to work a little bit on the end of his fingertips," yet their only major conflict involved *Wise* losing his temper over the actor persistently interrupting his attempt to set up a non-McQueen shot. "'For Christ's sake, Steve!' Wise exploded. 'Can't you see I'm tied up in the shot? Let's talk about it [McQueen's costume for another scene] at the end of the day.' Well, his feelings were so hurt he didn't talk to me for three days. When I was directing . . . [him] he was fine but he wouldn't say anything off the scene . . . [until he saw the

Candice Bergen (right), with (left to right) Marayat Andriane, Steve McQueen, and Richard Attenborough in The Sand Pebbles *(1966).*

weekly rushes] and was thrilled. Everything was fine from then on and he started speaking to me again."[8]

Wise had actually given McQueen his first feature-film experience—an unbilled part in *Somebody Up There Likes Me* (1956, with Newman). Though being a fellow Hoosier did not hurt, the part was more a courtesy of McQueen's wife, the then more famous dancer/singer/actress Neile Adams, one of the costars of Wise's *This Could Be the Night* (1957). Adams was again a factor in her husband being cast for *Sand Pebbles*, but in a different way. That is, as Adams later shared in her memoir: "I had read Richard McKenna's book and brought it to Steve's attention. He had immediately identified with the character of Seaman Jake Holman and was delighted when he was approached for the film version. We had been especially thrilled to learn that Robert Wise was directing. . . . We had eloped to Mexico while I had been in the middle of Bob's [*This Could Be the Night*] . . . and Steve had been steadily unemployed. Now, here he was, starring for this widely acclaimed director."[9]

Just as the delays in funding *Sand Pebbles* ultimately contributed to the movie's antiwar critical acclaim (as the United States became increasingly dovish about Vietnam), this same postponement aided McQueen's casting. When Wise had originally sought backing for the project in the early 1960s, his first choice for the lead was Newman, with whom he had so successfully teamed on *Somebody*. (Newman passed on the project at a time when *everyone* wanted Newman.) McQueen had been on Wise's short list, the studio moneymen felt he was not a big enough star to carry an expensive epic. For example, while Newman was consistently making the film industry's annual top-ten box office list throughout the 1960s, with the Hollywood Foreign Press giving him Golden Globes for "World Film Favorite—Male" multiple times (1963, 1965, and 1967), McQueen did not reach a comparable level of acclaim until the year *Sand Pebbles* came out, a status greatly assisted by his very commercially successful Western that same year, *Nevada Smith* (1966).[10] But with McQueen starting to appear consistently in commercially and/or critically recognized movies by late 1963, when both *The Great Escape* and *Love with a Proper Stranger* appeared, Twentieth-Century Fox was happy to sign McQueen for *Pebbles*.

The long-developing road to McQueen's casting was most fortuitous for *Sand Pebbles*. When the actor's first wife said he was just right for the part, she was a master of understatement. The real *Sand Pebbles* love story is not between McQueen's navy machinist and Candice Bergen's teacher/missionary but rather the sailor's fascination with the engine of his ship, the *San Pablo*. (The *Sand Pebbles* was the Chinese natives' name for the sailors, a linguistic misfire for *San Pablo*.) This was typical McQueen—in his best roles he embellished his minimalist acting style by an inspired relationship with props, large and small. As the actor's screenwriter for *The Getaway* (1972), Walter Hill observed, "He was wonderful at finding a physical piece of business that would extend his character."[11] Like the neglected paintings of Gerald Murphy, in which geometrically arranged objects, such as the precisely painted mechanism of a timepiece (*Watch*, 1924–25) suggest a sanctuary from human hurt, McQueen's engine room scenes provide the same escape in *Sand Pebbles*. These sequences, ranging from the reverential initial "meeting" in which he introduces himself to the machine, to the ongoing serenity of his maintenance of said engine, all disguise an individual damaged from personal relationships—a scenario that could also be used to explain the actor's real-life interest in all things mechanical.[12]

Wise poignantly uses Holman's (McQueen) normal instinctual resistance to the pain inherent in human contact/causes for *Pebbles'* devastating close. Like Ernest Hemingway's Robert Jordan in *For Whom the Bell Tolls* (1940), McQueen's character finds he must sacrifice his life in a delaying action against the enemy so that his love interest (Bergen) and others can escape. But while both these self-contained fictional figures do what they have to do, Holman's dying words have the modern ring of absurdist anger: "I was home. What happened? What the hell happened?" What the hell happened was he abandoned his principle of noninvolvement and paid the ultimate price. Ironically, just prior to this atypical for Holman action, he had broken away from

Steven McQueen and his actress wife Neile Adams, as his handprints and footprints are committed to history at Grauman's Chinese Theatre (March 21, 1967).

the hollow cause of his imperialistically patriotic commanding officer (Richard Crenna): "I ain't got no more enemies; shove off, Captain." Yet, this action, which aped the disillusionment of another Hemingway character closer to Holman's mindset (*A Farewell to Arms*' Frederic Henry, 1929, whose equally reluctant love affair also led to loss), still could not save McQueen's character. Holman had truly been "home"/ safe. But like a fatalistic film-noir figure, so central to Wise's early career, he lets himself get involved, and dies. Thus, his eleventh-hour questioning of this decision is reminiscent of lyrical Welsh poet Dylan Thomas's railing against death, "Do not go gentle into that good night," which contains the famous line, "Rage, rage against the dying of the light."[13] Like Thomas's poetry, Holman's "I was home. What happened? What the hell happened?" is a haunting tribute to mankind's short, misunderstood allotment of time.

Sand Pebbles is equally fatalistic about another lost cause, the marriage of McQueen's shipmate Frenchy (Richard Attenborough) to the young forced-into-prostitution Chinese girl Maily (Marayat Andriane). Consistent with Wise's signature sympathetic portrayals of both antiheroic women living on the fringes of society, to his racial colorblindness, the *Sand Pebbles* relationship ends badly, but realistically, given the director's background in "naturalistic" noir (realism carried to an extreme). Frenchy's attempt to see Maily involves his own farewell to arms—nightly long, cold swims from his ship to shore that result in a fatal case of pneumonia. The dying Frenchy, a good man simply trying to love someone, might also have been tempted to utter the tirade "What the hell happened?"

Another twist on a biracial *Sand Pebbles* couple keys upon Holman (McQueen) and his Chinese assistant Po-Han (Mako, in an Oscar-nominated performance.) Though it was common for American naval ships in the Pacific theater of the 1920s to take on Chinese laborers, there was often a racist attitude toward these workers. But McQueen's loner seamen and Po-Han bond over their shared fascination with the care of the ship's engine.

China's civil war involved Chiang Kai-shek's Nationalists, an embryonic Chinese Communist Party, and assorted regional warlords. The one thing these various factions agreed upon, however, was the need to rid China of foreign powers. American forces, such as McQueen's ship, were trying to be policemen yet somehow remain neutral. Late in the movie the Nationalists kidnap Po-Han and begin to torture him on the beach near the American ship hoping to provoke a military incident. The captain commands that nothing be done. But a distraught Jake disobeys, and taking a rifle from a fellow sailor, mercifully shoots and kills Po-Han. This violent death, predicated upon a rare instance of McQueen's character letting his emotional guard down, foreshadows Holman's own death. Like the horror and film-noir genres in which Wise started his career, survival in the *Sand Pebbles* world is contingent upon doing as little as possible. To get involved with someone and/or something is tantamount to a death sentence.

The Midwest *Sand Pebbles* premier was in Indianapolis (March 1, 1967), with Wise in attendance. While any such Hoosier homecoming was meaningful to the director, the site of this opening, the Lyric Theater, especially moved Wise. He had frequently attended Lyric Sunday screenings as a child, on those exciting after-church family movie outings to Indianapolis. Now, the boy once obsessed with iconic silent action hero Douglas Fairbanks Sr., had directed a comparable modern-day adventure star, McQueen, and was bringing the picture back to the Lyric.

The national reviews for the three-hour epic were uniformly excellent, such as *Variety*'s summary: "In 'Pebbles,' Wise has blended a series of conflicts, large and small, into a period drama that is, variously, exciting, tragic, stirring and romantic."[14] *Boxoffice* stated: "Wise, who spent almost a year shooting 'Pebbles' in Taiwan and Hong Kong locations which approximated the Chinese mainland, where filming is an impossibility today [1966–67], blended the many facets of his explosive story . . . into an absorbing drama of human beings of several races caught in the upheaval of a full-scale [1926] civil war."[15]

Cue suggested: "The film's point of view forces us [the United States] to think sharply about our present involvements with China and Vietnam."[16] The *Hollywood Reporter* added, "Robert Wise's 'Pebbles' takes a fragment of history, a tiny action in an obscure setting, and makes it high drama."[17] The *Los Angeles Herald-Examiner* reported: "The exciting new movie, producer-director Robert Wise's entry in the 1966 Oscar derby, had a gala benefit premiere last night [December 28, 1966] at the [Twentieth Century] Fox Wilshire Theater."[18] Some of the most laudatory critical comments came from film historian Arthur Knight's *Saturday Review* critique, including a link between the seemingly diverse *Sound of Music* and *Sand Pebbles*: "[In both] director Wise was speaking for human dignity and freedom of spirit."[19]

Paradoxically, Knight's greatest praise for Wise, from the essay's opening paragraph, also includes an unintended clue (the growing temptation of huge budgets) as to why the director's career would soon be sliding into decline: "It is said out in Hollywood that given a list of ten top directors, any studio would choose for its next multi-million dollar spectacular the mild, soft-spoken, unassuming Robert Wise."[20]

Sand Pebbles was essentially a 1967 release, the same year the Arthur Penn-directed *Bonnie and Clyde* (1967, produced by and starring Warren Beatty) "became the first shot in New Hollywood's war against Geezer Hollywood."[21] Well before this watershed film, Penn gave a prophetic prediction on old Hollywood (1963): "As far as I can see, the place is killing itself. Pretty soon it'll be churning out only big blockbusters and TV series. That's all, no more actual films."[22]

Sand Pebbles' antiwar theme eliminates the film from any "geezer" category. In fact, the movie's ugly, cruel, absurdist world violence, made more disturbing by another bullet suddenly ending Holman/McQueen's life just as he finishes his "What the hell happened?" monologue, actually foreshadows the new wave of deathly dark comedy in *Bonnie and Clyde*.[23] But the blockbuster nature of Wise's *West Side Story* (1961), *The Sound of Music* (1965), and such *Sand Pebbles* follow-ups as, *Star!* (1968), *The Hindenburg* (1975), and *Star Trek—The Motion Picture*

(1979), are consistent with Penn's premise that Hollywood had become too epic bloated. The artistry of *West Side Story* and *The Sound of Music* merits exemption from Penn's period claim that filmland was "killing itself." Yet, Wise's creative misfires on the overblown post-*Sand Pebbles* pictures is certainly fuel for an autopsy of old Hollywood. Hemingway once wrote, "the great fallacy . . . [is] the wisdom of old men. They do not grow wise. They grow careful."[24] Hollywood repeating itself was Hollywood growing careful, and old.

Sand Pebbles was the final creative peak in Wise's long career. Though he would intermittently direct for many more years (essentially retiring after *Rooftops*, 1989), his later projects rarely generated the critical and/or commercial clout that the public and critics had come to expect of him since *The Set-Up*'s (1949) international success. None of these movies, however, produced quite the thud of *Star!* At the time, it seemed like a promising project. *The Sound of Music* team of Wise and Julie Andrews would reunite on another epic musical biography—a picture profiling British stage star Gertrude Lawrence.

Although Andrews and Lawrence had both risen to stardom from English musical halls, they could not otherwise have been any different; therein lies part of the inherent problem in making *Star* a success. Red flags should have immediately surfaced on how Andrews's *Mary Poppins/Sound of Music* fans would respond to her playing what another age would have diplomatically called "a rounder." Noel Coward, Lawrence's best friend/confidant, greatest costar, and occasional public "beard" (Coward was gay), had severe reservations about casting Andrews as "Gertie." After meeting with Wise and his associates, in order to get Coward's blessings for a film in which the actor/playwright's work and presence (Daniel Massey plays the theatrical legend) is almost equal to Lawrence, Coward wrote in his diary: "I heartily disapprove [of the project]. . . . We argued back and forth. Julie Andrews is to play Gertie, about as suitable as casting the late Princess Royal as DuBarry [the trampish title character of the play *Dubarry Was a Lady*]. However, she's a clever girl and will at least be charming and sing well . . . Gertrude didn't have anything like that [Andrews's voice]."[25] To protect himself in what he felt was a mistake, Coward requested that only he would provide the dialogue for his character in the picture (Coward ultimately received a screen credit for this contribution).

Star was also potentially hampered by an audience's short-term memory. Though Lawrence had once been the theatrical toast of two cities (London and New York), for the general late-1960s movie fan, she had become an obscure figure. Andrews's biographer Les Spindle observed, "When *Star!* Opened its [American] roadshow engagements in October, 1968, it was massacred by several major critics."[26] Of course, *Music* had suffered the same fate. Yet, that film was critic-proof, with positive word of mouth keeping the picture in some theaters, such as London's Dominium, for four years. History did not repeat itself on *Star*.

The harshest and ever-so-brief review, for such a major production, came from the *New York Times*, which stated, in part, "There is some sort of clash between her [Andrews's] special niceness and . . . [how] Miss Lawrence is portrayed as a kind of monster."[27] *Variety*'s lengthy and more balanced critique, which recommended the film to readers, includes a passage that inadvertently reveals both a pivotal problem (the feature's survey nature), and potentially offensive material for period audiences (including the *New York Times* reviewer): "it is a somewhat superficial scamper through her [Lawrence's] life story . . . stressing her carefree bohemianism, and occasional bawdiness, her dedication, zest for work, delight in the bright lights and stardom, her madcap capriciousness and, quite candidly, her often maddening mixture of generosity and self-interest."[28]

Despite opposing axioms on the sources of success, rare is the failure without many fathers. When resurrecting figures from the past, one can always add *outdatedness* to the list of *Star* complaints about being "superficial," having an unsympathetic subject, and casting Andrews against type. For example, *Variety*'s review of this old-school musical appeared in the same issue (July 24, 1968) with a critique of the Beatles' groundbreaking animated rock 'n' roll feature, *Yellow Submarine*. Nothing then said geezer quicker than contrasting the "Fab Four" fighting Blue Meanies in [Sergeant] Pepperland with turn-of-the-century English music halls.

Regardless, the BOMB impact of *Star* was so great one is reminded of an observation by David Niven's theater critic in *Please Don't Eat the Daisies* (1960), "There are interesting failures. There are prestigious failures, and there are financial failures but this is the sort of failure that gives failures a bad name." With a final cost of $14 million, and a yield of only a *generously* credited $4 million, Wise expressed surprise about the film's results: "I was shocked. . . . I didn't expect that at all. I said, right, what happened here? You misjudge your audience sometimes . . . I [still] think it's a damn fine film, and it deserved better than it got. Julie did some of her best work in it; she told me she worked harder on that film than on *The Sound of Music*. I always thought *Funny Girl* [1968, opening before *Star*] took the edge off us, had a negative influence on our reception."[29]

Wise's comments about *Funny Girl*, for which Barbara Streisand later won a Best Actress Oscar (in a tie with Katharine Hepburn), are provocative on several levels. This superior picture was also a musical biography about another beloved stage star contemporary of Lawrence—American comedienne/singer Fanny Brice. But while both performers made only sporadic screen appearances, Brice was more of an American pop-culture phenomenon, given the mass appeal of her radio character "Baby Snooks," a precursor to such later popular precocious comic "youngsters" as Red Skelton's "Mean Widdle Kid" and Lily Tomlin's "Edith Ann."[30] Thus, while one could argue that *Funny Girl* stole the thunder of *Star*, the pictures really profiled radically different personalities, which is at the heart of both narratives, too. Though each entertainer worked their way up from modest roots, Brice seemed to maintain the "common [every woman] touch," especially with regard to love, while Lawrence was a relationship diva. To be more bitingly specific, a pivotal component of *Funny Girl*'s mass appeal was anchored in the bittersweet Brice-as-victim relationship with a gambler (Omar Sharif) who ultimately broke her heart. In *Star*, Lawrence is the heartbreaker. Is it any wonder Andrews had trouble selling this figure?

In spite of Wise's artistic derailment with *Star* (another project he had had on the backburner for years), the film's subject matter remained consistent with the director's background. Like so many Wise pictures, it falls under the umbrella of a "portrait" or biography, and keys upon yet another strong woman whose life choices invite melodramatic relationships. Lawrence's daughter, although a minor *Star* player, joined a long list of Wise's neglected cinema children. The director also recycled a storytelling device from his *Citizen Kane* (1941) days. As *Kane* opens with a newsreel thumbnail profile of its subject, *Star* begins with a 1940s Lawrence watching a documentary of her life, which becomes a transitional device for extended flashbacks of said life. But unlike *Kane*, *Star* periodically returns to the documentary (with Lawrence as its primary audience), something Wise might have repeated more throughout the film in order to help the audience better connect with/understand Lawrence.

Richard C. Keenan's book on Wise places a great deal of the film's failure on Andrews *not* being "equal to the challenge" of playing the sophisticatedly talented but "temperamental egocentric" Lawrence.[31] But that is overstating the point. Casting Andrews only explains why the movie failed commercially, not artistically. Just because Andrews's fans did not get another Mary Poppins/Maria von Trapp does not negate a critical hit. Cinema is full of great movies about less-than-likable entertainers, from Bob Fosse's autobiographical *All That Jazz* (1979) to Martin Scorsese's profile of boxer Jake La Motta, *Raging Bull* (1980). No, Wise just spread his Lawrence profile too thin. Besides, even if one keeps faulting Andrews, Wise would ultimately take the blame by default, since he felt directing was best defined by casting.

Twentieth Century Fox attempted to salvage something from *Star* by trimming over thirty minutes and reissuing it as *Those Were the Happy Times*. But these exercises produced no "happy times," though

Robert Wise at the time of Star! *(1968).*

viewers can rejoice over the studio's decision to not go with their first choice for a new title, *Gertie Was a Lady*. Either way, Wise, Andrews, and Fox still had a major flop.

Wise's next project, an adaptation of Michael Crichton's science-fiction novel *The Andromeda Strain* (1971), was a modest critical hit. Mining cautionary tale material explored in many mainstream science-fiction films, such as Stanley Kubrick's *2001: A Space Odyssey* (1968), *Andromeda* is about mankind going back to basics to counteract a threatening technology created to protect humans.

The "andromeda strain" of the title references a deadly micro-organism that has come to Earth via a contaminated satellite crashing near the desert village of Piedmont, New Mexico. The movie is at its noir-like thriller best in the opening half hour, as the government sends two scientists into what has become a dead small town. Doctors Stone (Arthur Hill) and Hall (James Olson), protective spacesuit attire notwithstanding, are not unlike Claire Trevor stumbling onto the dead bodies in Wise's celebrated film noir *Born to Kill* (1947). The Piedmont victims are even laid out in provocatively symbolic ways reminiscent of noir dead, such as a sexy bare-breasted girl adorned with a peace medallion, or an old army veteran inexplicitly wearing his World War I uniform—as if representing a delayed footnote/casualty to the first human conflict to introduce poison gas. Now, something similar to a poison gas has killed his small town. (There is an exhilaration in recognizing a signature genre scene and/or situation effectively replicated in a seemingly diverse film form. Such finesse suggests a major artist at work, able to tap into ancient/eternal creative springs which always engage viewers: danger, death, fear of the unknown, and the science-fiction mantra—fear of the future.)

Also along noir lines, a mystery exists among the *Andromeda* dead. Why did two such diverse Piedmont inhabitants survive: a crying baby and an old wino? (Later, we learn the alien strain had no impact on individuals with high or low blood acidity.) But the movie fails to maintain this adrenalin high. Once the action moves to a top-secret multilevel underground laboratory in Nevada, with a scientific team attempting to avert an earthly Armageddon by concocting an answer to the andromeda strain, the film flirts with C-Span talkiness. The narrative only picks up near the movie's conclusion, when the scientists must fight the laboratory's built-in nuclear self-destruct mechanism, originally designed to save civilization from an extraterrestrial epidemic. Ironically, the heat from such a blast would have compounded the problem. If science-fiction history teaches one thing, it is that man-made fail-safe systems inevitably fail man.

Andromeda's slight success was a result of several factors, starting with the bookend thriller scenes that bracket the otherwise lumbering narrative. Second, it never hurts to adapt a best seller. Whether fans of the book love or hate the film, they frequently see the cinema translation. And though one often hears the old chestnut, "the book was better," some reader/viewers preferred Wise's film. For example, the movie won by default with the *New York Times* critic Roger Greenspun, who described the source material as "Michael Crichton's dreadful novel."[32]

A third plus for the 1971 film was simply timing. Though fears over alien bacterial contamination are basic science-fiction components, there remained, for some individuals, lingering anxiety and/or anger at the National Aeronautics and Space Administration for the potential danger in retrieving "moon rocks" from the 1969 lunar landing. And the 1960s interest in all things space related would also have worked in *Andromeda*'s favor. Indeed, one of the winning elements of the novel, notwithstanding Greenspun's aside, is the mock-scientific foundation in which Crichton anchors the book. Though the work's think-tank foundations and "facts" are often pure fiction, it reads like a scientific documentary, which intrigued realist Wise.

The most obvious *Andromeda* link to Wise's oeuvre, however, is the film's suggestion that the U.S. military had more than merely the safety of humanity in mind concerning the containment of the "andromeda strain." Wise later said, "the bottom line of what interested me . . . was that I could make a film that was anti-biological warfare."[33] The director bolstered a message that had been mere subtext in the novel.

Unlike his previous run of big-budget pictures, Wise followed *Andromeda* with the modestly produced love story, *Two People* (1973). But as with *Sand Pebbles*, *People* had an antiwar message. An American Vietnam War deserter (Peter Fonda) has been in hiding overseas. Paralleling his decision to return home and face prison in the United States, he meets a model (Lindsay Wagner) on a train from Marrakech to Casablanca. Given this romantic setting and their diverseness, they naturally fall in love. During a brief Paris sojourn, their affair is consummated, and she lobbies unsuccessfully for him to remain abroad. The movie concludes with their return to an uncertain future in the United States.

As an admirer of Wise, antiwar films, and love stories in general, I wanted to admire *People*. And, as if recognizing the Penn message about "geezer Hollywood," Wise had again taken some story chances with a tightly budgeted message movie, as he periodically did throughout his career. That is the good news. The bad news is, as with *Two For the Seesaw* (1962), there is little chemistry between the romantic leads. Add stilted dialogue, and this slight picaresque road picture, despite a game attempt at cause célèbre-type bonding, seems, in *Variety*'s one-word summary: "interminable."[34]

Still, *People* might have played more effectively with a pared-down script and a less clichéd use of romantic settings and musical soundtrack cues. While the *New York Times* simply called it "a very silly movie," as if aping *Variety*'s comment, in which *People* is likened to "a parody of '50s foreign films," the Marx Brothers had spoofed both Casablanca the city, and the romantic Bogart movie, as early as *A Night in Casablanca* (1946).[35] Worse yet, *People*'s antiwar theme, as it related to Vietnam, was passé thanks to movies such as Wise's *Sand Pebbles*. As historian Gideon Rose later wrote, by 1973, "most Americans just wanted the whole subject [Vietnam] to go away—and few really cared if the South [Vietnamese] went with it."[36] Even Fonda's touching plan to somehow revisit Vietnam and apologize to the family of his victim, whose death was his responsibility, suggests melodramatic recycling. This story thread is reminiscent of Ernst Lubitsch's moving *Broken Lullaby* (1932, first called *The Man I Killed*). *Two People*, with poor reviews and a no longer timely Vietnam theme, received weak distribution and remains today one of Wise's least-seen movies.

The *Broken Lullaby* tie to *People* is fitting, however, for an antiwar liberal of Wise's generation. Just as he fleetingly linked a new age danger of biological warfare with his elderly *Andromeda* World War I veteran/victim, many artists have used this earlier conflict as an antiwar lightning rod. Naturally, all wars produce sad commentaries against armed conflict. That being said, several circumstances stack the deck in favor of World War I being the greatest fiction and film tutorial in any antiwar movement. So, what is there about the First World War? Critic Deirdre Donahue once summarized: "The extraordinary carnage of World War I did not just kill men. The violence destroyed accepted ideas about valor, duty, class, human behavior, and whether the future even mattered."[37]

Napoleon Bonaparte believed that "to understand the man you have to know what was happening in the world when he was twenty.[38] Wise, born the year World War I began (1914), approached and passed twenty in a 1930s artistic climate obsessed with watershed antiwar works filtered through the First World War. These included Erich Remarque's *All Quiet on the Western Front* (1928, adapted to the screen, 1930), Ernest Hemingway's *A Farewell to Arms* (1929, first adapted to the screen, 1932), Lubitsch's *Broken Lullaby* (1932), Humphrey Cobb's *Paths of Glory* (1935, adapted to the screen, 1957), director Jean Renoir's *Grand Illusion* (1937), and his fellow French filmmaker Abel Gance's *That They May Live* (1938).[39]

Appropriately, Wise's next movie would actually deal with this volatile between-the-world-wars period—the immediate events leading up to the famous *Hindenburg* disaster (1937), where the iconic Nazi dirigible of that name erupts into a fireball as it attempts to anchor at a Lakehurst, New Jersey, airport. Wise's film, *The Hindenburg* (1975), explores the still unsolved mystery of what caused the tragedy in which thirty-five of ninety-seven on board died. Recorded live by newsreel cameramen chronicling the ship's transatlantic crossing, the haunting footage of the burning dirigible is the historical hook of the movie, as well as the reason Wise became involved with the project.

Sadly, a more personal tragedy shattered the Wise household. The filmmaker's beloved wife died of cancer on September 22, 1975, after a ten-month illness. The former actress/dancer Patricia Doyle, who the then editor had met on the set of *My Favorite Wife* (1940), was sixty. Her very brief *Los Angeles Times* obituary (two short paragraphs) only cited one of her screen appearances: "a share-cropper's daughter in [director] John Ford's 'Grapes of Wrath' [1940]."[40] Her husband's career and their family, son Rob and two small grandchildren, Jenifer and Patrick (named for her), had swallowed up her life. Patricia's workaholic partner had turned the couple into movie gypsies during the last two decades of her life, with on-location shoots around the globe. But they loved to travel and frequently prolonged their time abroad after a picture wrapped. In fact, their extended Pacific production on *Sand Pebbles* kept them much closer to the Vietnam War than their navy son.

Ironically, Patricia's fatal illness came at a time when their only child was finally settling into a permanent career track. Now in his early thirties, Rob had pinballed through several jobs. In a letter to the Wises' friends, Monica and Jud Kinsberg, written two months before Patricia's diagnosis, the director reveals both a major positive development in Rob's life, and how Wise was a supportive but demanding father: "Rob is finally winding up his course at Brooks Photographic Institute up at Santa Barbara, and within a short time, we'll see about getting him into a camera department at one of the studios, starting at the bottom as a loader in the dark room. . . . He [Rob] talked at some length to Bob Surtees, my cameraman, and Bob told me later he was very impressed with Rob and his knowledge of photography, and predicted that he would do fine. So now we have to get him into the thing [Hollywood] in a professional manner."[41]

Prior to Patricia's illness, the Wises relaxed like many American couples, by watching films and entertaining friends. But both activities assumed a high-profile perspective if one was a multiple Oscar-winning director. For example, the following letter excerpt (November 25, 1974) is from director Blake Edwards, the husband of Julie Andrews: "Julie and I will arrive in Los Angeles on 7 December and will be there for 10 days. If possible, we would love to get together with you and Pat. We will be staying at the Bel Air Hotel. Julie sends her love."[42]

Screenings often involved borrowing private prints from equally prominent pals, such as producer/film executive Richard Zanuck, who sent Wise a copy of *The Sugarland Express* (1974, Steven Spielberg's first theatrical feature), prior to its release (December 1973). Zanuck's production company had just scored one of the biggest moneymaking movies of all time, *The Sting* (1973), and would soon light up the box office again with *Jaws* (1975). Though the Zanuck-produced *Sugarland Express* would not be a commercial smash, this based-on-fact melodrama about a young couple (Goldie Hawn and Michael Sacks) fleeing to Sugarland, Texas, to reclaim a son taken by welfare authorities, would go on to be critically acclaimed. Wise's prerelease thank-you note to Zanuck, besides being a dead-on critique of the picture, actually reveals more information on a subtextual level. In addition to demonstrating Wise is at home among the A-listers, the *Sugarland* story suggests the filmmaker enjoyed viewing movies very similar to the sort he made. *Sugarland* is a biography/family melodrama picture, with a strong nourish woman/child lead. and a true child as victim. *Sugarland* would not look out of place in a Wise filmography. The director's note to Zanuck said, in part: "I was particularly pleased with the range and scope of Goldie Hawn's performance. She is obviously on her way to becoming a major star and SUGARLAND will be an important step for her in that direction."[43]

Interestingly, as Wise's filmmaking career began to wind down, he watched even more films. There is a fascinating symmetry to this cinema life. As a boy back in Connersville, Indiana, he practically lived at his small-town movie theaters. And after a long career making pictures, he returned to nonstop viewing. But this is not an obvious evolution. When Red Skelton, a Hoosier contemporary, felt television was shutting him out, he declared a personal war on the medium and minimized his viewing.[44]

In addition to Wise's ongoing movie avocation/occupation, the filmmaker often acted as a Hollywood ambassador at large, from visiting Russia (1971) as part of a Soviet-United States cultural exchange, to serving as president of the Director's Guild from 1971 through 1975. Wise coupled these activities with generous gifts of time and money to several liberal charitable organizations, such as the American Civil Liberties Union; and in 1966 the director established the Robert E. Wise Foundation, which provided loans and monetary requests to worthy causes in the greater Los Angeles area. In addition, from Wise's first film as a director, *The Curse of the Cat People* (1944), he had been making his movies and himself available to various civic-minded organizations. These events ranged from psychiatrists fascinated by Wise's depiction of childhood anxiety in *Curse* to showing *The*

Red Skelton in Watch the Birdie *(1950). Robert Wise's fellow Hoosier struggled with the decline of his career.*

Haunting (1963) to a University of California at Los Angeles film class taught by historian Arthur Knight.[45] The Robert Wise Collection of private papers at the University of Southern California is a testament to the director's passionate belief in both pictures and people.

Unlike the a bitterness Skelton felt toward an entertainment industry he "read" as abandoning him, Wise remained optimistic about most new directions in Hollywood. And as he had done throughout his life, he constantly made himself available to fans and/or students of film, whatever their age or their profession. Many of these letters have been referenced in this book. (On a personal note: as a film professor in Wise's home state I can vouch for the director's patient correspondence with countless college students wanting to do an essay about this humble homegrown artist.)[46]

Wise was an upbeat person and rarely showed anger, unless he felt associates were not acting professionally. One such veiled complaint can be tied to a film-industry development about which even the passive Wise was bothered. In a letter from his longtime friend, director Mark Robson (his editing colleague from the RKO Val Lewton days), shared: "Frankly, many aspects of [the still in production] VON RYAN'S EXPRESS, 1965] are a pain in the ass."[47] Robson was both the director and executive producer of this World War II prisoner-of-war escape picture, which would be a critical and commercial hit. But the challenge of working with Frank Sinatra had soured things for Robson. Wise's response to Robson's letter covered several topics, including raising money to give the "[Barry] Goldwater gang a fight for their money."[48] (Goldwater was the extremely conservative Republican candidate for president in 1964. He lost to incumbent President Lyndon Johnson that fall.) With regard to the *Express*, Wise added knowingly: "Sorry to hear so many aspects of your picture are a pain in the ass . . . [But] I have some idea of what you're going through. It's a goddam shame; but I hear marvelous reports on the film you're getting, so that obviously helps to balance things somewhat."[49]

Wise was the ideal friend; he commiserated without burdening Robson with his own similar problems. Yes, Wise knew "pain in the

ass" interactions with stars, such as his clashes with Spencer Tracy on
Tribute to a Bad Man (1956), Burt Lancaster on *Run Silent, Run Deep*
(1958), Christopher Plummer on *The Sound of Music* (1965, which was
in production at the same time as *Von Ryan's Express*), and McQueen
on *The Sand Pebbles* (1967). More significantly, though Wise's batting
average was excellent in these situations, from having diva Tracy fired
to leveraging Lancaster's costar (Clark Gable) into the director's camp.
However, Wise recognized that modern stars were starting to thin the
veteran filmmaker ranks. For example, Frank Capra's problem with
Glenn Ford on *Pocketful of Miracles* (1961) was a key factor in Capra's
decision to retire. In the director's memoir, *Frank Capra: The Name
above the Title* (1971), he confessed to his public what Hollywood
insiders had long known: "*Miracles* was not the film that I set out to
make; it was the picture I chose to make for fear of losing a few bucks.
And by that choice I sold out the artistic integrity that had been my
trademark for forty years. . . . Glenn Ford made me lick his boots—I
had lost that precious quality that endows dreams with purport and
purpose. I had lost my courage."[50] Leo McCarey, who influenced young
Wise the RKO editor on *My Favorite Wife* (1940), also walked away
from directing after an intolerable situation with William Holden on
Satan Never Sleeps (1962).[51]

    While good filmmakers focus on stories over stars, these
developments had Wise keying even more on making his later movies
the star, or as he phrased it for a *Christian Science Monitor* article
headline on his dirigible disaster picture: "'Hindenburg'—Star of New
Spy Film."[52] Wise later "bristled" at the suggestion his *Hindenburg*,
this *Titanic* of the sky, was "getting on the cycle of disaster films," yet,
that is the most logical pigeonhole for the picture.[53] And the early
1970s were peppered with this genre, including *Airport* (1970), *The
Poseidon Adventure* (1972), *The Towering Inferno* (1974), and Robson's
Earthquake (1974). But as with Vietnam War subjects being passé
by the time of Wise's *Two People*, the 1970s disaster movie craze
was beginning to run its course prior to *The Hindenburg*'s release.

Earthquake had been the ultimate capstone for the genre. The decade's disaster hits had chronicled terror in the sky and below the sea; *Earthquake* allowed one to be terrorized in the discomfort of his/her own home.

For a midwestern take on the disaster cycle being over after *Earthquake*, note the following year's (1975) *Indianapolis News* review of the reissued French dark comedy, *King of Hearts* (1966), which ran three months before *The Hindenburg* opened: "Philippe de Broca's 'King of Hearts' is a delightful film demonstrating that movies don't have

Above: *A historical horror revisited—the finale of* The Hindenburgh *(1975).*
Left: *Robert Wise (right) and James Cagney on location for* Tribute to a Bad Man *(1956).*

to be horrible to be exciting . . . this eight-year-old film differs from today's disaster-centered movies in having perspective, some note of hope, instead of catastrophe and nihilism."[54]

Wise's picture was hammered by the critics, from the *New York Times* calling it "brainless" and "pricelessly funny at the wrong times," to *Variety* defining *Hindenburg* as a "total downer," going on to note: "Dull and formula scripting, a lack of real empathy and phoned-in acting shoot down some good though unspectacular special effects. Robert Wise's production is too little, too late."[55] Welles's comment on filmmaking, "A terribly expensive paint box," could again be applied to another late Wise movie that generated neither compensating box office nor solid reviews.

In the conspiracy-happy 1970s (the era of Watergate), Wise had initially been attracted to *Hindenburg's* backstory: Was this air tragedy the result of sabotage by an anti-Nazi crew member? But it became a special-effects movie. Granted, the film's final fiery ten minutes, which includes actual newsreel footage of the disaster, were stunning enough to help win Academy Awards for both Best Visual Effects (Albert Whitlock and Glen Robinson) and Best Sound Effects (Peter Berkos). Yet, as Wise author Richard C. Keenan summarized, "Whitlock and Robinson could not turn *Hindenburg* into a hit. In a film with a running time of 125 minutes, technical quality can't be expected to carry the entire picture."[56]

Patricia's battle against cancer for much of 1975 (she died three months before the Christmas season release of *Hindenburg*), made Wise's long involvement on the project, stretching back to 1973, all the more gut wrenching. But for the stoic workaholic filmmaker, the movie was also an escape/balm against the pain, and there was no marketing misuse of the tragedy (such as "grieving artist's latest work"). Just as the Wises had lived quietly, Patricia's passing was nearly invisible. Still, it seems odd when the longtime spouse of an active four-time Oscar winner dies and the normally very thorough *New York Times* and *Los Angeles Times* barely blink.[57] The logical "read" is that Wise's philosophy of avoid the limelight in order to better focus on film had played itself out yet again. But the media missed an opportunity. Wise, a perennial feminist filmmaker often operating out of a melodrama genre once designated as "women's pictures," loses the first lady of his life and it generates less verbiage than a family grocery list?

For all of Wise's lunch-bucket professional discipline, he and Patricia had lived the good life. The director's percentage deal on *The Sound of Music* (1965) had made him a millionaire. His 1960s cinema successes had given him final cut on his pictures, as well as a Universal Studio bungalow that was really a "mini-mansion that once belonged to Cary Grant."[58] Wise drove a Jaguar, the couple owned a specially designed California beach house, and were in a position to request special menu additions at their favorite local restaurant (Malibu's Sandcastle), asking that the catch-of-the-day "simply [be] charcoal-broiled [and] served with lemon and butter."[59]

Curiously, Wise's first film after his wife's death, *Audrey Rose* (1977), dealt with the subject of reincarnation. This melodramatic thriller chronicles the life of a married couple (Marsha Mason and John Beck) after a stranger (Anthony Hopkins) tells them their daughter (Susan Swift) is his twelve-year-old child reincarnated. Since Hopkins's daughter died in a fiery accident (shades of *Hindenburg*?), and the Mason/Beck girl is having horrific nightmares along these lines, the evidence seems to suggest that the child is reincarnated. Among Wise's late work, *Audrey Rose* is the director's only picture that feels like a reflection of his central credo as an artist: "In the constant search for material, the first point the picture maker has to consider is whether it excites him personally. It must be something he personally feels strongly about, something he wants to put on film."[60]

Though the reviews for the uneven thriller were decidedly mixed, this biographer would side with *Variety*'s critique, that "'Audrey Rose' is Wise's best film in some years."[61] Just as *Hindenburg* followed several signature disaster movies, *Rose* was sometimes criticized for being an *Exorcist* (1973) knockoff, given the film's phenomenal critical and

commercial success. For example, Vincent Canby's *New York Times'*
Rose review worked hardest at making this copycat claim: "The soul
of the movie is that of 'The Exorcist' instantly recycled. . . . It even
appears that Susan Swift . . . has been photographed to resemble [*The
Exorcist*'s young heroine] Linda Blair at her most bedeviled."[62] Canby's
comments are ludicrous. Yes, both pictures address disturbed preteen
girls in a horror/thriller context. Yet, neither the claims related to Blair,
nor *Rose* as a quick rip-off of *The Exorcist*, hold up. One might just as
well posit that Wise's film of an anxiety-ridden preteen in *The Curse of
the Cat People* (1944) spawned *The Exorcist*. *Rose* is a solid thriller about
a subject (reincarnation) that had been under explored at the time.

*A standard Robert Wise scenerio--a struggling mother/wife (Marsha Mason), a victimized
child (Susan Swift), and a stern father (John Beck) who cannot think outside the box in*
Audrey Rose *(1977).*

But the film suffers, at times, from slow or plodding pacing. *Rose*'s best attribute, after its quirky storyline, is Mason's performance.

A thorough examination of *Rose*'s plot points doubles as a Wise tutorial: a vulnerable child, a passionate mother feeling powerless, a father whose narrow-mindedness jeopardizes said child, and a family melodrama tucked into a horror/thriller. Also, the film's portrayal of the medical establishment is similar to Wise's typical take on the military complex—insensitivity to the rights of the individual. In addition, the director's proclivity for realism is showcased in such key scenes as the first-person camera footage of the car wreck/fire that kills Hopkins's daughter.

Just as Wise made *Haunting* (1963) at a time when he had tackled all the conventional genres, one could argue he again returned to the horror/thriller comfort zone of *Rose* after unsuccessful forays into the less-traveled realms of the antiwar love story (*Two People*) and the disaster picture (*Hindenburg*). Moreover, there would have been a pleasing symmetry to Wise's career (*Curse* to *Rose*), if he had retired after the latter movie. Instead, there would be two final directing projects, a decade apart: the bloated *Star Trek—The Motion Picture* (1979) and the modest *Rooftops* (1989), a compound genre mix of truly Wise dimensions: biracial love story/musical/problem film.

Star Trek was a television movie project that Paramount decided to turn into a theatrical release. Wise was only brought in after the scope of the movie necessitated a director with his epic film experience. Inspired by Gene Roddenberry's beloved television series of the same name, this movie adaptation would be the first of many feature films drawn from the small-screen program. *Star Trek* is now an American science-fiction entertainment franchise that has produced hundreds of novels, dozens of computer and video games, traveling museum exhibits of props, and several more television series follow-ups.

Paradoxically, given both Wise's disdain for television, and the fact he was frequently involved in overseas film productions during *Star Trek*'s original television run, he initially knew little about the series.

But just as the director's first wife had once advised him, Wise now received helpful input from his television-viewing bride of two years, Millicent Franklin, whom he married on January 29, 1977. She was a major "Trekkie" fan, with Wise even giving her a cameo in the picture, and sometimes lobbied for *Star Trek* basics. For example, with most of the series television stars reprising their roles in the movie (including William Shatner as now Admiral Kirk, DeForest Kelley as Doctor Leonard "Bones" McCoy, and James Doohan as Montgomery "Scotty" Scott), only Leonard Nimoy (Spock) balked at rejoining the USS *Enterprise* crew. Wise was fine with recasting the part. But according to Hollywood Hoosier historian David L. Smith, who interviewed Wise on the set of *Star Trek*, the director fully credited Millicent for insisting that Nimoy must return as Spock.[63] Consequently, negotiations continued with the actor, and he became an integral part of *Star Trek*'s big-screen rebirth, including directing one of the best subsequent sequels *Star Trek III: The Search for Spock* (1984).

Wise's *Star Trek* chronicles the reuniting of the "Starship Enterprise" crew to intercept a mysterious potentially lethal cloud-like entity approaching Earth. In the pop-culture aftermath of *Star War*'s (1977) homage to the 1930s B-movie serials, *Star Trek* was a special-effects driven epic even before Wise came onboard, and it proved a troubling shoot for the veteran filmmaker. With *Star Trek* creator Roddenberry producing the picture, and actors who had played their parts for several years voicing strong views on these characters, Wise felt like he had very little input. But his greatest sense of powerlessness was coupled to the picture's technical side: "*Star Trek* was a very trying experience because I had so many things that were beyond my control in terms of special effects."[64] Wise was even more candid in a later letter to an Ontario Film Institute official: "It was a very complex, 'messy' [the script was being rewritten throughout the shoot] kind of picture to make, as it turned out, and isn't one of my happiest film engagements of all-time; so when I hear some positive reaction to it, it is particularly rewarding."[65] What was worse for Wise, at the time, was that some critics, such as the *New York Time*'s Vincent Canby, zeroed in on the director's runaway helplessness: "I can't imagine what there was for him [Wise] to do after telling the actors where to stand."[66]

With special effects promised but not delivered by the original production house, a $15 million budget ballooned to $44 million! But over time, the loyalty of "Trekkies" (the fans actually prefer the designation "Trekkers") produced $56 million in rental fees.[67] Still, for an artist who once prided himself on economy, Wise was shocked by the runaway costs. There was also the irony that nearly thirty years before he had created a science-fiction classic memorial, in part, for its minimal special effects, *The Day the Earth Stood Still* (1951). Oddly enough, between the loyalty of "Trekkers," and Wise's picture being the first feature film installment of the franchise, the movie remains, when box office numbers are adjusted for inflation, the most financially successful *Star Trek* theatrical movie.[68]

The picture's opening reviews were mixed, with *Variety*'s critique actually championing Wise's direction.[69] But the general critical consensus, both then and now, is best summarized in pop-culture film historian Leonard Maltin's later capsule review: "Slow, talky, and derivative, somewhat redeemed by terrific special effects . . . still, mainly for purists."[70] Maltin's assessment would also be applicable to *Hindenburg*; without the special effects reference, one could recycle "slow, talky, and derivative" to much of Wise's post-*Sand Pebbles* productions.

Wise's career as a major director essentially ended with *Star Trek*. Ten years later his low-budget problem-film musical (New York gangs and drug abuse), *Rooftops*, opened and closed with no fanfare. As Roger Ebert's respectful but funereal *Chicago Sun Times* review suggested, while this was familiar Wise territory, the director's flair for mixing music and stylized realism was gone: "Wise [is] one of the great names in Hollywood history, and of his many films, *West Side Story* is the one that comes to mind [in conjunction with *Rooftops*] . . . [*Story*] was also a love story set against a slum war, with dance and music. But all the conventions worked together . . . *Rooftops* comes alive during the passages of music and dance, which feel like those moments in a musical when the characters burst into song but then it tries to fit those flights of fantasy into a melodrama about drugs. It's too tight a squeeze."[71]

Wise's service to the film community escalated as his directing career wound down. His post-1980s activities included serving as president of the Academy of Motion Picture Arts and Sciences (1984 to 1987), being on the board of directors for the American Film Institute (plus choiring AFI's Center for Advanced Studies), and serving on the National Council of the Arts and Sciences.

During these years, Wise, the Thalberg Award recipient (1967) and four-time Oscar-winner (1961, 1965), was frequently honored for his body of work. These awards included: the Directors Guild's D. W. Griffith Award for outstanding lifetime achievement (1988), the United States' National Medal of Arts (1992, presented by then President George H. W. Bush, in a White House ceremony), the AFI's Life Achievement Award (1998), and the Society of Motion Picture and Television Art Directors career award for "outstanding contribution to cinematic imagery" (1998). Throughout this period, Martin Scorsese, the AFI recipient from 1997, was a constant champion of the director's legacy.

The senior Wise also kept himself cinematically current in a host of other ways, from tirelessly responding to countless inquiries about movie history (be the researcher a college student or a documentary filmmaker), to supervising the directorial debut of twenty-three-year-old actor Emilio Estevez in *Wisdom* (1986, for which Wise was also the executive producer). Additional late credits included an acting cameo in John Landis's *The Stupids* (1996), and directing an award-winning television movie, *A Storm in Summer* (2000, Daytime Emmy category of Outstanding Children's Special).

Wise's passion for watching movies and travel continued with his second wife, Millicent. Their union was nearly as enduring as Wise's marriage to his beloved Patricia. But even before his Hollywood career waned, some of Wise's most personally satisfying trips brought him back to Indiana. On June 2, 1968, Franklin College awarded him an honorary Doctor of Fine Arts degree—three and a half decades after the Great Depression forced him to drop out of this same Hoosier college.

In conjunction with Franklin's recognition, there was a "Robert Wise Day" in both his nearby hometown of Connersville (June 4, 1968), and the following day in his birthplace of Winchester. The Indiana capstone, however, came November 3, 1990, when he attended the dedication of the Robert E. Wise Center for Performing Arts at the new Connersville High School. With friends, family, and former classmates present, he put this honor on the same level as the Best Director/Best Picture Academy Awards he won for *West Side Story* and *The Sound of Music.* (Another Indiana honor was bestowed on Wise in 1992, when he was named the first recipient of the Indianapolis-based annual Heartland Film Festival's Crystal Heart Career Achievement Award.) Novelist Thomas Wolfe was wrong—you can go home again.

Wise died on September 14, 2005, a few days after celebrating a joyous ninety-first birthday with friends and family. Ever the consummate yet unassuming artist, his movies are his memorial—a legacy embracing a litany of genres. The flavor of this often enigmatic man is best found in his films.

Epilogue

"Trust the tale, not the teller."
D. H. LAWRENCE

The *New York Times's* long, laudatory obituary of Robert Wise poignantly closed with a telling commentary on a quote by the director about Orson Welles, for whom he edited *Citizen Kane* (1941): "Wise said, 'And to think that Welles was 25, and it was his first film. Remarkable really.' (Mr. Wise neglected to mention that he was less than a year older than Welles.)"[1]

In Wise's lengthy memorable movie career, he never lost that humility. You can see it in his voluminous correspondence with everyone, from celebrities to schoolchildren; you can hear it in the voice-over commentary tracks to his classics on digital video disc; and you can feel it in the empathy with which he imbued so many of his disenfranchised screen characters.[2] A Wise biographer could wax too poetic about his lack of ego, but it would be a natural fault into which to fall. Even the most exaggerated "everyman" claim might be comically qualified by recycling a comment from Mark Twain, a humorist beloved by the filmmaker. In the opening of the *Adventures of Huckleberry Finn*, the title character says of his "biographer" ("Mr. Mark Twain"): "he told the truth, mainly. There were things which he stretched, but mainly he told the truth."[3] Still, it would be difficult for a Wise profiler to stretch the truly self-effacing nature of the man.

Wise's humbleness, and often intuitive approach to filmmaking, did not, however, always serve him well with auteur theory critics—a movement in cinema studies in which a director is seen as "author" of a film. Since the theory's 1960s popularization in the United States by Andrew Sarris, Wise's status as a true auteur (an artist with a consistent personal vision) has often been called into question. For example, while Sarris includes Wise in his auteur bible, *The American Cinema: Directors and Directions, 1929–1968*, it seems a reluctant inclusion: Sarris notes that Wise's "temperament is vaguely liberal, his style vaguely realistic; but after *The Sound of Music* [1965] and *The Sand Pebbles* [1966] the stylistic signature of Robert Wise is indistinct."[4] Sadly, Wise and many of his scholarly supporters have often seemed to acquiesce to a misguided left-handed compliment about his being a craftsman, *not* an auteur. For example, in a lengthy interview from 1998, here is Wise's response, in part, to the question, "Is there a Robert Wise style in films?": "I approach each genre in the cinematic style that I think is appropriate . . . for that genre. So I would no more have done *The Sound of Music* in the thinking and approach that I did in *I Want to Live!* [1958] for anything. So that's why I don't have a singular mark but I justify that by saying that it's just because of the number of genres I've done and the cinematic style that's proper for each one."[5]

But as novelist D. H. Lawrence suggests, sometimes one has to "trust the tale, not the teller." This study has documented an overall consistency to Wise's central characters, and to his cinematic world in general, that links the majority of his movies. Even as he juggled an assortment of genres, his filmography coalesced around a mix of noir, melodrama, and the profile picture. *Ironically*, as noted earlier in the book, French film critic/director Francois Truffaut, the 1950s *father* of the auteur theory, had always defined Wise in this manner. In fact, part of the original thrust to the "theory" was to celebrate neglected B directors of the 1940s (such as Wise) who managed to create a signature cinema despite being tied to a studio picture-by-assignment system.

While Wise's post-*Sand Pebbles* movies struggle to maintain the same grab-you-by-the-lapels intensity he brought to early works such as *The Set-Up* (1949) and *The Day the Earth Stood Still* (1952), the underlying characters and concerns therein still remain consistent. This is apparent in an interview he gave for one of his last films, the reincarnation thriller, *Audrey Rose* (1977). When asked whether he believed in reincarnation and other psychic phenomenon, Wise's open-ended answer applied equally to other films from the beginning of his directing career, where a departed spirit (Simone Simon) befriends a

The party girl phase of Barbara Graham's (Susan Hayward) short life, I Want to Live! *(1958)*

little girl (Ann Carter) in *The Curse of the Cat People* (1944), a guilt-ridden murderer (Henry Daniell) believes a victim (Boris Karloff) has returned in *The Body Snatcher* (1945), and a Christ-like alien called Carpenter/Klaatu (Michael Rennie) offers mankind a second chance in *The Day the Earth Stood Still*: "I'm a firm believer in the possibility [of reincarnation]. . . . Let me say that I'm a great believer that there is something beyond the reality that we have here on Earth, in the day to day things that we can see, feel, hear and touch."[6]

The somber fate of *Audrey Rose*'s title character, apparently to be played out in tragic variations throughout time, also mirrors Wise's standard nonpopulist, or dark movie, mindset about a malaise of life. That is, he often accents the *common* when examining the "common man." His child or childlike passionate protagonists are often fighting to make sense of a world that either does not care, or seems out to destroy them. While some Wise antiheroes succeed against the odds, such as boxer Rocky Graziano (Paul Newman) in *Somebody Up There Likes Me* (1956), or *The Sound of Music*'s Maria (Julie Andrews), more Wise characters are chewed up by the system. A list of his screen victims might start with another boxer, Robert Ryan's journeyman fighter in *The Set-Up*, and then most hauntingly include the Barbara Graham (Susan Hayward) execution of *I Want to Live!*, Jake Holman's (Steve McQueen) even more disturbing demise to end *Sand Pebbles*, and the concluding death (again) of the girl now known as Audrey Rose. Fittingly, the fate of many of these Wise shadowland, tormented characters could be drawn from the title of the first picture he also produced, *Odds Against Tomorrow* (1959). This is "Wise-ville."

Consistent with this naturalistic philosophy, one of feminist Wise's late unrealized projects was a Mae West biography film (to have starred Bette Midler).[7] Had such a profile picture been made, Wise would have had a field day choosing among such equally cynical West life lessons as, "When women go wrong, men go right after them" (*She Done Him Wrong*, 1933), or "It's not the men in my life but the life in my men" (*I'm No Angel*, 1933). (West was at the peak of her career when Wise first came to Hollywood; in 1968 the director attempted to produce a television special with the comedienne, *An Evening with Mae West*, but there was little network interest.)

Another unrealized Wise film, an adaptation of Jack Finney's time-travel novel, *Time and Again*, would have engaged the director in both his fascination with this subject, and his persistent subtext cinema question: "Is man capable of achieving permanent progress?" Earlier in the book (see chapter 8) I documented that Wise had written a telling note on his personal *The Day the Earth Stood Still* script— linking Klaatu to Twain's time-traveling title character in *A Connecticut*

A Mae West publicity still (circa 1933), the year Robert Wise arrived in Hollywood.

Yankee in King Arthur's Court.[8] Both enlightened individuals offer a
more primitive people a better life. Twain's tale ends in a bloodbath,
while Wise's story has a cliffhanger conclusion: Will the threat of an
alien Armageddon force Earth to change its violent ways? Probably
not, but Wise usually has a central figure, such as the narrator of H. G.
Wells's *The Time Machine*, who suggests that even if man's Darwinian
tendencies point the species toward negative and/or self-destructive
behavior, the individual should still strive to live as if he could make a
difference. Wise examples would stretch from the patriotic prostitute
(Simone Simon) in *Mademoiselle Fifi* (1944), to Anthony Hopkins's
father figure in *Audrey Rose*—attempting to reconnect with and comfort
each reincarnation of his daughter though she seems fated to forever be
the victim.

As a child, Wise thrilled to the silent swashbuckling adventure films
of Douglas Fairbanks Sr. Wise's more realistically grounded pictures,
and the man himself—described by David Robinson as having "less the
air of Hollywood than of an unusually kindly bank-manager"—seems
distant from the flashy, boy-hero Fairbanks.[9] Yet, the crusading spirit of
Fairbanks's films is more than alive in the problem-film attitude of so
many Wise movies. Borrowing a line from cinema producer/professor
James Schamus, Wise "tends to gravitate to the kid in the corner"[10]
But Wise's cornered kids often fail. The director's philosophy was in
accord with a paraphrasing of blacklisted writer Dalton Trumbo's ironic
comments on the U.S. Constitution: "The document only guarantees
the pursuit of happiness, not happiness itself."

Wise's often painful stories about the disenfranchised, exasperated
by age, gender and/or racial prejudice, chronicle why the more
hopeful Frank Capra pictures, such as *It's a Wonderful Life* (1946),
were called "*fantasies* of good will."[11] A more contemporary take
on Wise's bittersweet movie milieu might be taken from Annette
Bening's comments on her character in *The Kids Are All Right* (2010), a
melodramatic gay family comedy about an unfaithful partner. Bening
and her screen partner (Julianne Moore) decide to stay together. But

things are far from perfect. Bening observed: "You feel like, yeah, that's what a lot of people do. You either stay together or you don't. If you stay together, it's complicated and messy, and if you don't stay together, it's complicated and messy."[12] Complicated and messy—it is a fitting summation for realistic Wise at his minimalist best, and for any honest appraisal of life. But win or lose, Wise's characters fought against their fate.

Filmography

Robert Wise served a long Hollywood apprenticeship prior to becoming a feature-film director in 1944. Arriving in the movie capital in 1933, his early RKO cinema credits started with being an assistant sound editor on *Of Human Bondage* (1934). In this capacity, Wise worked on a series of film classics, from the Fred Astaire and Ginger Rogers musicals *The Gay Divorce* (1934) and *Top Hat* (1935), to George Stevens's *Alice Adams* (1935) and John Ford's *The Informer* (1935). Wise then graduated to assistant film editor on another watershed work, Gregory La Cava's *Stage Door* (1937). Wise moved up to editor status on *Bachelor Mother* (1939) and he achieved his greatest distinction in this role when his editing of *Citizen Kane* (1941) was Oscar nominated. (The following theaters-only filmography does not include Wise's Showtime picture, *A Storm in Summer*, 2000).

May 1944	*The Curse of the Cat People* (RKO, 70 minutes)
	Producer: Val Lewton. Codirectors: Gunther von Fritsch, replaced by Robert Wise. Screenplay: DeWitt Bodeen. Cast: Simone Simon, Kent Smith, Jane Randolph, Ann Carter, Elizabeth Russell, Julia Dean, Eve March, Sir Lancelot.
June 1944	*Mademoiselle Fifi* (RKO, 69 minutes)
	Producer: Val Lewton. Director: Robert Wise. Screenplay: Josef Mischel and Peter Ruric, from the Guy de Maupassant's stories "Mademoiselle Fifi" and "Boule de Suif." Cast: Simone Simon, John Emery, Kurt Kreuger, Alan Napier, Jason Robards Sr., Norma Varden, Romaine Callender, Fay Helm, Edmund Glover.
May 1945	*The Body Snatcher* (RKO, 77 minutes)
	Producer: Val Lewton. Director: Robert Wise. Screenplay: Philip MacDonald and Carlos Keith (Lewton), from Robert Louis Stevenson's story "The Body Snatcher." Cast: Boris Karloff, Bela Lugosi, Henry Daniell, Edith Atwater, Russell Wade, Rita Corday, Sharyn Moffett, Donna Lee, Mary Gordon.
November 1945	*A Game of Death* (RKO, 70 minutes)
	Producer: Herman Schlom. Director: Robert Wise. Screenplay: Norman Houston, from Richard Connell's story "The Most Dangerous Game." Cast: John Loder, Audrey Long, Edgar Barrier, Russell Wade, Russell Hicks, Jason Robards Sr.

November 1946   *Criminal Court* (RKO, 60 minutes)
                 Producer: Martin Rooney. Director: Robert Wise. Screenplay: Lawrence
                 Kimble. Cast: Tom Conway, Martha O'Driscoll, June Clayworth, Robert
                 Armstrong, Addison Richards, Pat Gleason, Steve Brodie.

April 1947   *Born to Kill* (RKO, 92 minutes)
                 Producer: Herman Schlom. Director: Robert Wise. Screenplay: Eve Greene
                 and Richard Macaulay, from James Gunn's novel *Deadlier Than the Male*.
                 Cast: Lawrence Tierney, Claire Trevor, Walter Slezak, Philip Terry, Audrey
                 Long, Elisha Cook Jr., Isabel Jewell, Esther Howard.

February 1948   *Mystery in Mexico* (RKO, 66 minutes)
                 Producer: Sid Rogell. Director: Robert Wise. Screenplay: Lawrence
                 Kimble, from a Muriel Roy Bolton story. Cast: William Lundigan,
                 Jacqueline White, Ricardo Cortez, Tony Barrett, Jacqueline Dalya, Walter
                 Reed.

November 1948   *Blood on the Moon* (RKO, 87 minutes)
                 Producer: Theron Warth. Director: Robert Wise. Screenplay: Lillie
                 Howard, from Luke Short's novel *Gunman's Choice*. Cast: Robert
                 Mitchum, Barbara Bel Geddes, Robert Preston, Walter Brennan, Phyllis
                 Thaxter, Frank Faylen, Tom Tully, Charles McGraw.

March 1949   *The Set-Up* (RKO, 72 minutes)
                 Producer: Richard Goldstone. Director: Robert Wise. Screenplay: Art
                 Cohn, from Joseph Moncure March's poem. Cast: Robert Ryan, Audrey
                 Totter, George Tobias, Alan Baxter, Wallace Ford, Percy Helton, Hal
                 Fieberling, James Edwards, Darryl Hickman.

October 1950   *Three Secrets* (Warner Brothers, 98 minutes)
                 Producer: Milton Sperling. Director: Robert Wise. Screenplay: Martin
                 Rackin and Gina Kaus. Cast: Eleanor Parker, Patricia Neal, Ruth Roman,
                 Frank Lovejoy, Leif Erickson, Ted de Corsia, Edmon Ryan, Larry Keating,
                 Katherine Warren.

October 1950   *Two Flags West* (Twentieth Century Fox, 92 minutes)
                 Producer/Screenplay: Casey Robinson, from a Frank S. Nugent and Curtis
                 Kenyon story. Director: Robert Wise. Cast: Joseph Cotton, Linda Darnell,
                 Jeff Chandler, Cornel Wilde, Dale Robertson, Noah Beery, Harry von Zell.

June 1951   *House on Telegraph Hill* (Twentieth Century Fox, 100 minutes)
                 Producer: Robert Bassler. Director: Robert Wise. Screenplay: Elick Moll
                 and Frank Partos from Dana Lyon's novel *The Frightened Child*. Cast:
                 Richard Basehart, Valentina Cortesa, William Lundigan, Fay Baker,
                 Gordon Gebert, Kei Thing Chung, John Burton.

September 1951   *The Day the Earth Stood Still* (Twentieth Century Fox, 92 minutes)
                 Producer: Julian Blaustein. Director: Robert Wise. Screenplay: Edmund H.
                 North, from the Harry Bates story "Farewell to the Master." Cast: Michael
                 Rennie, Patricia Neal, Hugh Marlowe, Sam Jaffe, Billy Gray, Frances
                 Bavier, Loch Martin, Drew Pearson.

March 1952   *The Captive City* (Aspen Productions, 90 minutes)
                 Producer: Theron Warth. Director: Robert Wise. Screenplay: Alvin M.

Josephy Jr. and Karl Kamb, from a Josephy story. Cast: John Forsythe, Joan Camden, Harold J. Kennedy, Marjorie Crossland, Victor Sutherland, Ray Teal, Martin Milner.

November 1952   *Something for the Birds* (Twentieth Century Fox, 81 minutes)
Producer: Samuel G. Engel. Director: Robert Wise. Screenplay: I. A. L. Diamond and Boris Ingster, from stories by Ingster, Alvin M. Josephy Jr., and Joseph Petracca. Cast: Victor Mature, Patricia Neal, Edmund Gwenn, Larry Keating, Gladys Hurlbut, Hugh Sanders, Christian Rub.

May 1952   *Destination Gobi* (Twentieth Century Fox, 88 minutes)
Producer: Stanley Rubin. Director: Robert Wise. Screenplay: Everett Freeman, from Edmund G. Love's story "Ninety Saddles for Kengtu." Cast: Richard Widmark, Don Taylor, Casey Adams, Murvyn Vye, Darryl Hickman, Martin Milner, Ross Bagdasarian.

May 1953   *The Desert Rats* (Twentieth Century Fox, 88 minutes)
Producer: Robert L. Jacks. Director: Robert Wise. Screenplay: Richard Murphy. Cast: Richard Burton, James Mason, Robert Newton, Robert Douglas, Torin Thatcher, Chips Rafferty, Michael Rennie (Narrator).

November 1953   *So Big* (Warner Brothers, 101 minutes)
Producer: Henry Blanke. Director: Robert Wise. Screenplay: John Twist, from Edna Ferber's novel. Cast: Jane Wyman, Sterling Hayden, Richard Beymer, Ruth Swanson, Roland Winters, Tommy Retting, Steve Forrest, Nancy Olson, Martha Hyer, Walter Coy.

April 1954   *Executive Suite* (MGM, 104 minutes)
Producer: John Houseman. Director: Robert Wise. Screenplay: Ernest Lehman, from Cameron Hawley's novel. Cast: William Holden, June Allyson, Barbara Stanwyck, Fredric March, Walter Pidgeon, Shelley Winters, Paul Douglas, Louis Calhern, Dean Jagger, Nina Foch, Tim Considine.

December 1955   *Helen of Troy* (Warner Brothers, 114 minutes)
Producer: Jack L. Warner. Director: Robert Wise. Screenplay: John Twist and Hugh Gray, adaptation from Homer by Gray, and N. Richard Nash. Uncredited second unit direction: Raoul Walsh and Yakima Canutt. Cast: Rossana Podesta, Jacques Sernas, Sir Cedric Hardwicke, Stanley Baker, Robert Douglas, Nora Swinburne, Torin Thatcher, Harry Andrews, Brigitte Bardot, Eduardo Ciannelli, Marc Lawrence, Janette Scott, Ronald Lewis.

March 1956   *Tribute to a Bad Man* (MGM, 95 minutes)
Producer: Sam Zimbalist. Director: Robert Wise. Screenplay: Michael Blankfort, from Jack Schaefer's story "Jeremy Rodock." Cast: James Cagney, Don Dubbins, Stephen McNally, Irene Papas, Vic Morrow, Royal Dano, James Bell, Jeanette Nolan, Lee Van Cleef.

August 1956   *Somebody Up There Likes Me* (MGM, 114 minutes)
Producer: Charles Schnee. Director: Robert Wise. Screenplay: Ernest Lehman, from Rocky Graziano's memoir (written with Rowland Barber). Cast: Paul Newman, Pier Angeli, Everett Sloane, Eileen Heckart, Sal Mineo, Harold J. Stone, Joseph Buloff, Arch Johnson, Robert Loggia.

May 1957   *This Could Be the Night* (MGM, 104 minutes)

Producer: Joe Pasternak. Director: Robert Wise. Screenplay: Isabel Lennart, from the Cordelia Baird Gross stories "Protection for a Tough Racket" and "It's Hard to Find Mecca." Cast: Jean Simmons, Paul Douglas, Anthony Franciosa, Julie Wilson, Joan Blondell, Neile Adams, J. Carroll Nash, Rafael Campos.

September 1957   *Until They Sail* (MGM, 94 minutes)
Producer: Charles Schnee. Director: Robert Wise. Screenplay: Robert Anderson, from a James A. Michener story in the collection *Return to Paradise*. Cast: Jean Simmons, Joan Fontaine, Paul Newman, Piper Laurie, Charles Drake, Sandra Dee, Wally Cassell, Alan Napier. Ralph Votrian.

March 1958   *Run Silent, Run Deep* (A Hecht-Hill Lancaster Production/United Artists, 93 minutes)
Producer: Harold Hecht. Director: Robert Wise. Screenplay: John Gay, from Commander Edward L. Beach's novel. Cast: Clark Gable, Burt Lancaster, Jack Warden, Brad Dexter, Don Rickles, Nick Cravat, Joe Maross, Mary LaRoche, Eddie Foy III.

November 1958   *I Want to Live!* (A Figaro Production/United Artists, 120 minutes)
Producer: Walter Wanger. Director: Robert Wise. Screenplay: Nelson Gidding and Don Mankiewicz, from reporter Ed Montgomery articles, and Barbara Graham letters. Cast: Susan Hayward, Simon Oakland, Virginia Vincent, Theordore Bikel, Wesley Lau, Philip Coolidge, Lou Krugman.

September 1959   *Odds Against Tomorrow* (A Harbel Production/United Artists, 95 minutes)
Producer/Director: Robert Wise. Screenplay: Nelson Gidding, John O. Killens, and uncredited blacklisted writer Abraham Polonsky, from William P. McGiven's novel. Cast: Harry Belafonte, Robert Ryan, Shelley Winters, Ed Begley, Gloria Grahame, Will Kuluva, Richard Bright, Kim Hamilton, Mae Barnes.

October 1961   *West Side Story* (The Mirisch Brothers/Seven Arts/United Artists, 155 minutes)
Producer: Robert Wise. Director: Wise, and Jerome Robbins. Screenplay: Ernest Lehman, from the musical (book by Arthur Laurents, lyrics by Stephen Sondheim, music by Leonard Bernstein, conceived/choreographed and directed for the stage by Jerome Robbins), from Shakespeare's *Romeo and Juliet*. Cast: Natalie Wood (vocals by Marni Nixon), Richard Beymer (vocals by Jimmy Bryant), Russ Tamblyn, Rita Moreno (vocals by Betty Ward), George Chakiris, Simon Oakland, Ned Glass.

October 1962   *Two for the Seesaw* (The Mirisch Brothers/Argyle Enterprises/Talbot Productions/Seven Arts/United Artists, 119 minutes)
Producer: Walter Mirisch. Director: Robert Wise. Screenplay: Isabel Lennart, from the William Gibson play. Cast: Shirley MacLaine, Robert Mitchum, Edmon Ryan, Elisabeth Fraser, Eddie Firestone, Billy Gray.

September 1963   *The Haunting* (MGM/Argyle Productions, 112 minutes)
Producer/Director: Robert Wise. Screenplay: Nelson Gidding, from Shirley Jackson's novel *The Haunting of Hill House*. Cast: Julie Harris, Claire

	Bloom, Richard Johnson, Russ Tamblyn, Lois Maxwell, Fay Compton, Rosalie Crutchley.
March 1965	*The Sound of Music* (Twentieth Century Fox, 176 minutes) Producer/Director: Robert Wise. Screenplay: Ernest Lehman, from the musical (book by Howard Lindsay and Russel Crouse, lyrics by Oscar Hammerstein II, and music by Richard Rodgers), from Maria von Trapp's memoir *The Trapp Family Singers*. Cast: Julie Andrews, Christopher Plummer (vocals by Bill Lee), Eleanor Parker, Richard Haydn, Peggy Wood (vocals by Margery MacKay), Charmian Carr, Heather Menzies, Nicholas Hammond, Duane Chase, Angela Cartwright, Debbie Turner, Kym Karath, Daniel Truhitte, Norma Varden, Marni Nixon.
December 1966	*The Sand Pebbles* (Twentieth Century Fox/Argyle-Solar Productions, 174 minutes) Producer/Director: Robert Wise. Screenplay: Robert Anderson, from Richard McKenna's novel. Cast: Steve McQueen, Richard Attenborough, Richard Crenna, Candice Bergen, Marayat Andriane, Mako, Larry Gates, Charles Robinson, Simon Oakland, Ford Rainey, Gavin Macleod, Joe Turkel, Richard Loo.
July 1968	*Star!* (Twentieth Century Fox, 174 minutes) Producer: Saul Chaplin. Director: Robert Wise. Screenplay: William Fairchild, from, in part, Richard Aldrich's *Gertrude Lawrence as Mrs. A,* with Noel Coward's dialogue (played by Daniel Massey) provided by Coward. Cast: Julie Andrews, Michael Craig, Robert Reed, Richard Crenna, Daniel Massey, John Collin, Bruce Forsyth, Beryl Reid.
March 1971	*The Andromeda Strain* (Universal, 137 minutes) Producer/Director: Robert Wise. Screenplay: Nelson Gidding, from Michael Crichton's novel. Cast: Arthur Hill, David Wayne, James Olson, Kate Reid, Paula Kelly, George Mitchell, Ramon Bieri, Kermit Murdock.
March 1973	*Two People* (Universal/Filmmakers Group Picture, 100 minutes) Producer/Director: Robert Wise. Screenplay: Richard De Roy. Cast: Peter Fonda, Lindsay Wagner, Estelle Parsons, Alan Fudge, Philippe March, Frances Sternhagen, Brian Lima, Geoffrey Horne.
December 1975	*The Hindenburg* (Universal/Filmmakers Group Picture, 120 minutes) Producer/Director: Robert Wise. Special Visual Effects: Albert Whitlock. Screenplay: Nelson Gidding, from the Michael M. Mooney novel. Cast: George C. Scott, Anne Bancroft, William Atherton, Roy Thinnes, Gig Young, Burgess Meredith, Charles Durning, Richard A. Dysart, Robert Clary.
April 1977	*Audrey Rose* (United Artists, 113 minutes) Producer: Joe Wizan and Frank De Felitta. Director: Robert Wise. Screenplay: De Felitta, from his novel. Cast: Marsha Mson, Anthony Hopkins, John Beck, Susan Swift, Norman Lloyd, John Hillerman, Robert Walden.
December 1979	*Star Trek—The Motion Picture* (Paramount, 132 minutes) Producer: Gene Roddenberry. Director: Robert Wise. Special Effects

Director: Douglas Trumbull. Screenplay: Harold Livingston, from the television series created by Roddenberry. Cast: William Shatner, Leonard Nimroy, DeForest Kelley, James Doohan, George Takei, Stephen Collins, Walter Koenig, Majel Barrett, Grace Lee.

March 1989   *Rooftops* (New Visions, 98 minutes)

Producer: Howard Koch Jr. Director: Robert Wise. Screenplay: Terence Brennan, from an Allan Goldstein and Tony Mark story. Cast: Jason Gedrick, Troy Beyer, Eddie Velez, Alexis Cruz, Tisha Campbell, Allen Payne, Steve Love, Rafael Baez.

Notes

Preface

1. Jonathan Cott, "The Last [John Lennon] Interview," *Rolling Stone*, December 23, 2010–January 6, 2011, p. 95.

2. See Richard C. Keenan, *The Films of Robert Wise* (Lanham, MD: Scarecrow Press, 2007); Sergio Leeman, *Robert Wise on His Films* (Los Angeles: Silman-James Press, 1995); Frank Thompson, *Robert Wise: A Bio-Bibliography* (Westport, CT: Greenwood Press, 1995).

3. John Baxter, *Hollywood in the Sixties* (New York: A. S. Barnes, 1972), 52.

4. Charles Higham and Joel Greenberg, *Hollywood in the Forties* (New York: A. S. Barnes, 1968), 48.

5. Richard Schickel, *Elia Kazan: A Biography* (New York: HarperCollins, 2005), 262.

6. David Orr, "The Formalist," *New York Times Book Review*, January 9, 2011, p. 17.

7. C. S. Lewis, *Surprised by Joy: The Shape of My Early Life* (New York: Harcourt, 1955), x.

Prologue

1. George Bernard Shaw, *The Art of Rehearsal* (1922; repr., New York: P. F. Collier and Son, 1928), 1.

2. George Bernard Shaw, "Make Them Do It Well," *Collier's Weekly*, June 24, 1922.

3. Shaw, *Art of Rehearsal*, 7.

4. Ibid., 8.

5. Douglas Fairbanks, "One Reel of Autobiography," *Collier's Weekly*, June 18, 1921.

Chapter 1

1. "Robert Wise," in *Current Biography 1989*, Charles Moritz, ed. (New York: H. W. Wilson Company, 1990), 630.

2. Garnet R. Donieker and W. A. Richards, *Living in Connersville* (Connersville: privately published, 1950), 162.

3. *Connersville News-Examiner*, September 5, 1922.

4. Frank Miller, *Leading Men: The 50 Most Unforgettable Actors of the Studio Era* (San Francisco: Chronicle Books, 2006), 75.

5. Harry Kreisler, "Robert Wise Interview: Conversations with History," Institute of International Studies, University of California, Berkeley, February 28, 1998, http://globetrotter.berkeley.edu/conversations/Wise/wise-con01.html.

6. Frank S. Nugent, "A Man and an Illusion," *New York Times*, December 17, 1939.

7. Douglas Fairbanks, "One Reel of Autobiography," *Colliers*, June 18, 1921, p. 11.

8. Leonard Klady, "AFC Decides to Wise Up," *Variety*, February 23, 1998.

9. Douglas Fairbanks (with uncredited ghostwriter Kenneth Davenport), *Laugh and Live*

(New York: Britton Publishing Company, 1917), 41.

10. Ibid., 92, 151.

11. Sergio Leeman, *Robert Wise on His Films* (Los Angeles: Silman-James Press, 1995), 107.

12. *Laugh Clown Laugh* movie advertisement, *Connersville News-Examiner*, July 3, 1928; *The Crowd* movie advertisement, ibid., July 17, 1928.

13. *Winchester Journal-Herald*, March 2, 1967, p. 1.

14. See Wes D. Gehring, *Carole Lombard: The Hoosier Tornado* (Indianapolis: Indiana Historical Society Press, 2003).

15. Robert Wise, "Wise Crax," *The Clarion*, February 9, 1932.

16. Robert Benchley, "Ill Will Towards Men," in *No Poems or Around the World Backwards and Sideways* (New York: Harper and Brothers, 1932), 220.

17. "Wise Crax," April 26, 1932.

18. Ibid., February 9, 1932.

19. Ibid., April 26, 1932.

20. Benchley, "Matinées—Wednesday and Saturdays," *No Poems*, 329.

21. "Wise Crax," May 17, 1932.

22. Benchley, "The Murder without Interest," *No Poems*, 265.

23. Wise Crax," March 22, 1932.

24. Author interview with Jackie Mabee Heck and Charles Heck, September 18, 2009.

25. Robert Wise letter, June 15, 1962, in the Jackie and Charles Heck private family collection, Connersville, IN.

26. Jackie Heck letter, September 26, 2009, in the collection of the author.

27. E. I. Higgs, "Golden Voice and the Woman Make Schumann-Heink Truly Great Artist," *Connersville News-Examiner*, November 15, 1924.

28. Ibid.

29. William H. Miller, ed., *The 150th Year of Connersville, Indiana: 1963* (Connersville: Sesquicentennial Book Club, 1964), 190.

30. Mike Selke, "Wise Dies at 91," *Connersville News-Examiner*, September 16, 2005.

31. Robert Wise voice-over *The Body Snatcher*, directed by Robert Wise (1945; Turner Entertainment Company and Warner Brothers Entertainment, 2005), DVD.

32. Michael Ringlespaugh, "School Board Considers Naming Auditorium for Robert Wise," *Connersville News-Examiner*, June 4, 1990.

33. *Senior Siren* (Connersville, Indiana: Connersville High School, 1932), 2.

34. *Connersville News-Examiner*, May 1, 1989.

35. Charles and Jackie Mabee Heck interview.

36. Author telephone interview with Kim Giesting, October 16, 2009.

37. Ibid.

38. Wise voice-over.

39. "Robert Wise."

40. *Connersville News-Examiner*, June 1, 3, 1932.

41. Ibid., June 1, 1932.

42. Ibid., May 28, 1932.

43. David Thomson, *Try to Tell the Story: A Memoir* (New York: Alfred A. Knopf, 2009), 56.

44. Anthony Lane, "Looking for Heroes," *The New Yorker*, June 6, 2005, p. 106.

45. H. G. Wells, *The Time Machine* (1895), in *The Favorite Short Stories of H. G. Wells* (Garden City, NY: Doubleday, Doran and Company, 1937), 86.

Chapter 2

1. Sergio Leeman, *Robert Wise on His Films* (Los Angeles: Silman-James Press, 1995), 17.

2. David L. Smith, *Hoosiers in Hollywood* (Indianapolis: Indiana Historical Society Press, 2006), 404.

3. Albert Marrin, *Years of Dust: The Story of the Dust Bowl* (New York: Dutton's Children's Books, 2009).

4. John M. Blum, "The End of an Era," in *The National Experience: A History of the United States*, John M. Blum, ed. (New York: Harcourt Brace, 1968), 674.

5. Frank Thompson, *Robert Wise: A Bio-Bibliography* (Westport, CT: Greenwood Press, 1995), 5.

6. Harry Kreisler, "Robert Wise Interview: Conversations with History," Institute of International Studies, University of California, Berkeley, February 28, 1998, http://globetrotter .berkeley.edu/conversations/wise/wise-con01.html.

7. Francois Truffaut, foreword to *Orson Welles*, by Andre Bazin (New York: Harper and Row, 1972), 3.

8. Joseph Epstein, *Fred Astaire* (New Haven, CT: Yale University Press, 2008), 15.

9. Ralph Appelbaum, "Audrey Rose in Search of a Soul: Robert Wise Interviewed," *Films and Filming* (November 1977): 21.

10. Lewis Jacobs, *The Rise of the American Film* (1939; repr., New York: Teachers College Press, Columbia University, 1971), 532–33.

11. George Eells and Stanley Musgrove, *Mae West: A Biography* (New York: William Morrow and Company, 1982), 270.

12. Ibid.

13. See Wes D. Gehring, *Screwball Comedy: A Genre of Madcap Romance* (Westport, CT: Greenwood Press, 1986), and *Romantic vs. Screwball Comedy: Charting the Difference* (Lanham, MD: Scarecrow Press, 2002).

14. Author interview with Pandro S. Berman, June 1975.

15. Leeman, *Robert Wise on His Films*, 19.

16. Samuel Stark, "Robert Wise," *Films in Review*, January 1963, p. 6.

17. David Thomson, *The New Biographical Dictionary of Film* (New York: Alfred A. Knopf, 2003), 503–4.

18. "A Portrait of Michael Crichton," bonus material, *The Andromeda Strain*, directed by Robert Wise (1971; Universal, 2003), DVD.

19. Kreisler, "Robert Wise Interview."

20. Thompson, *Robert Wise*, 6–7.

21. Stark, "Robert Wise."

22. See Wes D. Gehring, *Leo McCarey: From Marx to McCarthy* (Lanham, MD: Scarecrow Press, 2005).

23. Marino Amoruso and John Gallagher, "Robert Wise: Part One 'The RKO Years,'" *Grand Illusion* (Winter 1977).

Chapter 3

1. Bernard Weinraub, "A Life in Hollywood, but Never a Niche," *New York Times*, February 9, 1998.

2. Allen Barra, "The Rise and Fall of Orson Welles," *Biography Magazine* (January 2002).

3. Mark W. Estrin, ed., *Orson Welles Interviews* (Jackson: University Press of Mississippi, 2002), 135.

4. Frank Thompson, *Robert Wise: A Bio-Bibliography* (Westport, CT: Greenwood Press, 1995), 7.

5. Joseph McBride, *Orson Welles* (New York: Viking Press, 1972), 26.

6. Barbara Leaming, *Orson Welles: A Biography* (1985; repr., New York: Penguin Books, 1986), 287.

7. Budd Schulberg, *The Disenchanted* (New York: Random House, 1950), 51.

8. See Wes D. Gehring, *Mr. Deeds Goes to Yankee Stadium: Baseball Films in the Capra Tradition* (Jefferson, NC: McFarland and Company, 2004).

9. Gerald Mast, *A Short History of the Movies*, revised by Bruce F. Kawin (New York: Macmillan Publishing, 1992), 272.

10. Leaming, *Orson Welles*, 249.

11. Arthur Knight, *The Liveliest Art: A Panoramic History of the Movies*, rev. ed. (New York: Macmillan Publishing, 1978), 158.

12. "The Battle over *Citizen Kane*," bonus material, *Citizen Kane*, directed by Orson Welles (1941; Turner Entertainment Company and WGBH Educational Foundation's *American Experience*, 2001), DVD.

13. Ibid.

14. Sergio Leeman, *Robert Wise on His Films* (Los Angeles: Silman-James Press, 1995), 57.

15. Otis Ferguson, "Citizen Welles," *New Republic*, June 2, 1941.

16. Gilbert Seldes, "Radio Boy Makes Good," *Esquire*, August 1941.

17. See Wes D. Gehring, *Film Classics Reclassified: A Shocking Spoof of Cinema* (Davenport, IA: Robin Vincent Publishing, 2001).

18. "Battle over *Citizen Kane*."

19. *Indianapolis News*, February 27, 1942.

20. See Wes D. Gehring, *American Dark Comedy: Beyond Satire* (Westport, CT: Greenwood Press, 1996).

21. Andre Bazin, *What Is Cinema?*, Hugh Gray, trans. (1967; repr., Los Angeles: University of California Press, 1971), 33.

22. Leeman, *Robert Wise on His Films*, 21.

23. Ibid.

24. "Battle over *Citizen Kane*."

25. David Denby, "Wild Nights," *The New Yorker*, November 30, 2009.

26. Nahma Sandrow, introduction to *The Magnificent Ambersons*, by Booth Tarkington (1918; repr., New York: Barnes and Noble Classics, 2005), xv.

27. Ibid.

28. Andrew Sarris, ed., *Interview with Film Directors* (1967; repr., New York: Avon Books, 1972), 544.

29. David L. Smith, *Hoosiers in Hollywood* (Indianapolis: Indiana Historical Society Press,

2006), 405.

30. Donald J. Gray, introduction to *The Magnificent Ambersons*, by Booth Tarkington (1919; repr., Bloomington: Indiana University Press, 1989), xix.

31. Orson Welles and Peter Bogdanovich, *This Is Orson Welles* (New York: HarperCollins, 1992), 115.

32. McBride, *Orson Welles*, 55.

33. Welles and Bogdanovich, *This Is Orson Welles*, 122.

34. Leaming, *Orson Welles*, 293.

35. Ibid.

36. *It's All True*, unfinished Orson Welles film (1942; Paramount Pictures, 2004), DVD.

37. Ibid.; Chris Welles Feder, *In My Father's Shadow: A Daughter Remembers Orson Welles* (Chapel Hill, NC: Algonquin Books, 2009).

38. Joel E. Siegel, *Val Lewton: The Reality of Terror* (New York: Viking Press, 1973), 20.

39. *The Magnificent Ambersons* review, *Variety*, July 1, 1942.

40. Ibid.

41. Thomas M. Pryor, "'The Magnificent Ambersons,' Welles' Film from Novel by Tarkington, Opens at Capitol," *New York Times*, August 14, 1942.

42. "'Magnificent Ambersons' Magnificent Welles Film: A Prestige Picture When RKO Needs It." *Hollywood Reporter*, July 1, 1942.

43. Ibid.

44. Allan Hunter, ed., *Movie Classics* (New York: Chambers, 1992), 136.

45. Jeremy McCarter, "Me and Orson Welles: The Boy-Wonder Years," *Newsweek*, December 7, 2009.

46. *Indianapolis Star*, January 2, 2011.

47. Chris Nashawaty, "The Film That Broke Orson Welles' Heart ['Mr. Arkadin']," *Entertainment Weekly*, April 14, 2006.

48. Duane Byrge, ed., *Private Screenings: Insiders Share a Century of Great Movie Moments* (Atlanta: Turner Publishing, 1995), 75.

49. Weinraub, "A Life in Hollywood," 6.

50. See Wes D. Gehring, *W. C. Fields: A Bio-Bibliography* (Westport, CT: Greenwood Press, 1984), 80.

Chapter 4

1. David Thomson, "Val Lewton," in *The New Biographical Dictionary of Film* (New York: Alfred A. Knopf, 2003), 522.

2. Susan Wloszczyna, "Wise: The 'Spielberg of His Time,'" *USA Today*, September 16, 2005.

3. Selise Eiseman, "Wise, Beyond His Years: A Life's Hard Work," *Editors Guild Magazine* (November/December 2005): 49.

4. Marino Amoruso and John Gallagher, "Robert Wise: Part One 'The RKO Years,'" *Grand Illusions* (Winter, 1977): 10.

5. Michael Ringlespaugh, "School Board Considers Naming Auditorium for Robert Wise," *Connersville News-Examiner*, June 4, 1990.

6. Author telephone interview with Anthony Slide, December 23, 2009.

7. Arthur Knight, "Wise in Hollywood," *Saturday Review*, August 8, 1970, p. 25.

8. Robert Wise letter to Glenna Boltuck, May 28, 1965, Robert Wise Collection, Cinema Arts Library, Doheny Memorial Library, University of Southern California, Los Angeles (hereafter cited as Wise Collection).

9. Wise letter to Stewart L. Udall, February 14, 1967, Wise Collection.

10. Wise letter to Jeffrey Dane, August 15, 1973, ibid.

11. Wise letter to Florence Mischel, February 8, 1967, ibid.

12. Ralph Appelbaum, "*Audrey Rose*: Robert Wise Seeking the Innermost Crisis in an Interview," *Films and Filming* (November 1977): 19–20.

13. Joel E. Siegel, *Val Lewton: The Reality of Terror* (New York: Viking Press, 1973), 56.

14. Ibid., 21.

15. Robert Wise voice-over, *The Body Snatcher*, directed by Robert Wise (1945; Turner Entertainment Company and Warner Brothers Entertainment, 2005), DVD.

16. Manny Farber, *Movies* (New York: Hillstone, 1971), 47.

17. Wise voiceover, *Body Snatcher*.

18. Peter Bogdanovich, *Pieces of Time* (New York: Dell Publishing Company, 1974), 41.

19. Wise voiceover, *Body Snatcher*.

20. Sergio Leeman, *Robert Wise on His Films* (Los Angeles: Silman-James Press, 1995), 65.

21. James Agee, *The Curse of the Cat People* review, *Nation*, April 1, 1944.

22. John T. McManus, "A Blessing in Disguise," *PM*, March 5, 1944.

23. Siegel, *Val Lewton*, 140.

24. Bosley Crowther, "A Child's Mind," *New York Times*, March 4, 1944.

25. Rose Pelswick, "'Cat People' Sequel on Rialto Screen," *New York Journal American*, March 4, 1944.

26. James Agee, "[The Year 1944 in Review]," *Nation*, January 20, 1945.

27. Siegel, *Val Lewton*, 136.

28. George Brown, "Dark Knight," *Village Voice,* July 6, 1993.

29. David Riesman, *The Lonely Crowd* (1950; repr., New Haven, CT: Yale University Press, 1965), 52.

30. Robert Wise voice-over, *The Curse of the Cat People*, directed by Robert Wise (1944; Warner Brothers Entertainment Company, 2005), DVD.

31. Irving Hoffman, "Tales of Hoffman," *Hollywood Reporter*, September 8, 1944, p. 3.

32. Appelbaum, "*Audrey Rose*," 21.

33. Manny Farber, "A Director's Skill with Terror, Geography, and Truth," *The New Leader*, November 23, 1959.

34. J. P. Telotte, *Dreams of Darkness: Fantasy and the Films of Val Lewton* (Chicago: University of Illinois Press, 1985), 113.

35. Thomson, "Boris Karloff," *New Biographical Dictionary of Film*, 453.

36. Cynthia Lindsay, *Dear Boris: The Life of William Henry Pratt, a.k.a. Boris Karloff* (New York: Alfred A. Knopf, 1975), 111.

37. Paul M. Jensen, *Boris Karloff and His Films* (New York: A. S. Barnes and Company, 1974), 140.

38. Wise letter to Gordon B. Shriver, September 10, 1973, Wise Collection.

39. Elliott Stein, "Arty Monster [Karloff]," *Village Voice*, February 1–7, 2006, p. 56.

40. "'Body Snatcher' All Horror Fans Want; Lewton, Wise Hit," *Hollywood Reporter*, February 14, 1945.

41. Bert McCord, "'The Body Snatcher'—Rialto [Theater]," *New York Herald Tribune*, May 26, 1945.

42. John T. McManus, "Grave-Robbing Neatly Done," *PM*, May 27, 1945.

43. *The Body Snatcher* review, *Variety*, February 21, 1945.

44. *The Body Snatcher* review, *Motion Picture Daily*, February 16, 1945.

45. William K. Everson, *Classics of the Horror Film* (1974; repr., New York: Citadel, 1990), 2.

46. *The Body Snatcher* review, *The New Yorker*, June 4, 1945.

47. Farber, "Director's Skill with Terror, Geography, and Truth."

48. David Anderson, "The Jets Hope Ryan's Confidence Is as Good as a Guarantee," *New York Times*, January 19, 2010.

Chapter 5

1. William Grimes, "Ihor Sevcenko, 87, a Byzantine Historian," *New York Times*, January 5, 2010.

2. J. P. Telotte, *Dreams of Darkness: Fantasy and the Films of Val Lewton* (Chicago: University of Illinois Press, 1985), 154.

3. "'Mlle. Fifi' Intriguing Pic," *Hollywood Reporter*, July 27, 1944.

4. Guy de Maupassant, "Mademoiselle Fifi" (1882), in *Best Short Stories of Guy de Maupassant* (New York: World Publishing Company, 1944), 258.

5. Guy de Maupassant, "Boule de Suif" (1880), in *Boule de Suif Monsieur Parent and Other Stories* (New York: Edition de Trianon, 1909), 43, 52.

6. *Best Short Stories of Guy de Maupassant*, xi.

7. Joel E. Siegel, *Val Lewton: The Reality of Terror* (New York: Viking Press, 1973), 146.

8. Bruce Weber, "C. Bryan, 73, 'Friendly Fire' Writer, Dies," *New York Times*, December 18, 2009, p.5.

9. Antoine de Saint Exupéry, *The Little Prince* (1943; repr., New York: Harcourt Brace and World, 1971), 4.

10. J. D. Salinger, *The Catcher in the Rye* (Boston: Little, Brown and Company, 1951), 14.

11. See Wes D. Gehring, *James Dean: Rebel with a Cause* (Indianapolis: Indiana Historical Society Press, 2005).

12. Maupassant, "Boule de Suif," 45.

13. See Wes D. Gehring, *Leo McCarey: From Marx to McCarthy* (Lanham, MD: Scarecrow Press, 2005).

14. Toni Bentley, "Faithless Love," *New York Times*, January 31, 2010.

15. "'Mlle. Fifi' Intriguing Pic"; James Agee, *Mademoiselle Fifi* review, *Nation*, December 2, 1944.

16. *Mademoiselle Fifi* review, *Time*, November 27, 1944.

17. *Mademoiselle Fifi* review, *Motion Picture Herald*, July 29, 1944.

18. Manny Farber, *Destination Gobi* review, *Nation*, April 11, 1953.

19. Siegel, *Val Lewton*, 147.

20. "*The Set-Up* (RKO) at the Criterion," *CUE*, April 2, 1949.

21. Robert Wise, voice-over, *The Body Snatcher*, directed by Robert Wise (1945; Turner Entertainment Company and Warner Brothers Entertainment, 2005), DVD.

22. Steve Slosarek, "Wise Attributes Success to Hoosier Boyhood," *Indianapolis Star*, April 23, 2004.

23. Wise voice-over, *Body Snatcher*.

24. Vanessa Grigoriadis, "He's So Vain," *New York Times*, February 7, 2010.

25. "Val Lewton Dies Following Illness," *Hollywood Reporter*, March 15, 1951.

26. *Val Lewton: The Man in the Shadows*, film by Kent Jones, produced by Martin Scorsese, 2007.

27. *Shadows in the Dark: The Val Lewton Legacy*, a film by Steve Haberman and Constantine Nasr, 2005.

28. *Mademoiselle Fifi*, script (1944, Robert Wise's copy), Robert Wise Collection, Cinema Arts Library, Doheny Memorial Library, University of Southern California, Los Angeles.

Chapter 6

1. *USA Today*, December 14, 2009.

2. Sergio Leeman, *Robert Wise on His Films* (Los Angeles: Silman-James Press, 1995), 74.

3. Charlotte Chandler, *Nobody's Perfect: Billy Wilder* (New York: Simon and Schuster, 2002), 285.

4. Ibid., 284.

5. Frank Eng, "'Game of Death' Masterful . . . Direction Makes Everything Count," *Hollywood Reporter*, November 23, 1945.

6. *A Game of Death* review, *Variety*, November 28, 1945.

7. *Criminal Court* review, *Variety*, August 14, 1946.

8. Joelyn R. Littauer, "Court in Session," *New York Times*, November 16, 1946.

9. Kevin Jackson, ed., *Schrader on Schrader* (Boston: Faber and Faber, 1990), 89.

10. Martin Scorsese and Michael Henry Wilson, *A Personal Journey with Martin Scorsese through American Movies* (New York: Miramax Books, 1997), 110, 117.

11. Carlos Clarens, *Crime Movies* (New York: W. W. Norton and Company, 1980), 193.

12. *Born to Kill* script, April 22, 1946, Robert Wise Collection, Cinema Arts Library, Doheny Memorial Library, University of Southern California, Los Angeles (hereafter cited as Wise Collection).

13. Longhand notation at the *Born to Kill* script's conclusion, wise Collection.

14. Raymond Chandler, *The Big Sleep* (1939; repr., New York: Vintage Books, 1992), 9.

15. *Born to Kill* script, Wise Collection.

16. Selise Eiseman, "Wise beyond His Years," *Editor's Guild Magazine* (November/December 2005): 52.

17. Leeman, *Robert Wise on His Films*, 78.

18. Ibid.

19. Bosley Crowther, *Born to Kill* review, *New York Times*, May 1, 1947.

20. Pauline Kael, *I Lost It at the Movies* (Boston: Little, Brown and Company, 1965), 206.

21. Rose Pelswick, "'Born to Kill' Shown at Palace Theatre," *New York Journal American*,

May 1, 1947.

    22. Ann Helming, *Born to Kill* review, *Hollywood Citizen News*, July 3, 1947.

    23. *Born to Kill* review, *Film Daily*, April 17, 1947.

    24. *Born to Kill* review, *Variety*, April 16, 1947.

    25. "'Born to Kill' above 'B' Par," *Hollywood Reporter*, April 16, 1947.

    26. Virginia Wright, *Born to Kill* review, *Los Angeles Daily News*, July 3, 1947.

    27. See Wes D. Gehring, *Charlie Chaplin: A Bio-Bibliography* (Westport, CT: Greenwood Press, 1983), and the *Monsieur Verdoux* chapter in Wes D. Gehring, *Forties Film Funnymen: The Decade's Great Comedians at Work in the Shadow of War* (Jefferson, NC: McFarland and Co., 2010).

    28. Wheeler Winston Dixon, *The Early Film Criticism of Francois Truffaut* (Bloomington: Indiana University Press), 15.

    29. *Born to Kill* program notes for the "Melbourne [Australia] Film Festival of 1995," *Born to Kill* clipping files, Margaret Herrick Library, Academy of Motion Picture Arts and Sciences, Beverly Hills, CA; Kevin Thomas, "In Noir Heaven," *Los Angeles Times*, April 1, 1999.

    30. Leeman, *Robert Wise on His Films*, 80.

    31. *Mystery in Mexico* review, *Variety*, June 23, 1948.

    32. "Atmosphere Touch Puts Budgeter Over," *Hollywood Reporter*, June 23, 1948.

    33. Robert Wise letter to Monica and Jud Kinsberg, October 16, 1974, Wise Collection.

Chapter 7

    1. Voice-over, *The Set-Up*, directed by Robert Wise (1949; Warner Brothers Entertainment Company, 2004), DVD.

    2. Justin Spring, *The Essential Edward Hopper* (New York: Harry N. Abrams, 1998), 95.

    3. David Thomson, *The New Biographical Dictionary of Film* (New York: Alfred A. Knopf, 2003), 721.

    4. Tom Hiney, *Raymond Chandler: A Biography* (New York: Grove Press, 1997), 101.

    5. Raymond Chandler, *The Big Sleep* (1939; repr., New York: Vintage Books, 1992), 230.

    6. *Until They Sail* script (1957, Robert Wise copy), Robert Wise Collection, Cinema Arts Library, Doheny Memorial Library, University of Southern California, Los Angeles (hereafter cited as Wise Collection).

    7. For a tongue-in-cheek look at "real-time" and on-screen clocks, see Wes D. Gehring, *Film Classics Reclassified: A Shocking Spoof of Cinema* (Davenport, IA: Robin Vincent Publishing, 2001), 128–45.

    8. Sergio Leeman, *Robert Wise on His Films* (Los Angeles: Silman-James Press, 1995), 84.

    9. Philip K. Scheuer, "Mitch, Preston Takes Sides in War on Range," *Los Angeles Times*, January 1, 1949.

    10. Ibid.

    11. "'Blood' Brutal Western . . . Adult Yarn, Thesp Names Are Lures," *Hollywood Reporter*, November 10, 1948.

    12. Eileen Creelman, *Blood on the Moon* review, *New York Sun*, November 12, 1948.

    13. Alvin H. Marill, *Robert Mitchum on the Screen* (New York: A. S. Barnes, 1978), 104, 106.

    14. Frank Thompson, *Robert Wise: A Bio-Bibliography* (Westport, CT: Greenwood Press,

1995), 9.

15. *Blood on the Moon* script (1948, Robert Wise copy), Wise Collection.

16. See, Rose Pelswick, "A Horse Opera in Slow Walk," *New York Journal American*, November 12, 1948.

17. *Blood on the Moon* review, *Variety*, November 10, 1948.

18. *Blood on the Moon* review, *Pacific Film Archive*, February 20, 1998, *Blood on the Moon* clipping file, Margaret Herrick Library, Academy of Motion Picture Arts and Sciences, Beverly Hills, CA.

19. Christopher Frayling, *Sergio Leone: Something to Do with Death* (London: Faber and Faber, 2000), 69.

20. Ibid., 206.

21. David Thomson, *The New Biographical Dictionary of Film* (New York: Alfred A. Knopf, 20003), 604.

22. Virginia MacPherson, "Fans Cheer as Mitchum Finishes Jail Term," *New York World-Telegram*, March 30, 1949.

23. Leeman, *Robert Wise on His Films*, 170.

24. Joe Collura, "Robert: His Sense of Direction—Part 1," *Classic Images* 153 (1987).

25. John Belton, *Robert Mitchum* (New York: Pyramid Publications, 1976), 29.

26. Richard C. Keenan, *The Films of Robert Wise* (Lanham, MD: Scarecrow Press, 2007), 43.

27. Edwin Schallert, "Ryan Packs Terrific Wallop as 'Set-Up' Star," *Los Angeles Times*, March 31, 1949.

28. Leeman, *Robert Wise on His Films*, 87.

29. Ibid.

30. Carl Sandburg, "Limited" (1916), in *Harvest Poems: 1910-1960* (New York: Harcourt, Brace and World, 1960), 38.

31. Thompson, *Robert Wise*, 9.

32. Robert Wise letter, May 6, 1981, Wise Collection.

33. Thomas M. Pryor, "At the Criterion," *New York Times*, March 30, 1949.

34. *New York World Telegram*, March 29, 1949.

35. *The Set-Up* review, *Variety*, March 23, 1949.

36. Eileen Creelman, *The Set-Up* review, *New York Sun*, March 30, 1949.

37. "'Set-Up' . . . Story of Pug Has Action and Drama," *Hollywood Reporter*, March 21, 1949.

38. Schallert, "Ryan Packs Terrific Wallop as 'Set-Up' Star."

39. Wanda Hale, *The Set-Up* review, *New York Daily News*, March 30, 1949.

40. "'Set-Up' Knocks Out 'Champ' As Court Orders UA Film Cut," *Hollywood Reporter*, May 6, 1949.

41. *The Set-Up* File, Herrick Library.

42. Mile Hale, "A Fight Film Makes a Two-Week Comeback," *New York Times*, September 18, 2009.

Chapter 8

1. Stephen Michael Shearer, *Patricia Neal: An Unquiet Life* (Lexington: University of

Kentucky Press, 2006), 90.

    2. Sergio Leeman, *Robert Wise on His Films* (Los Angeles: Silman-James Press, 1995), 94.

    3. Patricia Neal, with Richard DeNeut, *Patricia Neal: As I Am* (New York: Simon and Schuster, 1988), 117.

    4. Robert Wise letter to Rita Moreno, February 14, 1964, Robert Wise Collection, Cinema Arts Library, Doheny Memorial Library, University of Southern California, Los Angeles (hereafter cited as Wise Collection).

    5. Wise letter to Patricia Neal, January 3, 1967, Wise Collection.

    6. *Good Housekeeping* folder 89367, *Three Secrets* file 367, box 2, Warner Brothers Archive, School of Cinematic Arts, University of Southern California.

    7. *Three Secrets* folder "U.S. Pic," in the *Three Secrets* file 367, box 2, ibid.

    8. *House on Telegraph Hill* review, *Los Angeles Examiner*, June 9, 1951.

    9. *The Haunting* script (1963, Robert Wise copy), Wise Collection.

    10. *The Curse of the Cat People* script (September 3, 1943, Robert Wise copy), ibid.

    11. Justin Spring, *The Essential Edward Hopper* (New York: Harry N. Abrams, 1998), 72.

    12. Jean-Dominique Bauby, *The Diving Bell and the Butterfly* (1997; repr., New York: Vintage Books, 1998), 82.

    13. Leeman, *Robert Wise on His Films*, 107.

    14. *The Day the Earth Stood Still* script (1951, Robert Wise copy), Wise Collection.

    15. Mark Twain, *A Connecticut Yankee in King Arthur's Court* (1889; repr., New York: Signet Classics, 1963), 289.

    16. Peter Biskind, *Seeing Is Believing: How Hollywood Taught Us to Stop Worrying and Love the Fifties* (1983; repr., New York: Henry Holt and Company, 2000), 151.

    17. Tom Weaver, "Years after Stillness," *Starlog* (February 1995): 25.

    18. Neal, *Patricia Neal*, 136.

    19. Ibid.

    20. Weaver, "Years after Stillness," 26.

    21. "Robert Wise to Direct 20th 'Earth Stood Still,'" *Hollywood Reporter*, March 19, 1951, and James Otten, "Some Notes about a Secret Movie Plot," *New York Times*, March 18, 1951. See also Wes D. Gehring, *Leo McCarey: From Marx to McCarthy* (Lanham, MD: Scarecrow Press, 2005).

    22. Richard C. Keenan, *The Films of Robert Wise* (Lanham, MD: Scarecrow Press, 2007), 69.

    23. "Out of this World," *The New Yorker*, December 7, 1992.

    24. *The Day the Earth Stood Still* script (1951, Robert Wise copy), Wise Collection.

    25. "The New Pictures," *Time*, October 1, 1951.

    26. Edwin Schallart, "'Earth Stood Still' Advanced Thriller," *Los Angeles Times*, September 29, 1951.

    27. "Excitement, Tense Drama Mark 'Earth Stood Still,'" *Hollywood Reporter*, September 4, 1951.

    28. Darr Smith, *The Day the Earth Stood Still* review, *Los Angeles Daily News*, September 29, 1951.

    29. Rose Pelswick, "Don't Miss This Thriller," *New York Journal American*, September 19, 1951, p. 23.

    30. Schallert, "'Earth Stood Still' Advanced Thriller."

31. Biskind, *Seeing Is Believing*, 153.

32. *The Day the Earth Stood Still* revisionist review, *Pacific Film Archive*, February 14, 1998, *The Day the Earth Stood Still* file, Margaret Herrick Library, Academy of Motion Picture Arts and Sciences, Beverly Hills, CA.

33. Steven Jay Schneider, *101 Sci-Fi Movies You Must See Before You Die* (New York: Barron's Educational Series, 2009), 45.

34. "Walt Kelly," in *The World Encyclopedia of Comics* Maurice Horn, ed. (New York: Avon Books, 1976), 422–23.

35. Leeman, *Robert Wise on His Films*, 111.

36. Wise Collection.

Chapter 9

1. For example, see David Denby, "Guilt Trips," *The New Yorker*, May 3, 2010, p. 83.

2. See war's darker side in Michael C. C. Adams, *The Best War Ever: America and World War II* (Baltimore: John Hopkins University Press, 1994).

3. Otis L. Guernsey, Jr., *The Desert Rats* review, *New York Herald Tribune*, May 9, 1953, p. 9.

4. Richard C. Keenan, *The Films of Robert Wise* (Lanham, MD: Scarecrow Press, 2007), 80.

5. Evan Thomas, "The War beneath the Sea," *New York Times*, May 16, 2010, "Book Review" section, 25.

6. Keenan, *Films of Robert Wise*, 113.

7. Robert Harris, *The Ghost Writer*, previously published as *The Ghost* (2007; repr., New York: Gallery Books, 2010), 228.

8. Michael Munn, *Richard Burton: Prince of Players* (New York: Skyhorse Publishing, 2008), 76–77.

9. Keenan, *Films of Robert Wise*, 115.

10. Doris Klein, "Bob Wise Makes Pics for People, Not Himself or Other Filmmakers," *Hollywood Reporter*, April 29, 1968.

11. Charles Champlin, "Brainstorms Pay Off for Hollywood's Wise Men," *Los Angeles Times*, December 25, 1966.

12. Tom Dardis, *Some Time in the Sun* (1976; repr., New York: Penguin Books, 1981), 153.

13. Sergio Leeman, *Robert Wise on His Films* (Los Angeles: Silman-James Press, 1995), 144.

14. Robert Wise letter dated June 29, 1982, Robert Wise Collection, box 46: "Wise Corresp. 1979–1983," Cinema Arts Library, Doheny Memorial Library, University of Southern California, Los Angeles.

15. Shawn Levy, *Paul Newman: A Life* (New York: Harmony Books, 2009), 112.

16. Ibid., 234.

17. Rose Pelswick, "Stirring Tale of Girls Who Wait on War," *New York Journal American*, October 9, 1957, p. 26.

18. *Until They Sail* review, *Variety*, September 25, 1957.

19. *Run Silent, Run Deep* review, *New York Times*, March 28, 1958, p. 29.

20. Alton Cook, "Lancaster and Gable Clash in Submarine," *New York World Telegram and Sun*, March 28, 1958, p. 20.

21. Ronald Johnson, "Moving with the Movies," *Toronto Globe and Mail*, May 29, 1958.

22. *Helen of Troy* review, *Variety*, December 21, 1955.

23. "Young Dean's Legacy," *Newsweek*, October 22, 1956, p. 112.

24. David Denby, "Loners," *The New Yorker*, August 8, 15, 2005, p. 101.

25. Henry Gaggiotini, "Helen of Troy," *Chicago Tribune Magazine*, June 27, 1954, p. 28; "Helen of Troy, 1954," *Des Moines Register Magazine*, August 1, 1954, p.15.

26. Christopher Marlowe, *Doctor Faustus*, act 5, scene 1.

27. Robert Wise and *Helen of Troy* material, "Robert Wise," boxes 1, 4, 5, Warner Brothers Archives, School of Cinema Arts, University of Southern California, Los Angeles.

28. Todd McCarthy, *Howard Hawks: The Grey Fox of Hollywood* (New York: Grove Press, 1997), 538.

29. Leeman, *Robert Wise on His Films*, 125–26.

30. Keenan, *Films of Robert Wise*, 87.

31. Alvin H. Marill, *Katharine Hepburn* (New York: Pyramid Publications, 1973), 31.

32. John Hillcoat voice-over, *The Road*, directed by John Hillcoat (2009; Sony Pictures/Weinstein Company, 2009), DVD.

33. Christopher Frayling, *Sergio Leone: Something to Do with Death* (New York: Faber and Faber, 2000), 69.

34. Jack Warner telegram to Robert Wise, December 16, 1953, "Robert Wise/*Helen of Troy*" collection, box 5, Warner Brothers Archives.

35. Wise telegram to Warner, December 18, 1953, ibid.

36. T. C. Wright letter to Jack Warner, May 1, 1954, "Robert Wise/*Helen of Troy*" collection, "Production Department Folder," box 1, Warner Brothers Archives.

37. Wright letter to Warner, May 4, 1954, ibid.

38. Wright letter to Warner, June 8, 1954, ibid.

39. Ephraim Katz (revised by Fred Klein and Ronald Dean Nolen), "Yakima Canutt," in *The Film Encyclopedia* (New York: HarperCollins, 2001), 218.

40. Wright letter to Warner, June 22, 1954, "Robert Wise/*Helen of Troy*" collection, "Production Department Folder," box 1, Warner Brothers Archives.

41. Warner letter to Wright, April 10, 1954, ibid.

42. Raoul Walsh, *Each Man in His Own Time: The Life Story of a Director* (New York: Farrar, Straus and Giroux, 1974), 360.

43. Warner letter to Wright, April 5, 1954, in the "Robert Wise/*Helen of Troy*" collection, "Production Department Folder," box 1, Warner Brothers Archives.

44. Wise letter to Warner, September 29, 1954, ibid.

45. David Carr, "English Legends: That Rubin Guy and Sir Ridley," *New York Times*, May 9, 2010, Arts & Leisure Section, 8.

Chapter 10

1. Frank Litsky and John Branch, "John Wooden, Who Built an Incomparable Dynasty at U.C.L.A., Dies at 99," *New York Times*, June 6, 2010.

2. Wheeler Winston Dixon, *The Early Film Criticism of Francois Truffaut* (Bloomington:

Indiana University Press, 1993), 137.

3. Carolyn Anderson, "Biographical Film," in *Handbook of American Film Genres*, Wes D. Gehring, ed. (Westport, CT: Greenwood Press, 1988), 331.

4. *Run Silent, Run Deep* clipping file, Margaret Herrick Library, Academy of Motion Picture Arts and Sciences, Beverly Hills, CA.

5. Richard C. Keenan, *The Films of Robert Wise* (Lanham, MD: Scarecrow Press, 2007), 80.

6. Bosley Crowther, *So Big* review, *New York Times*, October 22, 1953.

7. *So Big* review, *Variety*, September 30, 1953.

8. Robert Wise voice-over, *The Body Snatcher* (1945; Turner Entertainment Company and Warner Brothers Entertainment, Inc., 2005), DVD.

9. *So Big* review, *Variety*.

10. *So Big* review, *Newsweek*, November 9, 1953, p. 99; *So Big* review *Time*, November 9, 1953, p. 112.

11. Harrison Carroll, "Jane Wyman Shines as Heroine of 'So Big,'" *Los Angeles Herald Express*, November 4, 1953.

12. Frances Melrose, "'So Big' Is Picture Everyone Should See," *Denver Rocky Mountain News*, November 19, 1953.

13. *Indianapolis News*, October 20, 1953.

14. Ibid., October 22, 1953.

15. Author conversation with Conrad Lane, June 11, 2010.

16. Mrs. Robert F. Iott letter to Warner Brothers, October 30, 1953, Warner Brothers Archives, School of Cinema Arts, University of Southern California, Los Angeles.

17. Cobbett Steinberg, *Reel Facts: The Movie Book of Records* (New York: Vintage Books, 1978), 406.

18. Don Jones, Rough draft of a United Press wire story on *So Big* (1953), Warner Brothers Archives.

19. Lawrence J. Quirk, *Jane Wyman: The Actress and the Woman* (New York: Dembner Books, 1986), 156.

20. Joe Morella and Edward Z. Epstein, *Jane Wyman: A Biography* (New York: Delacorte Press, 1985), 173.

21. Quirk, *Jane Wyman*, 156.

22. Paul Guest, *One More Theory about Happiness: A Memoir* (New York: Ecco/Harper-Collins, 2010).

23. Christopher R. Beha, "The Art of Pain," *New York Times*, June 13, 2010.

24. Interoffice Warner Brothers communication to Jerry Wald from Jo Pagano, October 12, 1943, Warner Brothers Archives.

25. Interoffice Warner Brothers communication to Wald from Pagano, July 19, 1945, ibid.

26. Peter Biskind, *Seeing Is Believing: How Hollywood Taught Us to Stop Worrying and Love the Fifties* (1983; repr., New York: Henry Holt and Company, 2000), 306.

27. Alton Cook, "Stars a Team in Executive Suite," *New York World Telegram and Sun*, May 7, 1954.

28. *Executive Suite* review, *Variety*, February 24, 1954.

29. Otis L. Guernsey Jr., "'Executive Suite' Takes a Look at Big Business," *New York*

Herald Tribune, May 16, 1954.

    30. Arthur Knight, "Mr. Houseman's 'Executive Suite,'" *Saturday Review*, May 1, 1954, p. 33.

    31. Ibid., 34.

    32. Alton Cook, "Bellicose Cagney in Palace Film," *New York World Telegram and Sun*, March 31, 1956.

    33. Sergio Leeman, *Robert Wise on His Films* (Los Angeles: Silman-James Press, 1995), 132.

    34. Bill Davidson, *Spencer Tracy: Tragic Idol* (New York: E. P. Dutton, 1987), 128.

    35. Charles Higham, *Kate: The Life of Katharine Hepburn* (1975; repr., New York: Signet Book, 1981), 158.

    36. Christopher Anderson, *An Affair to Remember* (New York: William Morrow and Company, 1997), 248.

    37. Davidson, *Spencer Tracy*, 134.

    38. James Cagney, *Cagney by Cagney* (Garden City, NY: Doubleday and Company, 1976), 119.

    39. Patrick McGilligan, *Cagney: The Actor as Auteur* (1975; repr., New York: Da Capo Press, 1979), 139.

    40. Jesse Zunser, "Rocky Graziano's Movie, Too, Scores a K.O.," *Cue* magazine, July 14, 1956, p. 16.

    41. "Let Us Now Praise Famous Men," *Saturday Review*, July 14, 1956.

    42. Phil Berger, "Rocky Graziano, Former Boxing Champion, Dies," *New York Times*, May 24, 1990.

    43. ["Robert Wise Interview"], *American Film*, November 1975, p. 47.

    44. Berger, "Rocky Graziano, Former Boxing Champion, Dies."

    45. Shawn Levy, *Paul Newman: A Life* (New York: Harmony Books, 2009), 111.

    46. *Somebody Up There Likes Me* script (1956, Robert Wise's copy), Robert Wise Collection, Cinema Arts Library, Doheny Memorial Library, University of Southern California, Los Angeles (hereafter cited as Wise Collection).

    47. Bosley Crowther, *Somebody Up There Likes Me* review, *New York Times*, July 6, 1956.

    48. *Somebody Up There Likes Me* review, *Variety*, July 4, 1956.

    49. "A Fine Part for Pier," *Life*, July 30, 1956, p. 41.

    50. Crowther, *Somebody Up There Likes Me* review.

    51. *Somebody Up There Likes Me* review, *Variety*.

    52. John Beaufort, "Portrait of a Fighter," *Christian Science Monitor*, July 31, 1958.

    53. William K. Zinsser, *Somebody Up There Likes Me* review, *New York Herald Tribune*, July 6, 1956.

    54. Frank Thompson, *Robert Wise: A Bio-Bibliography* (Westport, CT: Greenwood Press, 1995), 70.

    55. See Wes D. Gehring, *James Dean: Rebel with a Cause* (Indianapolis: Indiana Historical Society Press, 2005).

    56. Robert Wise letter to Dore Schary, March 2, 1959, Wise Collection.

    57. Leeman, *Robert Wise on His Films*, 151.

    58. Ibid.

    59. Robert Wise letter to Joe Mankiewicz, February 20, 1958, Wise Collection.

60. Rose Pelswick, "Susan Sparks Taut Shocker," *New York Journal American*, November 19, 1958.

61. Robert Wise letter to Joe Mankiewicz, January 28, 1958, Wise Collection.

62. Robert Wise letter to Walter Schmidt, October 10, 1963, ibid.

63. *I Want to Live!* script (1958, Robert Wise copy), ibid.

64. Ibid., 172.

65. Roberta Smith, "Carving with Color on Canvas," *New York Times*, July 16, 2010.

66. Dudley Nichols letter to Walter Wanger, October 11, 1958, Wise Collection.

67. James Mason letter to Wanger, October 17, 1958, ibid.

68. Robert Wise letter to Arthur Krim (UA), October 8, 1958, ibid.

69. Bosley Crowther, *I Want to Live!* review, *New York Times*, November 19, 1958.

70. Alton Cook, "She Tried to Go Straight but . . .," *New York World Telegram and Sun*, November 19, 1958.

71. Paul V. Beckley, "The New Movie: *I Want to Live!*," *New York Herald Tribune*, November 19, 1958.

72. Cobbett Steinberg, *Reel Facts: The Movie Book of Records* (New York: Vintage Books, 1978), 348.

73. Richard Stern, *Still on Call* (Ann Arbor: University of Michigan Press, 2010).

Chapter 11

1. Bill Shaikin (syndicated, *Los Angeles Times*), "Yankees' Boss Dies at 80 after Seven World Titles," *Des Moines Register*, July 14, 2010.

2. Robert Wise letter to Hilda and Nels Gidding, August 12, 1964, Robert Wise Collection, Cinema Arts Library, Doheny Memorial Library, University of Southern California, Los Angeles (hereafter cited as Wise Collection).

3. See Wes D. Gehring, *Steve McQueen: The Great Escape* (Indianapolis: Indiana Historical Society Press, 2009), 205.

4. Wise letter to Christopher Plummer, August 8, 1973, Wise Collection.

5. Wise letter to Amos Vogel, April 24, 1961, ibid.

6. John McCabe, *Mr. Laurel and Mr. Hardy* (1961; repr., with additions, New York: Signet, 1966), 148. See also Wes D. Gehring, *Laurel & Hardy: A Bio-Bibliography* (Westport, CT: Greenwood Press, 1990).

7. Wise letter to Rock Hudson, September 5, 1973, Wise Collection.

8. Wise letter to E. Gregory Hookstratten, December 17, 1974, ibid.

9. Wise letter to Rita Moreno, February 14, 1964, ibid.

10. Wise letter to the Screen Extras' Guild, December 10, 1963, ibid.

11. *Odds Against Tomorrow* review, *Variety*, October 7, 1959.

12. Ibid.

13. Alton Cook, "Shocker Opens at Victoria," *New York World Telegram and Sun*, October 6, 1959.

14. Bosley Crowther, *Odds Against Tomorrow* review, *New York Times*, October 16, 1959.

15. Ibid. See also Rose Pelswick's "Belafonte Venture Gripping," *New York Journal American*, October 16, 1959.

16. Gerald Eskenazi, *The Lip: A Biography of Leo Durocher* (New York: William Morrow,

1993), 206.

17. James S. Hirsch, *Willie Mays: The Life, the Legend* (New York: Scribner, 2010), 87–88.

18. Leo Durocher's "Nice guys finish last" is cited in countless sources, such as Arnold Rampersad's *Jackie Robinson: A Biography* (New York: Alfred A. Knopf, 1997), 229–30.

19. William Grimes, "Tony Judt, Polemical Chronicler of History and Government, Is Dead at 62," *New York Times*, August 8, 2010.

20. David P. Thelen, *Robert M. LaFollette and the Insurgent Spirit* (Boston: Little, Brown and Company, 1976), 16.

21. Psalms 51:1.

22. Richard C. Keenan, *The Films of Robert Wise* (Lanham, MD: Scarecrow Press, 2007), 116.

23. Sergio Leeman, *Robert Wise on His Films* (Los Angeles: Silman-James Press, 1995), 166.

24. E. H. Gombrich, *The Story of Art* (1950; repr., with additions, New York: Phaidon, 1972), 456.

25. Leeman, *Robert Wise on His Films*, 167.

26. Mason Wiley and Damien Bona, *Inside Oscar* (1986; repr., New York: Ballantine Books, 1993), 339.

27. Ibid., 338.

28. Quoted in Alec Guinness, *Blessings in Disguise* (1985; repr., Glasgow, Scot.: Fontana/Collins, 1986), 312.

29. Susan Sackett, *Box Office Hits* (New York: Billboard Books, 1990), 156.

30. Cobbett Steinberg, *Reel Facts: The Movie Book of Records* (New York: Vintage Books, 1978), 349.

31. Sackett, *Box Office Hits*, 154.

32. Bosley Crowther, *West Side Story* review, *New York Times*, October 19, 1961.

33. *West Side Story* review, *Variety*, September 27, 1961.

34. James Power, "'West Side Story' Hailed as B.O. Smash, Great Film Work," *Hollywood Reporter*, September 22, 1961.

35. Paul V. Beckley, "'West Side Story' and 4 others," *New York Herald Tribune*, October 19, 1961.

36. James W. Seymore Jr., ed., *The* Entertainment Weekly *Guide to the Greatest Movies Ever Made* (1994; repr., New York: Warner Books, Inc., 1996), 130.

37. Rose Pelswick, "An Interesting but Talky Film," *New York Journal American*, November 23, 1962.

38. Paul V. Beckley, *Two for the Seesaw* review, *New York Herald Tribune*, November 22, 1962.

39. *Two for the Seesaw* review, *Variety*, October 24, 1962.

40. Bosley Crowther, *Two for the Seesaw* review, *New York Times*, November 22, 1962.

41. Shirley MacLaine, *My Lucky Stars: A Hollywood Memoir* (New York: Bantam Books, 1995), 304.

42. Alvin H. Marill, *Robert Mitchum on the Screen* (New York: A. S Barnes, 1978), 180; Keenan, *Films of Robert Wise*, 119.

43. MacLaine, *My Lucky Stars*, 296.

44. Marill, *Robert Mitchum*, 180.

45. "'Two for Seesaw' Rated One of the Year's Best Pix," *Hollywood Reporter*, October 30, 1962.

46. Ibid.

47. *Two for the Seesaw* review, *Variety*.

48. Terrence Rafferty, "Her Darkest Places," *New York Times*, August 29, 2010.

49. William K. Everson, *Classics of the Horror Film* (1974; repr., New York: Citadel Press, 1990), 183.

50. Francois Truffaut, ed., *Hitchcock* (New York: Simon and Schuster, 1983), 201.

51. Jeff VanderMeer, "Science Fiction Chronicle," *New York Times*, September 5, 2010.

52. Wise letter to Russell Ciccone, September 21, 1964, Wise Collection.

53. *The Haunting* review, *Variety*, August 21, 1963; Bosley Crowther, *The Haunting* review, *New York Times*, August 19, 1963.

54. Keenan, *Films of Robert Wise*, 125.

55. William Peper, "'The Haunting' Is Genuinely Ghostly, *New York World-Telegram*, September 19, 1963.

56. Rose Pelswick, "Bang-Up Thriller Full of Suspense," *New York Journal American*, September 19, 1963.

57. Judith Crist, "'Haunting'—Of Ghosts & Ghouls," *New York Herald Tribune*, September 19, 1963.

58. Richard Howard (translation and introduction) to "A Cruel Country: Notes on Mourning [by Roland Barthes]," *The New Yorker*, September 13, 2010, p. 26.

59. Rafferty, "Her Darkest Places."

60. *The Sound of Music* (film) listing, Wikipedia, http://en.wikipedia.org/.

61. Frank Thompson, *Robert Wise: A Bio-Bibliography* (Westport, CT: Greenwood Press, 1995), 14.

62. Leeman, *Robert Wise on His Films*, 180.

63. Robert Windeler, *Julie Andrews: A Biography* (New York: Saint Martin's Press, 1983), 100.

64. Ibid., 102.

65. Richard Sterling, *Julie Andrews: An Intimate Biography* (New York: Saint Martin's Press, 2007), 141.

66. Ibid.

67. Ibid., 144.

68. Christopher Plummer, *In Spite of Myself* (New York: Alfred A. Knopf, 2008), 394.

69. Ibid., 394, 395.

70. Wise to Plummer, August 8, 1973.

71. Sterling, *Julie Andrews*, 139.

72. Charmian Carr, with Jean A. S. Straus, *Forever Liesel: A Memoir of "The Sound of Music"* (New York: Viking, 2000), 63.

73. Windeler, *Julie Andrews*, 98.

74. Carr, *Forever Liesl*, 14.

75. Judith Crist, "Sugar Spice, but *Not* Everything Nice," *New York Herald Tribune*, March 3, 1965.

76. Stanley Kauffmann, *The Sound of Music* review, *New Republic*, March 20, 1965,

26–27.

77. Pauline Kael, *The Sound of Music* review, in *Kiss, Kiss, Bang Bang* (New York: Bantam, 1969), 214.

78. Bosley Crowther, *The Sound of Music* review, *New York Times*, May 3, 1965.

79. Windeler, *Julie Andrews*, 108.

80. *The Sound of Music* review, *Variety*, March 3, 1965.

81. Sackett, *Box Office Hits*, 179.

82. Alton Cook, "'Sound of Music' Comes in Sweetly," *New York World Telegram and Sun*, March 3, 1965.

83. Rose Pelswick, "Julie Andrews Is Wonderful," *New York Journal American*, March 3, 1965, 23.

84. Philip K. Scheuer, *The Sound of Music* review, *Los Angeles Times*, March 7, 1965.

85. Thompson, *Robert Wise*, 90.

86. Shirley Jackson, "Colloquy," in *Shirley Jackson: Novels and Stories*, Joyce Carol Oates, ed. (New York: Library of America, 2010), 118.

87. Philip Norman, *John Lennon: The Life* (New York: HarperCollins, 2008), 348.

88. Stephen King, *Dance Macabre* (1979; repr., New York: Berkley Books, 1982), 270, 37.

89. Ibid., 380.

Chapter 12

1. Orson Welles, from the documentary film, *The Battle over "Citizen Kane"* (1996), made for the American Experience, WGBH Education Experience.

2. Sergio Leeman, *Robert Wise on His Films* (Los Angeles: Silman-James Press, 1995), 202.

3. For example, see Michael C. C. Adam's *The Best War Ever: America and World War II* (Baltimore: John Hopkins University Press, 1994).

4. Quoted in David S. Reynold's "Learning to Be Lincoln," *New York Times*, October 3, 2010.

5. Cobbett Steinberg, *Reel Facts: The Movie Book of Records* (New York: Vintage Books, 1978), 350.

6. Candice Bergen, *Knock Wood* (1984; repr., New York: Ballantine Books, 1985), 166.

7. See Wes D. Gehring, *Steve McQueen: The Great Escape* (Indianapolis: Indiana Historical Society Press, 2009).

8. Leeman, *Robert Wise on His Films*, 187–88.

9. Neile McQueen Toffel, *My Husband, My Friend* (New York: Atheneum, 1986), 137.

10. Steinberg, *Reel Facts: The Movie Book of Records*, 171, 172, 173, 175, 350, 406–7.

11. Marshall Terrill, *Steve McQueen: Portrait of an American Rebel* (1993; repr., London: Plexus Publishing, 2005), 238.

12. See Gehring, *Steve McQueen*.

13. Julian Patrick, ed., *501 Great Writers* (London: Barron's, 2008), 424.

14. *The Sand Pebbles* review, *Variety*, December 21, 1966.

15. Frank Leyendecker, *The Sand Pebbles* review, *Boxoffice*, January 2, 1967, p. 11.

16. *The Sand Pebbles* review, *Cue*, December 31, 1966, p. 57.

17. James Power, "'Sand Pebbles' Has All the Elements," *Hollywood Reporter*, December

21, 1966.

18. George H. Jackson, "A Massive Film Saga," *Los Angeles Herald-Examiner*, December 29, 1966.

19. Arthur Knight, "Unsentimental Gentleman," *Saturday Review*, December 24, 1966, p. 62.

20. Ibid.

21. Manohla Dargis, "Arthur Penn, a Director Attuned to His Country," *New York Times*, October 10, 2010.

22. Ibid.

23. See Wes D. Gehring, *American Dark Comedy: Beyond Satire* (Westport, CT: Greenwood Press, 1996).

24. Ernest Hemingway, *A Farewell to Arms* (1929; repr., New York: Charles Scribner's Sons, 1957), 261.

25. Richard Stirling, *Julie Andrews: An Intimate Biography* (New York: Saint Martin's Press, 2008), 200, 201.

26. Les Spindle, *Julie Andrews: A Bio-Bibliography* (Westport, CT: Greenwood Press, 1989), 15.

27. Renata Adler, *Star!* Review, *New York Times*, October 23, 1968.

28. *Star!* review, *Variety*, July 24, 1968.

29. An uncredited Robert Wise interview, Robert Wise clipping files at the Performing Lincoln Center Arts Library, New York, NY.

30. See, Wes D. Gehring, *Red Skelton: The Mask Behind the Mask* (Indianapolis: Indiana Historical Society Press, 2008).

31. Richard C. Keenan, *The Films of Robert Wise* (Lanham, MD: Scarecrow Press, 2007), 136.

32. Roger Greenspun, "Screen: Wise's 'Andromeda Strain,'" *New York Times*, March 22, 1971, p. 40.

33. Leeman, *Robert Wise on His Films*, 200.

34. *Two People* review, *Variety*, March 14, 1973.

35. Roger Greenspun, "The Cast," *New York Times*, March 19, 1973; *Two People* review, *Variety*.

36. David E. Sanger, "Get Me Out of Here," *New York Times*, November 7, 2010.

37. Deirdre Donahue, "'Truth' Wrapped in Mystery in Postwar London," *USA Today*, August 29, 2006.

38. R. F. Foster, *W. B. Yeats: A Life,* vol. 1 (New York: Oxford University Press, 1997), xxviii.

39. See, Wes D. Gehring, "A War by Any Other Name," *USA Today Magazine* (September 2009): 71.

40. *Los Angeles Times*, September 25, 1975.

41. Robert Wise letter to Monica and Jud Kinsberg, October 16, 1974, Robert Wise Collection, Cinema Arts Library, Doheny Memorial Library, University of Southern California, Los Angeles (hereafter cited as Wise Collection).

42. Blake Edwards letter, November 25, 1974, Wise Collection, ibid.

43. Robert Wise letter to Richard Zanuck, December 26, 1973, ibid.

44. See Gehring, *Red Skelton.*

45. Robert Wise letter, October 18, 1963, Wise Collection.

46. The best Robert Wise student paper I supervised was Nicholas W. Chandler "Robert Wise in Indiana" (honor thesis, April 30, 2003), author's private papers.

47. Mark Robson letter, August 24, 1964, Wise Collection.

48. Mark Robson's letter is cited in a Robert Wise letter to Robson, August 24, 1964, ibid.

49. Ibid.

50. Frank Capra, *Frank Capra: The Name above the Title* (New York: Macmillan, 1971), 486.

51. See Wes D. Gehring, *Leo McCarey: From Marx to McCarthy* (Lanham, MD: Scarecrow Press, 2005).

52. Nora E. Taylor, "'Hindenburg'—Star of New Spy Film," *Christian Science Monitor*, December 18, 1975.

53. Leeman, *Robert Wise on His Films*, 209.

54. Henry Butler, "'King of Hearts' Delightful Film," *Indianapolis News*, September 23, 1975.

55. Vincent Canby, *The Hindenburg* review, *New York Times*, December 26, 197; "'The Hindenburg': Dull Disaster Pic[ture]," *Variety*, December 24, 1975.

56. Keenan, *Films of Robert Wise*, 148.

57. *New York Times*, September 24, 1975;" *Los Angeles Times*, September 24, 1975.

58. Natalie Gittelson, "Robert Wise: Mythmaker," *Harper's Bazaar*, May 1971, p. 63.

59. Robert Wise letter to Sandcastle restaurant, 1974, Wise Collection.

60. Robert Wise, "Costs Must Come Down . . .," *Variety*, undated, Robert Wise files, Margaret Herrick Library, Academy of Motion Picture Arts and Sciences, Beverly Hills, CA.

61. *Audrey Rose* review, *Variety*, April 6, 1977.

62. Vincent Canby, "Poor Little Girl," *New York Times*, April 7, 1977.

63. David L. Smith telephone interview with the author, November 13, 2010.

64. Leeman, *Robert Wise on His Films*, 217.

65. Robert Wise letter to an Ontario Film Institute official, March 31, 1981, Wise Collection.

66. Vincent Canby, *Star Trek—The Motion Picture* review, *New York Times*, December 8, 1979.

67. Susan Sackett, *Box Office Hits* (New York: Billboard Books, 1990), 266.

68. Ibid.

69. *Star Trek—The Motion Picture* review, *Variety*, December 12, 1979.

70. Leonard Maltin, ed., *Leonard Maltin's Movie Guide: 2006* (New York: Signet Books, 2005), 1226.

71. Roger Ebert, *Rooftops* review, *Chicago Sun Times*, March 17, 1989.

Epilogue

1. *New York Times*, September 15, 2005.

2. Robert Wise Collection, Cinema Arts Library, Doheny Memorial Library, University of Southern California, Los Angeles.

3. Mark Twain, *Adventures of Huckleberry Finn* (1885; repr., New York: W. W. Norton

and Company, 1962), 7.

4. Andrew Sarris, *The American Cinema: Directors and Directions, 1929–1968* (New York: Dutton, 1968), 203.

5. Robert Wise Interview: Conversations with History, Institute of International Studies, University of California Berkeley, http://globetrotter.berkeley.edu/conversations/Wise/wise-con06.html.

6. Ralph Appelbaum, "Audrey Rose in Search of a Soul: Robert Wise Interviewed," *Films and Filming* (November 1977): 18.

7. Frank Thompson, *Robert Wise: A Bio-Bibliography* (Westport, CT: Greenwood Press, 1995), 154. (All subsequent references to unrealized projects are drawn from Thompson's text.)

8. *The Day the Earth Stood Still* script (1951, Robert Wise copy), Wise Collection.

9. John Wakeman, ed., *World Film Directors, Volume I: 1890–1945* (New York: H. W. Wilson Company, 1987), 1219.

10. Carlo Rotella, "The Professor of Micro Popularity," *New York Times Magazine*, November 28, 2010, p. 53.

11. See Wes D. Gehring, *Populism and the Capra Legacy* (Westport, CT: Greenwood Press, 1995).

12. Constance Rosenblum, "Hedda Gabler to Medea to Frazzled Mom," *New York Times*, January 2, 2011.

Select Bibliography

Special Collections

Robert Wise Clipping Files. Connersville Public Library, Connersville, IN.

Robert Wise Clipping Files. Margaret Herrick Library, Academy of Motion Picture Arts and Sciences, Beverly Hills, CA.

Robert Wise Clipping Files. Performing Arts Library, New York Public Library at Lincoln Center, New York, NY.

Robert Wise Collection. Cinema Arts Library, Doheny Memorial Library, University of Southern California, Los Angeles.

Robert Wise Files for each of the director's films at both the Academy Library and New York's Performing Arts Library. These clipping folders were also supplemented by the microfilm "Tombs" (dead newspaper) section of New York City's Main Library at Fifth Avenue and Forty-second Street.

Warner Brothers Archive. School of Cinema Arts, University of Southern California, Los Angeles.

Books

Adam, Michael C. C. *The Best War Ever: America and World War II.* Baltimore: John Hopkins University Press, 1994.

Anderson, Carolyn. "Biographical Film." In *Handbook of American Film Genres.* Edited by Wes D. Gehring. Westport, CT: Greenwood Press, 1988.

Anderson, Christopher. *An Affair to Remember.* New York: William Morrow and Company, 1997.

Bauby, Jean-Dominique. *The Diving Bell and the Butterfly.* 1997. Reprint, New York: Vintage Books, 1998.

Bazin, Andre *What Is Cinema? I.* Translated by Hugh Gray. 1967. Reprint, Los Angeles: University of California Press, 1971.

Belton, John. *Robert Preston.* New York: Pyramid Publications, 1976.

Benchley, Robert. *No Poems or Around the World Backwards and Sideways.* New York: Harper and Brothers, 1932.

Bergen, Candice. *Knock Wood.* 1984. Reprint, New York: Ballantine Books, 1985.

Biskind, Peter. *Seeing Is Believing: How Hollywood Taught Us to Stop Worrying and Love the Fifties.*1983. Reprint, New York: Henry Holt and Company, 2000.

Blum, John M. "The End of an Era." In *The National Experience: A History of the United States.* New York: Harcourt Brace, 1968.

Bogdanovich, Peter. *Pieces of Time.* New York: Dell Publishing Company, 1974.

Byrge, Duane, ed. *Private Screenings: Insiders Share a Century of Great Moments.* Atlanta: Turner Publishing, 1995.

Cagney, James. *Cagney by Cagney.* Garden City, NY: Doubleday and Company, 1976.

Capra, Frank. *The Name above the Title.* New York: Macmillan, 1971.

Carr, Charmian. *Forever Liesel: A Memoir of "The Sound of Music."* With Jean A. S. Straw. New York: Viking 2000.

Chandler, Charlotte. *Nobody's Perfect: Bill Wilder.* New York: Simon and Schuster, 2002.

Chandler, Raymond. *The Big Sleep.* 1939. Reprint, New York: Vintage Books, 1992.

Clarens, Carlos. *Crime Movies.* New York: W. W. Norton and Company, 1980.

Dardis, Tom. *Some Time in the Sun.* 1976. Reprint, New York: Penguin Books, 1981.

Davidson, Bill. *Spencer Tracy: Tragic Idol.* New York: E. P. Dutton, 1987.

Dixon, Wheeler Winston. *The Early Film Criticism of Francois Truffaut.* Bloomington: Indiana University Press, 1993.

Donieker, Garnet R., and W. A. Richards, *Living in Connersville.* Connersville, IN: privately published. 1950.

Eells, George, and Stanley Musgrove. *Mae West: A Biography.* New York: William Morrow and Company1982.

Epstein, Joseph. *Fred Astaire.* New Haven: Yale University Press, 2008.

Eskenazi, Gerald. *The Lip: A Biography of Leo Durocher.* New York: William Morrow, 1993.

Estrin, Mark W., ed. *Orson Wells Interviews.* Jackson: University Press of Mississippi, 2002.

Evans, R. Tripp. *Grant Wood: A Life.* New York: Alfred A. Knopp, 2010.

Everson, William K. *Classics of the Horror Film.* 1974. Reprint, New York: Citadel Press, 1990.

Exupéry, Antoine de Saint. *The Little Prince.* 1943. Reprint. New York: Harcourt Brace and World, 1971.

Fairbanks, Douglas. With Kenneth Davenport (uncredited). *Laugh and Live.* New York: Britton Publishing Company, 1917.

Farber, Manny. *Movies.* New York: Hillstone, 1971.

Feder, Chris Welles. *In My Father's Shadow: A Daughter Remembers Orson Welles.* Chapel Hill, NC: Algonquin Books 2009.

Foster, R. F. *W. B. Yeats: A Life,* vol. 1. New York: Oxford University Press, 1997.

Frayling, Christopher. *Sergio Leone: Something to Do with Death.* London: Faber and Faber, 2000.

Gehring, Wes D. *American Dark Comedy: Beyond Satire.* Westport, CT: Greenwood Press, 1996.

_____. *Carole Lombard: The Hoosier Tornado.* Indianapolis: Indiana Historical Society Press, 2003.

_____. *Charlie Chaplin: A Bio-Bibliography.* Westport, CT: Greenwood Press, 1983.

_____. *Film Classics Reclassified: A Shocking Spoof of Cinema.* Davenport, IA: Robin Vincent Publishing, 2001.

_____. *Forties Film Funnymen: The Decade's Great Comedians at Work in the Shadow of War.* Jefferson, NC: McFarland and Company, 2010.

_____. *James Dean: Rebel with a Cause.* Indianapolis, Indiana Historical Society Press, 2005.

_____. *Laurel & Hardy: A Bio-Bibliography.* Westport, CT: Greenwood Press, 1990.

_____. *Leo McCarey: From Marx to McCarthy.* Lanham, MD: Scarecrow Press, 2005.

_____. *Mr. Deeds Goes to Yankee Stadium: Baseball Films in the Capra Tradition.* Jefferson, NC: McFarland and Company, 2004.

_____. *Red Skelton: The Mask Behind the Mask.* Indianapolis: Indiana Historical Society Press, 2008.

_____. *Romantic vs. Screwball Comedy: Charting the Difference.* Lanham, MD: Scarecrow

Press, 2002.

_____. *Screwball Comedy: A Genre of Madcap Romance.* Westport, CT: Greenwood Press, 1986.

_____. *W. C. Fields: A Bio-Bibliography.* Westport, CT: Greenwood Press, 1984.

Gombrich, E. H. *The Story of Art.* 1950. Reprint, with additions, New York: Phaidon, 1972.

Guest, Paul. *One More Theory about Happiness: A Memoir.* New York: Ecco/HarperCollins, 2010.

Gray, Donald J. Introduction to *The Magnificent Ambersons*, by Booth Tarkington. Bloomington: Indiana University Press. 1989.

Guinnes, Alec. *Blessings in Disguise.* 1985. Reprint, Glasgow, Scotland: Fontana/Collins, 1986.

Harris, Robert. *The Ghost Writer.* Previously published as *The Ghost.* 2007. Reprint, New York: Gallery Books, 2010.

Hemingway, Ernest. *A Farewell to Arms.* 1929. Reprint, New York: Charles Scribner's Sons, 1957.

Higham, Charles. *Kate: The Life of Katharine Hepburn.* 1975. Reprint, New York: Signet Book, 1981.

Hiney, Tom. *Raymond Chandler: A Biography.* New York: Grove Press, 1997.

Hirsch, James S. *Willie Mays: The Life, the Legend.* New York: Scribner, 2010.

Horn, Maurice, ed. "Walt Kelly." *The World Encyclopedia of Comics.* New York: Avon Books, 1976.

Hunter, Allan, ed. *Movie Classics.* New York: Chambers, 1992.

Jackson, Kevin, ed. *Schrader on Schrader.* Boston: Faber and Faber, 1990.

Jackson, Shirley. "Colloquy." In *Shirley Jackson: Novels and Stories.* Edited by Carol Oates. New York: Library of America, 2010.

Jensen, Paul M. *Boris Karloff and His Films.* New York: A. S. Barnes and Company, 1974.

Kael, Pauline. *I Lost It at the Movies.* Boston: Little, Brown and Company, 1965.

——. "The Sound of Music Review." In *Kiss Kiss, Bang Bang.* New York: Bantam, 1969.

Katz, Ephraim "Yakima Canutt." In *The Film Encyclopedia.* Revised by Fred Klein and Ronald Dean Nolen. New York: HarperCollins, 1960.

Keenan, Richard C. *The Films of Robert Wise.* Lanham, MD: Scarecrow Press, 2007.

King, Stephen. *Dance Macabre.* 1979. Reprint, New York: Berkley Books, 1982.

Knight, Arthur. *The Liveliest Art: A Panoramic History of the Movies.* Rev. ed. New York: Macmillan Publishing, 1978.

Leaming, Barbara. *Orson Welles: A Biography.* 1985. Reprint, New York: Penguin Books, 1986.

Leeman, Sergio. *Robert Wise on His Films.* Los Angeles: Silman-James Press, 1995.

Levy, Shawn. *Paul Newman, A Life.* New York: Harmony Books, 2009.

Lindsey, Cynthia. *Dear Boris: The Life of William Henry Pratt, a.k.a. Boris Karloff.* New York: Alfred A. Knopf, 1975.

MacLaine, Shirley. *My Lucky Stars: A Hollywood Memoir.* New York: Bantam Books, 1995.

Maltin, Leonard, ed. *Leonard Maltin's Movie Guide: 2006.* New York: Signet Books, 2005.

Marill, Alvin H. *Katharine Hepburn.* New York: Pyramid Publications, 1973.

——. *Robert Mitchum on the Screen.* New York: A. S. Barnes, 1978.

Marrin, Albert. *Years of Dust: The Story of the Dust Bowl.* New York: Dutton's Children's Books, 2009.

Mast, Gerald. *A Short History of the Movies.* 1971. Revised by Bruce F. Kawin. New
    York: Macmillan Publishing, 1992.
Maupassant, Guy de. "Boule de Suif" (1880). In *Boule de Suif Monsieur Parent and Other
    Stories.* New York: Edition de Triaon, 1909.
———. "Mademoiselle Fifi" (1882). In *Best Short Stories of Guy de Maupassant.*
    New York: World Publishing Company, 1944.
McBride, Joseph. *Orson Welles.* New York: Viking Press, 1972.
McCabe, John. *Mr. Laurel and Mr. Hardy.* 1961. Reprint, with additions, New York: Signet,
    1966.
McCarthy, Todd. *Howard Hawks: The Grey Fox of Hollywood.* New York: Grove Press, 1997.
McGilligan, Patrick. *Cagney: The Actor as Auteur.* 1975. Reprint, New York: Da Capo Press,
    1979.
Miller, Frank. *Leading Men: The 50 Most Unforgettable Actors of the Studio Era.* San Francisco:
    Chronicle Books, 2006.
Miller, William H., ed. *The 150th Year of Connersville, Indiana: 1963.* Connersville, IN: Sesqui-
    centennial Book Club, 1964.
Morella, Joe, and Edward Z. Epstein. *Jane Wyman: A Biography.* New York: Delacorte Press,
    1985.
Munn, Michael. *Richard Burton: Prince of Players.* New York: Skyhorse Publishing, 2008.
Neal, Patricia. With Richard DeNeut. *Patricia Neal: As I Am.* New York: Simon and Schuster,
    1988.
Norman, Philip. *John Lennon: The Life.* New York: HarperCollins, 2008.
Patricia, Julian, ed. *501 Great Writers.* London: Barron's, 2008.
Plummer, Christopher. *In Spite of Myself.* New York: Alfred A. Knopf, 2008.
Quick, Lawrence J. *Jane Wyman: The Actress and the Woman.* New York: Dembner Books,
    1986.
Rampersad, Arnold. *Jackie Robinson: A Biography.* New York: Alfred A. Knopf, 1997.
Riesman, David. *The Lonely Crowd.* 1950. Reprint, New Haven: Yale University Press, 1965.
"Robert Wise." In *Current Biography, 1989.* New York: H. W. Wilson Company, 1990.
Sackett, Susan. *Box Office Hits.* New York: Billboard Books, 1990.
Salinger, J. D. *The Catcher in the Rye.* Boston: Little, Brown and Company, 1951.
Sandburg, Carl. "Limited." In *Harvest Poems: 1910–1960.* New York: Harcourt, Brace and
    World, 1960.
Sandrow, Nahma. Introduction to *The Magnificent Ambersons,* by Booth Tarkington. Reprint,
    New York: Barnes and Noble Classics, 2005.
Sarris, Andrew. *The American Cinema: Directors and Directions, 1929–1968.* New York:
    Dutton, 1968.
———, ed. *Interviews with Film Directors.* 1967. Reprint, New York: Avon Books,
    1972.
Schickel, Richard. *Elia Kazan: A Biography.* New York: HarperCollins, 2005.
Schneider, Steven Jay. *101 Sci-Fi Movies You Must See before You Die.* New York: Barron's
    Educational Series, 2009.
Schulberg, Budd. *The Disenchanted.* New York: Random House, 1950.
Scorsese, Martin, and Michael Henry Wilson. *A Personal Journey with Martin Scorsese through
    American Movies.* New York: Miramax Books, 1997.

Seymore, James W., Jr. *The Entertainment Weekly Guide to the Greatest Movies Ever Made.* 1994. Reprint, New York: Warner Books.

Shearer, Stephen Michael. *Patricia Neal: An Unquiet Life.* Lexington: University of Kentucky Press, 2006.

Siegel, Joel E. *Val Lewton: The Reality of Terror.* New York: Viking Press, 1973.

Smith, David L. *Hoosiers in Hollywood.* Indianapolis: Indiana Historical Society Press, 2006.

Spindle, Les. *Julie Andrews: A Bio-Bibliography.* Westport, CT: Greenwood Press, 1989.

Spring, Justin. *The Essential Edward Hopper.* New York: Harry N. Abrams, 1998.

Steinberg, Cobbett. *Reel Facts: The Movie Book of Records.* New York: Vintage Books, 1978.

Sterling, Richard. *Julie Andrews: An Intimate Biography.* New York: St. Martin's Press, 2007.

Stern, Richard. *Still on Call.* Ann Arbor: University of Michigan Press, 2010.

Symons, Arthur. Introduction to *Best Short Stories of Guy de Maupassant.* New York: World Publishing Company, 1944.

Teachout, Terry. *Pops: A Life of Louis Armstrong.* New York: Houghton Mifflin Harcourt, 2009

Telotte, J. P. *Dreams of Darkness: Fantasy and the Films of Val Lewton.* Chicago: University of Illinois Press, 1985.

Terrill, Marshall. *Steve McQueen: Portrait of an American Rebel.* 1993. Reprint, London: Plexus Publishing, 2005.

Thelen, David P. *Robert M. LaFollette and the Insurgent Spirit.* Boston: Little, Brown and Company, 1976.

Thompson, Frank. *Robert Wise: A Bio-Bibliography.* Westport, CT: Greenwood Press, 1995.

———. *The New Biographical Dictionary of Film.* New York: Alfred A. Knopf, 2003.

Thomson, David. "Boris Karloff" and "Val Lewton." In *The New Biographical Dictionary of Film.* New York: Alfred A. Knopf, 2003.

———. *Try to Tell the Story: A Memoir.* New York: Alfred A. Knopf, 2009.

Toffell, Neil McQueen. *My Husband, My Friend.* New York: Atheneum, 1986.

Trapp, Maria Augusta. *The Story of the Trapp Family Singers.* 1949. Reprint, New York: Scholastic Book Services, 1971.

Truffaut, Francois. Foreword to *Orson Welles,* by Andre Bazin. New York: Harper and Row, 1972.

———, ed. *Hitchcock.* New York: Simon and Schuster, 1983.

Twain, Mark. *Adventures of Huckleberry Finn.* 1885. Reprint, New York: W. W. Norton and Company, 1962.

———. *A Connecticut Yankee in King Arthur's Court.* 1889. Reprint, New York: Signet Classics, 1963.

———. "The Man That Corrupted Hadleyburg." (1899). In *The Complete Stories of Mark Twain.* Edited by Charles Neider. 1957. Reprint, New York: Bantam Books, 1964.

Walsh, Raoul. *Each Man in His Own Time: The Life Story of a Director.* New York: Farrar, Straus and Giroux, 1974.

Wells, H. G. *The Time Machine* 1895. In *The Favorite Short Stories of H. G. Wells.* Garden City, NY: Doubleday, Doran and Company, 1937.

Welles, Orson, and Peter Bogdanovich. *This Is Orson Welles.* New York: HarperCollins, 1992.

Wiley, Mason, and Damien Bona. *Inside Oscar.* 1986. Reprint, New York: Ballantine Books,

1993.

Windeler, Robert. *Julie Andrews: A Biography.* New York: Saint Martin's Press, 1983.

Articles, Reviews, and Other Media

Agee, James. *The Curse of the Cat People* review. *Nation*, April 1, 1944.

———. "[The Year 1944 In Review]." *Nation*, January 20, 1945.

Amoruso, Marino, and John Gallagher, "Robert Wise: Part One 'The RKO Years.'" *Grand Illusion* (Winter 1977).

Appelbaum, Ralph. "Audrey Rose in Search of a Soul: Robert Wise Interviewed." *Films and Filming* (November 1977).

Born to Kill review. *Film Daily*, April 17, 1947.

Collura, Joe. "Robert Wise: His Sense of Direction—Part I." *Classic Images* 153 (1987).

Cott, Jonathan. "The Last [John Lennon] Interview," *Rolling Stone*, December 23, 2010–January 6, 2011.

Denby, David. "Guilt Trips." *The New Yorker*, May 3, 2010.

———. "Loners." *The New Yorker*, August 8, 15, 2005.

———. "Wild Nights." *The New Yorker,* November 30, 2009.

Eiseman, Selise. "Wise beyond His Years." *Editor's Guild Magazine* (November/December 2005).

Fairbanks, Douglas. "One Reel of Autobiography." *Colliers*, June 18, 1921.

Farber, Manny. *Destination Gobi* review. *Nation*, April 11, 1953.

———. "A Director's Skill with Terror, Geography, and Truth." *The New Leader,* November 23, 1959.

Ferguson, Otis. "Citizen Welles." *New Republic*, June 2, 1941.

"A Fine Part for Pier." *Life,* July 30, 1956.

Gittelson, Natalie. "Robert Wise: Mythmaker." *Harper's Bazaar,* May 1971.

Howard, Richard, "A Cruel Country: Notes on Mourning [by Roland Barthes]." *The New Yorker*, September 13, 2010.

Kaufman, Stanley. *The Sound of Music* review. *New Republic*, March 20, 1965.

Knight, Arthur. "Mr. Houseman's 'Executive Suite.'" *Saturday Review*, May 1, 1954.

———. "Unsentimental Gentleman." *Saturday Review*, December 24, 1966.

———. "Wise in Hollywood." *Saturday Review*, August 8, 1970.

Kreisler, Harry. "Robert Wise Interview: Conversations with History." Institute of International Studies, University of California at Berkeley, February 28, 1998. http://globetrotter .berkeley.edu/conversations/Wise/wise-con0l.html.

Lane, Anthony. "Looking for Heroes." *The New Yorker*, June 6, 2005.

"Let Us Now Praise Famous Men." *Saturday Review*, July 14, 1956.

Leyendecker, Frank. *The Sand Pebbles* Review. *Boxoffice*, January 2, 1967.

Mademoiselle Fifi review. *Motion Picture Herald*, July 29, 1944.

Mademoiselle Fifi review. *Time*, November 27, 1944.

Nashaway, Chris. "The Film That Broke Orson Welles' Heart [:'Mr. Arkin']." *Entertainment Weekly*, April 14, 2006.

"The New Picture [*The Day the Earth Stood Still*]." *Time*, October 1, 1951.

"Out of This World." *The New Yorker*, December 7, 1992.

"[Robert Wise Interview]. *American Film*, November 1975.

The Sand Pebbles review. *Cue*, December 31, 1966.

Seldes, Gilbert. "Radio Boy Makes Good." *Esquire*, August 1841.

"*The Set-Up* (RKO) At the Criterion." *Cue*, April 2, 1949.

Shaw, George Bernard. "Make Them Do It Well." *Colliers Weekly*, June 24, 1922 (Published in pamphlet form as *The Art of Rehearsal* in 1928.)

So Big review. *Newsweek,* November 9, 1953.

So Big review. *Time*, November 9, 1953.

Stark, Samuel. "Robert Wise." *Film in Review*, January 1963.

Weaver, Tom. "Years after Stillness." *Starlog* (February 1995).

"Young Dean's Legacy." *Newsweek*, October 22, 1956.

Zunser, Jesse. "Rocky Graziano's Movie, Too, Scores a K.O." *Cue*, July 14, 1956.

Interviews

Author conversation with Conrad Lane, June 11, 2010.

Author interview with Jackie Maybee Heck and Charles Heck, September 18, 2009.

Author interview with Kim Giesting, October 16, 2009.

Author interview with Pandro S. Berman, June 1975.

Author telephone conversation with Anthony Slide, December 23, 2009.

Newspapers (see individual citations in Notes)

Chicago Sun Times.

Chicago Tribune.

Christian Science Monitor.

The Clarion (Connersville High School).

Connersville News-Examiner.

Denver Rocky Mountain News.

Des Moines Register.

Hollywood Citizen News.

Hollywood Reporter.

Indianapolis News.

Indianapolis Star.

Los Angeles Daily News.

Los Angeles Examiner.

Los Angeles Herald Express.

Los Angeles Herald-Examiner.

Los Angeles Times.

New York Daily News.

New York Journal American.

New York Sun.

New York Times.

New York World-Telegram.

New York World Telegram and Sun.

PM (New York City).

Senior Siren (Connersville High School Year Book.

Toronto Globe and Mail.

USA Today.
Variety.
Winchester (IN) Journal-Herald.

Documentaries and Voice-over Material

"The Battle over *Citizen Kane.*" Bonus material on *Citizen Kane*, DVD. Directed by Orson
    Welles. Turner Entertainment Company and WGBH Educational Foundation's *American
    Experience*, 2001.

John Hillcoat voice-over on *The Road*, DVD. Sony Pictures/Weinstein Company, 2009.

"A Portrait of Michael Crichton." Bonus material on "*The Andromeda Strain*, DVD.
    Universal, 2003.

Robert Wise voice-over on *The Body Snatcher*, DVD. Turner Entertainment, 2005.

Robert Wise voice-over on *The Set-Up*, DVD. Warners Brothers Entertainment Company,
    2004.

Shawdows in the Dark: The Val Lewton Legacy. A film by Steve Haberman and Constantine Nasr,
    2005.

Val Lewton: The Man in the Shadows. A film by Kent Jones, 2007.